CHANGE AND CONTINUITY IN TRIBAL VILLAGES

A Sociological Study

CHANGE AND CONTINUITY IN TRIBAL VILLAGES

A Sociological Study

J. LONGKUMER

AKANSHA PUBLISHING HOUSE
NEW DELHI-110002 (INDIA)

AKANSHA PUBLISHING HOUSE
4649-B/21, Ansari Road
Darya Ganj, New Delhi - 110 002
Ph.: 23263193 / 9811582579 / 09435116718
Fax: 011-23263193
Email: ektabooks@yahoo.com

Change and Continuity in Tribal Villages: A Sociological Study

First Published 2009
ISBN–978–81–8370–129-7

PRINTED IN INDIA

Published by Akansha Publishing House, New Delhi and Printed at Aryan Enterprises, Delhi.

CONTENTS

FOREWORD

Village studies have a long and established tradition in Indian anthropology and sociology. The tradition was only briefly abandoned during 1970s and 1980s, as the authority of such studies to speak for the entire societies wa questioned and even contested. The emphasis during those decades of lull in village studies was on representativeness of such studies rather than on indepth understanding of the functioning of societies. That every village is a microcosm of the society it belongs to was temporarily forgotten, and that the norms and values of one village are shared by other neighbouring villages as well was ignored. Fortunately, the faith in village studies never completed died out and the fact that communities come truly alive only in the villages was never ever forgotten.

Incidentally, such studies in India have been conducted mostly in caste-based societies and there are indeed countable few that have been done on tribal societies. This is a little strange because study of tribal societies is as old as the existence of anthroplogy and sociology in India. One possible reason for this omissions is the great interest anthropologists and sociologists doing village studies in India shared, that is understanding Indian civilization. Tribal societies being on the edge of Indian civilization were lower in the priority of those whose challenge was to grapple with the complexity of Indian civilization.

In this backdrop the book Change and Continuity in Tribal Villages: A Sociological Study by Dr. Ms. Jungmayangla Longkumer is a welcome publication. The book is divided into seven chapters. Four major themes discussed in the book are kinship and marriage, political institution, economy, and religious organization. In short, the book is modeled on the classical village studies where the primary focus has been to understand the traditional social structure and institutions as well as the forces of change that have shaken them or failed to shake them. Among the forces of such change discussed by Dr. Longkumer Christianity nd education rightly occupy the most important position. The book also deals with the rapid changes taking place in the village and shows the oncern of the author about some of the fast-disappearing heritages of the village.

The book, however, shows that changes noticed in the village are only one side of the coin, the other side being marked by the resolve of the Changki villagers to hang on to their traditions. Despite being converted into Christianity and adopted western values the author shows that the people of the village are still traditional in many respects such as their kinship structure, village council, age-set system and even their pre-Christian religious beliefs and values. The author explains why certain changes took place rather easily while certain other aspects did not change at all.

Dr. Longkumer must be credited for maintaining the delicate balance between the construction of the village as a self-contained social, religious and economic entity and its construction as one in constant interaction with other neighbouring villages belonging or not to the Ao Naga community. She also maintains a fine balance between the image of the village as a functionally inter-dependent unit and that of the village characterized by factions and conflicts between hamlets and clans.

It is further desirable to point out that the book brings out the migratory character of the Nagas quite clearly through various narratives, which might go well with those Naga clans who claim aboriginality of a particular village, as is common in Naga-inhabited village including Changki. Generally speaking, all communities that practised shifting cultivation till recently have been migratory till years after they came in contact with the British. That is why oral history of almost every tribe of Northeast India shows that its ancestors passed through the land of several other tribes before finally settling in the place where their descendants are found today.

I strongly believe that this book written in a lucid language should be read by all those who are interested in village studies in general and Naga Society in particular.

T B Subba
Professor of Anthropology
North-Eastern Hill University
Shillong.

PREFACE

The present work is based on one village located in the Ao area of Mokokchung district and as a case study it is restricted by the local differences because even among the Ao Naga villages there are variations in the institutions found in the villages. But the significance of case studies is by no means diminished. A necessary step in understanding the different tribes of Nagaland divided by local variations is to establish the local types; and adequate study of each divergent part is an obvious requisite for the proper understanding of the whole. This is even more so as there have been very few studies conducted on single villages in Nagaland.

Changki was chosen for the simple reason that as such no studies have been carried out in this village although Changki is well known for its high literacy rate and its people have been pioneers in various fields such as in the administrative and academic fields as well as in sports and politics in Nagaland. Another motivation was that the traditions and cultural traits of Changki village are fast being forgotten and as no records are available of such, it was felt that whatever has been preserved and is being practiced, need to be recorded and hence this book is a humble endeavor in that direction. This work attempts to highlight the village as the most important entity in the lives of the people and to show the continuity of traditions through various institutions as found in the village despite the forces of changes.

This work would never have seen the light of day if it had not been for my Supervisor Prof. P. M. Chacko. I am immensely indebted to him. His kindness, generosity of spirit, patience and sense of humour has been a great source of strength and encouragement for me. Prof. P. M. Chacko's valuable suggestions and intellectual inputs have contributed much to this work. Words are inadequate to express my heartfelt gratitude for his active support and meticulous guidance.

My heartfelt thanks also go to former Vice Chancellor of NEHU Prof. Mrinal Miri for his support and especially for going out of his way to help me in my endeavor. I also take this opportunity to thank Prof. Sujata Miri for her loving support, help and many acts of kindness.

I am thankful to Prof. T B Subba for writing the foreword and for his valuable suggestions.

Without the support and cooperation of the respondents I would have been unable to gather the data required and I take this opportunity to thank all the respondents at Changki. I am grateful especially to Mr. Imlimeren Amri ex-Gaon Bura (upper *khel)*, Mr. Tajenyuba Changkiri, former Changki Village Council Chairman, Mr. Lanusüja Longkumer (lower *khel*), Mr Imtinochet Changkiri (lower *khel*), Ms. Temendangla Amlari (upper *khel)*, Mr. Temjenwati Amri (upper *khel*), Mr. Longriniken Longchari, ex-Gaon Bura (upper *khel)*, Mr. Moachuchang Aonok (lower *khel)* and Mr. Allen Amri, Secretary, Baptist Church Changki for giving every assistance. I am particularly grateful to Ms. Imnalemla Longkumer of Tsüngli kiong, Changki, who provided a home away from home throughout my research work in Changki.

I am grateful to Monalisa Changkija, Editor, Nagaland Page, as well as Makentoshi (IAS) and Ayo Aier for giving me free access to their personal libraries. Thank you.

To my friend Anita P Jyrwa, thank you for helping me stay sane and happy! I owe you big.

A big thank you goes to my brother Taliaküm Longkumer and my sisters Imlinungla and Süngtiyenla Longkumer for their unfailing encouragement and belief in me.

My deepest gratitude goes to Temjenmenba Changkiri for his patient and loving care, support and encouragement. Without him I would have been lost.

Most of all I am eternally grateful to my mother Prof. Temsüla for being with me every step of the way. You have shaped and moulded my life and all I can say is thank you Mom. I also take this opportunity to pay respect to the memory of my father Late Assamwati Longkumer. He always took pride in all my achievements and he would have been very pleased with this one.

Above all I am thankful to God for all the blessings He has showered on me.

Jungmayangla Longkumer

1

INTRODUCTION

Nagaland has a total population of 1,988,636, out of which the rural population is 1,635,815, that is, 82:26% of the total population is rural. The majority of the Nagas still lives in some 1,278 villages and make their living from agriculture (Census 2001). The villages are usually established on high ridges with populations ranging from a hundred to more than ten thousand people and where the houses are huddled close to each other with the agricultural fields located away from the village – these are the physical aspects of the Naga village, in which a life of simplicity, hardship and stability is lived, founded on a traditional social order.

Nagaland is a wholly tribal state with each tribe having its own territory, language and customs. The present study is based on one village located in the Ao area of Mokokchung district and as a case study it is restricted by the local differences because even among the Ao Naga villages there are variations in the institutions found in the villages. But the significance of case studies is by no means diminished. A necessary step in understanding the different tribes of Nagaland divided by local variations is to establish the local types; and adequate study of each divergent part is an obvious requisite for the proper understanding of the whole. This is even more so as there have been very few studies conducted on single villages in Nagaland.

Village studies in India have been conducted over a long period and especially so since the establishment of the British colonial rule. The idea that the Indian village was a monolithic, atomistic, unchanging entity as articulated by the early British administrators was the commonly held view but later empirical studies especially in the fifties on village communities not only refuted and questioned such views but also proved that most Indian villages have ties of an extensive nature and rectified the myth that the Indian village was a self-sufficient isolated unit. Each village is connected through a variety of crucial horizontal linkages with other villages and with urban areas both near and far. Most villages are characterized by a multiplicity of economic, caste, kinship, occupational, and even religious groups linked vertically within each settlement. Factionalism is a typical feature of village politics. In one of the first modern anthropological studies of Indian village life, anthropologist Oscar Lewis (1965:324) called this complexity "rural cosmopolitanism." The various studies also showed that a village is usually an administrative and revenue unit.

The saying that India live in its villages is as close to reality now as it was in the pre-independence period. Even with five decades of economic planning after independence, the bulk of the country's population live in the rural areas. Agriculture and its allied activities still provide employment and income to a substantial segment of the rural work force. During the post-independent period, rural India had absorbed the impact of institutional, structural and technological improvements leading to multi-faceted transformations and changes.

Singh (1988:187) stated that 'institutional changes introduced through land reforms, community development programmes, panchayat elections and national elections have considerably changed the structure of community cohesion and its pattern of inter-group relationship and power structure. But none of these factors has completely eroded the sense of village identity nor do they portend to do so in future. Since independence, many government-sponsored schemes of development and reform have been introduced having the village as a unit of administration and communication of change-producing values and techniques. The significance of village as a social micro-cosm has thereby been further reinforced.'

In traditional India there were continual instances of change without implying modernization, (ibid:192) and the changes were initiated both through orthogenetic and heterogenetic causal sources, and related to social structure as well as culture, but these were essentially pre-modern in nature and quality (ibid:192). Before the western influence permeated the traditional Indian society, many changes had already been introduced through orthogenetic sources such as Buddhism, Jainism, Sikhism and so on leading to differentiation within the traditional framework of traditional social structure and values. The Islamic tradition came from a heterogenetic source the establishment of which was by conquest. Endogenous changes in the cultural tradition of Hinduism were mainly confined to Sanskritisation before the beginning of Western contact (ibid:194). Srinivas (1972:6) defined sanskritisation as the 'process by which a "low" Hindu caste, or tribal or group, changes its customs, ritual, ideology, and way of life in the direction of a high and frequently, "twice-born" caste'. However he pointed out that the sanskritisation results only in *positional* changes in the system and does not lead to any *structural* changes. The traditional caste system remains stable and the system itself does not change. Exogenous changes were mainly brought with the Western contact through the establishment of the British rule. Singh stated that 'this contact had a special historicity which brought about many far reaching changes in culture and social structure of the Indian society. Not all of them, however, could be called modernizing. The basic direction of this contact was towards modernization, but in the process a variety of traditional institutions also got reinforcement.' (op.cit.:202). Mandelbaum (1974:464) stated that the village society was not static under the colonial regime; there were some systemic adjustments, but generally villagers tended to assimilate the main innovations in government, technology, and communication into the established pattern of *jati* relations. British culture was too alien from the village world to provide a new reference category and British society in India was far too isolated and aloof from village life to yield a new reference group for mobility. Eisenstadt (1973:287) noted that 'the reactions of Indian civilization, of the major social and cultural groups in India, to these various changes were throughout history characterised by a relatively great variety of responses with what we have called the "adaptive" response the most predominant.' He wrote that despite the heterogeneity of Indian society there was continuity of identity and postulated that 'the root of the explanation of this paradox of continuity of cultural identity in the face of great heterogeneity or variety, as well as of the predominance of the adaptive response in situations of change in the very central core of Indian tradition, can be found, first, in he structure of centers of Indian society and civilization, and second, in some of the major aspects of the contents of the Indian value system and of its structural repercussions – that is, in the nature of the Brahminic value system and especially of the structure of the caste system.' This was so because 'the basic religious and cultural orientations were not necessarily tied to any particular political or Imperial framework, and the cultural identity of Indian civilization was not bound to any given political framework.' (ibid:288) Eisenstadt explained this by saying that the caste system was not organized as a homogenous, unified center as it constituted of a series of networks and many organizational-ritual sub-centers in the form of temples, sects and so forth. On the other hand, the various political centers although themselves organizationally more compact, were not continuous, nor did they serve as major foci of Indian cultural identity. He further elaborated by stating that 'parallel to the relative independence of the cultural traditions from the political center (*sic*), the complex of castes, the villages, and the various networks of cultural communication were also to a very high degree autonomous and self-regulating in terms of their own cultural and social identity, with but limited recourse to the political center or centers (*sic*).' (ibid:288).

The continuity of cultural and social identity is exemplified best by the Indian village, inspite of the tremendous external changes that were impinged on its internal arrangements; as a territorial unit, it has endured and continues to be most important point of reference for individual prestige and identification. The vast literature on the Indian village gives credence to this assertion and 'the Indian villages as a micro-structure has thus not only been recognised, but has gradually become a vital aspect of national developmental planning and politico-consciousness' (Singh:op.cit:184). In the light of this we may say the villages of India are subsystems within greater systems and serves as the focal point of individual identification within a greater field. The villages of India were never isolates nor were they static. Although changes from various sources were introduced, incorporated and diffused into the traditional social structure, such changes did not diminish the importance and necessity of villages for the people. The simple reason being that from the village stemmed the roots of one's cultural background and most importantly one's identity.

The Naga villages may be discussed as a distinct universe of social arrangements significantly different from other Indian villages because the Naga villages are wholly tribal and they differ vastly in social, cultural and politico-jural institutions. The Nagas as a whole do not form one homogenous tribe but comprises of fifteen major tribes each with its own territory, language and identity. Each Naga village has their own local customary laws and traditions and its internal affairs are managed internally. Smith (1980:179) stated that 'the Ao Nagas, as well as the other Naga tribes, made very few changes during their long residence in these hills. Their non-migratory ways and their head-hunting habits kept them insulated from all other influences...' However with the establishment of British colonial administration and rule from 1866, when a new district in the Naga Hills with its headquarters at Samaguting was established, changes were brought about especially in 'improved methods of travel and communication and the development of commerce which have annihilated distances and the world has grown smaller...' (ibid:179). Under British control headhunting was abolished and this had an impact on the agricultural sector, mainly jhum cultivation, as the men could go farther from the villages to grow crops in safety, thus improving the economic condition. The construction of bridle paths through the Naga territories also improved conditions of travel and inter- connections between villages and free access to the markets in the Brahmaputra valley was also opened.

The introduction of Christianity (1872) and in its wake, education, proved to be the most important and influential instrument of change for the Nagas in general and the Ao in particular. Education opened new vistas of opportunities for the Nagas like employment as teachers, pastors and low-level administrative clerks in the district offices. People began to migrate to newly established towns and a new elite emerged. The changes brought about were exogenous, mostly through imposition of new ideas and new set of rules and regulations. From a pre-literate society the Naga society became a 'modern' society, the changes being sudden and rather drastic. The social, psychological and ideological changes in Naga culture were manifested in myriad ways but they also influenced in the formation and crystallization of cultural identity. The British policy of not interfering in the internal affairs of the villages under their control and their utilization of the prevailing local systems albeit with certain modifications, as well as giving the tribes a nomenclature - Naga – and popularizing it to identify the various tribes in Nagaland, contributed in the formation of a united cultural identity among the Nagas. The British introduced the *Dobashi* (interpreters) and *Gaon Bura* (village headmen/elders) institutions but these were meant mostly to facilitate the British administrators in maintaining law and order and in collection of household taxes. The traditional village government 'still acted as a tribunal for the adjucation of petty cases, and the district officers intervened only in cases which the village authorities could not settle at their level of administration...'...'furthermore the British introduced the Innerline Regulation in 1873 and with this 'the possible socio-economic exploitation of the Nagas by the plains people was effectively warded off" and 'on the whole the colonial administrative policy of keeping Naga Hills isolated benefited the Nagas in so far as it helped to preserve and promote Naga identity...' and ... 'Nagas maintained an exclusive socio-political entity in a classical colonial situation.' (Sema, 1992:54-56).

Nagaland became the sixteenth state of the Indian Union in 1963 and under the Constitution of India, provisions for safeguarding social and religious practices, customary justice and landed property of the Nagas were included in Article 371 A (1). This Act states that the processes of dispensing justice, administration of the villages and land ownership and transfer will be according to the Naga customary laws. In effect the customary laws are recognised as legal and binding. Only the State Legislative Assembly can amend the Act. Thus the Naga people were protected and their traditional village governments according to customary usages remained intact.

Many books have been written about the Nagas in general and about particular tribes, but single village studies are few, the most notable among them being Das' study of the Zounou-Keyhonou (Angami tribe) living in Viswema village in Kohima district (1993). Another study is by Sanyu (1996) of two Angami villages: Kohima and Khonoma. With regard to the Ao tribe apart from monographs written by Mills (1926), Smith (1925) and Majumdar (1926); and except for a village survey by Roy Burman on Waromong village, an Ao village in the Changkikong range under Mokokchung district as part of the Census Monograph series (1961), single village studies have not been carried out.

In the preface to the first edition of *The Angami Nagas* (1921) Hutton cites Mr. S.E. Peal who in his book "Fading Histories" lamented the delay in the study of the eastern Naga tribes, and the consequent loss of much material out of which their past histories might have been recovered, pointing out the remarkable rapidity with which the Nagas were changing and had already changed. Hutton reiterated this by stating that the changes taking place among the western Nagas such as the Angami, Lotha, Ao and so on was even more rapid. He wrote that 'it is barely forty years since Captain Butler wrote, but many customs of the Angami at war which he records are almost entirely forgotten by the sons of those from whom he learnt them.' (Hutton:1969). If in the early part of the twentieth century changes had already taken place among the Nagas, the changes over almost a century after would be overwhelming. Despite the changes it is also important to take cognizance of the fact that continuities exist and this study aims to highlight this factor – that is, although changes have been pervasive in the traditional village society, there are continuities of institutions and traditions that binds the village society and contributes to its survival. The importance that Nagas attach to their village is still very relevant, for it is from the village that the Nagas get their identity and their cultural roots stem from the village.

Review of Literature

The Indian village has been a subject of intense study for a very long time. The first account of the Indian village appeared in the *Fifth Report from the Select Committee on the Affairs of the East Indian Company (1812),* authored by Munro, whose authorship was traced by Dumont. The study of Indian villages began with the intensive survey work conducted by the British administration for the collection of revenue and the data collected have been valuable sources of information of that period.

Among the social scientists, economists first undertook the village studies. In the early 20th century, the efforts of the economists' surveys of individual villages have been of significant importance as it was based on first hand empirical investigations. However the drawback of such investigations was that although the economic life of the villages was given in detail, the socio-economic and cultural relationships of the villages were not examined.

Among the early anthropological studies, the work of American missionary Wiser based on intensive field work gave some insights into village life and his works are considered important in the sense that these were the first studies of village life in the Anthropological tradition.

The idea that the Indian village was a monolithic, atomistic and unchanging entity as was reported by Metcalfe, one of the founding administrators of British colonial rule stated that 'the village communities are little republics having nearly everything that they want within themselves and almost independent of any foreign relations.' (*quoted in* Mandelbaum:1972,327). Maine (1974, reprint) depicted the

Indian village communities as having communal land ownership, where the 'village community' known for its immense antiquity and great stability comprised of a group of people connected by common descent owning the land in common or collectively which was perfect' and where the 'clearest signs of an original proprietary equality between all the families composing the group' (1974,reprint: 125) was shown. The village council was viewed as a representative body and not as an inherently authoritarian body. He viewed the Indian village-community as an 'organised and self acting' 'brotherhood' where there was political and economic self sufficiency, completely removed from outside influence and interference. He also stated that the village-community 'include a nearly complete establishment of occupations and trades for enabling them to continue their collective life without assistance from any person or body external to them.' (1974, reprint: 123)

But later empirical studies especially in the fifties on village communities not only refuted and questioned such views but also proved that most Indian villages have ties of an extensive nature and rectified the myth that the Indian village was a self-sufficient isolated unit. Marriage affiliations, the jajmani system and the caste system are some of the important ties. Srinivas (op.cit.:60) rebutted the idea that the Indian village was self-sufficient for economically, socially and religiously the villages were anything but independent and self-contained. 'Even a basic commodity like salt was not produced by most villages. Iron, indispensable for ploughs and other agricultural implements, was not available everywhere, and iron smelting was a localized industry.' Even the essential artisan and servicing castes were not found in every village. He concluded that 'caste ties stretch across villages and in a great part of northern India the concept of village exogamy, and the existence of hypergamy on a village basis, constitute an advertisement for inter-village interdependence. The partiality of peasants for pilgrimages and fairs also highlights the fact that the Indian village was always a part of a wider network.' (ibid:63)

Mandelbaum (op.cit.:327) also stated that no *jati* stands alone. 'Its people necessarily cooperate with some people of other *jatis*; commonly they compete with still others. The main locale of this cooperation and competition is the village. The groups involved are primarily the families and *jati* groups of the same village and its vicinity; rather than whole *jatis* of a region. To a villager then, his village is far more than just a collection of houses, lanes and fields; it is a prime social reality.' He regarded the village as an important and viable social entity, which is 'not a neatly separable social and conceptual package but it is nonetheless a fundamental social unit.' (ibid:329)

Mandelbaum focused on the roles, groups and systems of village society and the rules of the social game and considered these important in the study of villages for a better understanding of the whole system enabling us to get a better idea of the Indian village. 'The village, in sum, is a basic feature of civilisation and continues to be a viable community for its inhabitants. A person's village provides him with one source of his self-identification, with a nexus of his activities, a stage for his status, and an area of conflict. Observers can view it as a system comprising component *jati* groups and functional activities, and also as a subsystem of larger social systems.' (ibid:421)

Desai (1961) also reiterated that civilisation began with the development of agriculture and the village became the first settled form of human habitation. The growth and development of the village according to him was the outcome of development of agriculture: 'the rise of the village is bound up with the rise of agricultural economy in history. The emergence of the village signified that man passed from the nomadic mode of collective life to that of the settled one. This was basically due to the improvement of tools of production which made agriculture and hence settled life in a fixed territorial zone possible and necessary' (Desai,1961:13).

Dube (1967:5) stated that 'no village in India is completely autonomous and independent, for it is always one unit in a wider social system and is a part of an organized political society. Dube described the Indian village in terms of its features: ' i) as a territorial, as well as social, economic and ritual unit, the village is a separate and distinct entity. The residents of this settlement recognize their corporate identity, and it is recognized as such by others; ii) These settlements have a composite population comprising a number of groups belonging to different Hindu castes, and in some cases to tribes as well as to other religious groups; iii) The members of this local group are bound together by ties of mutual and reciprocal obligations. Interpersonal and inter-group relations in several spheres of village affairs are governed by established usage and social ethics.' (1967:7-8)

Dube argued that the village settlement, as a unit of social organization, represented a solidarity different from that of the kin, caste, and the class, and played a vital role as an agency of socialization and social control. He also stated that each village was a distinct entity having individual mores and usages and thus possesses a corporate unity. Mutual and reciprocal obligations sanctioned by the caste system also integrate economic, social and ritual patterns within the village. Thus he viewed the village as a corporate entity, which represented a solidarity, characterised by economic, social and ritual co-operation existing between different castes.

However Dube also pointed out that the Indian village does not have a similar pattern all over the country. The ethnic and linguistic composition of a village, as well as its caste constitution, also determines its character. Dube classified the villages into distinguishable types based on i) size, population, ii) ethnic composition and caste constitution, iii) pattern of land ownership, iv) structure of authority and power hierarchy, v) degree of isolation and vi) local traditions. He felt that classifying the villages on these criteria would give a better understanding of their social structure.

About the tribal village Dube pointed out 'the structure, ethos and problems of a wholly tribal village will be very different from those of a village with a mixed or homogeneous population. A tribal village is often unitary in respect of its authority structure, the tribal authority, itself being supreme in secular, ritual and cultural village matters' (Dube, op.cit.:4).

According to Srinivas 'each village has a pattern and mode of life, which is to some extent unique. Villages next door to each other differ considerably and this fact is recognized by the rural folk'.(Srinivas, ed, 1969:2). He made a distinction between two types of village: the nucleated village and the dispersed village. The nucleated village is one where the houses and huts are huddled in the middle with the farmland surrounding it, while the dispersed village is one where the house or hut is surrounded by the farmland and is independent of the other houses and huts. The organisation of the two types of village was based on defence. In the nucleated village the defence against wild animals and dacoits lay with all the people of the village, while in the dispersed village, the responsibility lay with the kin groups and servants.

In the essay *The Social Structure of a Mysore village,* Srinivas defined the village of Rampura as 'an interdependent unit, largely self-sufficient, having its own village assembly, watch and ward, officials and servants. Inside each village each caste lives its own life, though it is dependent on other castes within and without the village' (quoted in Mandelbaum, op.cit.329). The Indian village was thus viewed as a vertical entity made up of several horizontal layers, each of which was a caste.

McKim Marriott (1955 ed) conveys a general impression of great variety within prevailing similarity. Attention is drawn to the rapid changes taking place and the inter-relation of an Indian village with the larger society and with the civilization of which it is a small and focal part. In his study of Kishan Garhi Marriott (1955:191) stated that 'viewed from the perspective of Kishan Garhi, the village which are the little communities of India today may be conceived as relative structural nexuses, as subsystems within greater systems, and as foci of individual identification within a greater field.' He went on to say that the villages cannot be conceived as entities in themselves in their organisation of marriage and kinship, residence patterns, modes of conflict, or caste organisation. India's villages were never isolates and the greater community of India cannot be understood apart from the continuing existence of the little communities. Both little communities and greater communities are mutually necessary conditions of each other's existence in their present forms. One must consider both in order thoroughly to understand each other.

The various empirical studies show that marriage affiliations, the *jajmani* system and the caste system are some of the important ties that link a village to a wider social sphere. Marriage affiliations were made commonly between families of different villages thus setting a lifelong relationship between the villagers. The inter dependence of the villages was reflected on the fact that resident specialists were not found in a single village and in this context, specialists and skilled workers go from village to village for work and trade. In examining Senapur, near Benares, Opler (quoted in Mandelbaum, op.cit:329) wrote that the articulations of Senapur people with other communities and far-flung places are 'not a recent development or a consequence of modern systems of communication or transportation. They rest on ancient practices and patterns.' Each village is connected through a variety of crucial horizontal linkages with other villages and with urban areas both near and far.

Even if it is true that the Indian village is not a 'little republic', yet it is an important and viable social entity. Village even today exists as a territorial cohesive unit. 'Village identity, solidarity and loyalty cut across caste and community, but divisive factors also exist simultaneously. Land reforms, changes in power structure and social and cultural mobility could be witnessed within a given village as well as village of a given area in terms of new form of stratificational relations' (Sharma, 1985:18)

Beteille (1996:237) in his study of Sripuram sought to systematically describe the different dimensions of social stratification in the community, to examine the relations among them and to explore the changes taking place in those relations. For Beteille, the physical structure of a village reflected its social structure so much so that the distribution of population in the village in territorial divisions depicted characteristics of similarities and differentiation in structural terms. The contradictions and conflicts inherent in the Indian village is given a wider meaning by examining the interrelations of the three principle dimensions of social stratification – caste, class and power – in the context of change. Social mobility, economic change, and political modernization lead to the creation not only of new relations, but also of new values, new attitudes and new aspirations. The simple traditional structure was thus open to changes due to external forces, which brought about new articulations in the social, political and economic spheres.

The various village studies have focused on the internal structure and dynamics of inter-relationships of the population within the village. These studies show that the village in general has been analyzed in terms of the unity of the village and different types of solidarity other than that of caste. Caste stresses on the ties between members of the same caste scattered in different villages (horizontal solidarity), whereas the village stresses on the ties of the different castes living in the same village (vertical solidarity). The extension of the village into the outside world and the inter- penetration of the wider world into the village (e.g., through the market forces); kinship networks; affinal ties; and the changes that have been brought about in the village due to external forces and hence the changes in traditional inter- relationships in the community.

The term 'village' as defined in the Census reports shows that the villages have clearly demarcated boundaries that are distinct social entities having administrative functionaries and recognised as a 'village' not only by the inhabitants themselves but also by others.

With regard to Nagaland the village is defined in the *Nagaland Code Volume III*, under the chapter on The Nagaland Village and Area Councils Act, which extends to the whole of Nagaland, in the following:

'Village means and includes an area recognised as a village as such by the Government of Nagaland. An area in order to be a Village under the Act shall fulfil the following conditions namely:

a) The land in the area belong to the population of that area or given to them by the Government of Nagaland, if the land in question is a Government land or is given to them by the lawful owner of the land; and

b) The Village is established according to the usage and customary practice of the population of the area.'(Government of Nagaland, 1971:61)

Under this provision the villages in Nagaland have ownership of the land as well as land transfer rights. The establishment of the village as well as the administrative set up according to the usage of customary practices is recognised by the Government of Nagaland. The land ownership and customary practices of Naga villages are protected and safeguarded under this provision.

The village as defined in the Nagaland Village and Area Councils Act has been accepted as the general definition of Naga village for it has never been amended. This could be interpreted to mean that it provides the prerequisites for protecting and safeguarding the traditional village in its entirety and is therefore accepted by all sections of Naga society.

Under the Constitution of India, provisions for safeguarding social and religious practices, customary justice and landed property of the Nagas are included in Article 371 A (1). This article deals with the special provisions with respect to the state of Nagaland. The religious, social, customary laws and procedure, administration of civil and criminal justice involving decisions according to Naga customary law and ownership and transfer of land and its resources of the Nagas are protected under this article.

In the villages in present day Nagaland, we find that physically they are invariably built either on the summit of a hill, on a high saddle, or perhaps more frequently on the ridge of some spur running down from a high range. The village sites were selected mainly for defence purposes as the Nagas practiced headhunting in the olden days. The village sites were positioned in a location that made them highly defensible, if not impregnable from the point of view of Naga warfare.

Naga village have been regarded as a 'village- state' for they are independent of external forces and within its own jurisdiction every village was autonomous and free from any outside interference making each village distinctly different from the other. Ganguli (1984:99) asserted that 'every village is an independent, self-contained administrative unit.' Without exception, none of the Naga villages recognised the authority of another village when it came to internal matters.

The Ao Naga villages are independent administrative units which function according to customary laws and traditions. The Ao villages are independent of outside forces and the village administration and the maintenance of law and order is taken at the clan and Village Council level.

A typical Ao village is characterized by: (i) multi- clan population, (ii) the Village Council, (iii) the age set grades, and (iv) the khels.

The villages are organized on two main principles. The whole village is divided into age-set grades to which various communal duties are assigned. Secondly the control of village affairs lies with the Village Council, represented by elders of the respective clans residing in the village, the tenure of which varies from village to village, or represented by the age-set grades, the tenure of which is fixed. The Ao have two dialects; Mongsen and Chungli, based on which local traditions and customary laws have been formulated. Among the Mongsen speaking villages, the village government is called *Samen Menchen* (literally- meat share rule) and among the Chungli speaking villages, the village government is called *Putu Menden* (literally- generation rule). The tenure of these two types of local traditional government is not fixed as each village follows its own system of village rule. The local village government based on age-set system is called *Yanga Menchen* (age-set rule) and the tenure is fixed.

A review of literature with regard to the Ao Nagas of Nagaland might be useful to understand the Ao village and to help define the Ao village. The review reveals that three major monographs on the Ao have been written; namely *The Ao Nagas* by James Phillip Mills (1926), *The Ao Naga Tribe of Assam* by William C. Smith (1927) and *Ao Nagas* by Surendra Nath Majumdar (1926). While Mills was a British administrator, Majumdar was an Indian doctor and Smith an American Sociologist. Along with these three, a few other authors are also reviewed.

Smith, an American sociologist and missionary, wrote a detailed comparative study of the Ao tribe. He traced the similar characteristics of the Aos with the Dyaks of Borneo and Igorots of the Philippines such as (1) headhunting; (2) common sleeping-houses for the unmarried men, which are taboo to women; (3) dwelling-houses built on posts or piles; (4) disposal of dead on raised platforms; (5) a sort of trial marriage or great freedom of intercourse between the sexes before marriage; (6) betel chewing; (7) aversion to milk as an article of diet; (8) tattooing by pricking; (9) absence of any powerful political organisation; (10) the double –cylinder vertical forge (double barreled air-forcing pump); (11) the simple loom for weaving cloth; (12) a large quadrangular or hexagonal shield; (13) residence in hilly regions and a crude form of agriculture. He traced the immigration of the Aos based on these facts and the process of acculturation that the Aos presented then.

Smith stated that 'among the Aos there is no tribal organization of any kind, although the geographic boundaries of the tribe are rather distinctly marked. It is difficult to find any unifying principle on which the tribe might be said to depend; yet it is not difficult to recognize people not of their fold.'(1980, reprint:52) He goes on to say that the physical appearance, language and customs are markedly different from the other Naga tribes and observes that the 'Aos believe they have a common origin, and this feeling of kinship tends to hold them together. So far as the tribe is concerned they hold fairly well to the rules of endogamy' (1980, reprint:53).

About the Ao village, Smith wrote that 'in the land of the Ao Nagas the villages are some distance apart and are always entirely distinct. The Ao Naga villages are large. Intense love for the ancestral village site seems to be a characteristic of the people, which keeps the villages from breaking up easily.' He says that among the Ao the largest unit is the village, and that is bound together by social, political and religious ties. Theoretically the village acts as a unit in all things, and if anybody fails to attend a village function he is punished. Thus in these small homogeneous communities there is but little room for any individualistic tendencies. It was mandatory for every man to contribute their quota of work for clearing the village paths to the rice fields and water reservoirs and to attend the religious festivals and to observe the *gennas* (taboos).

For convenience of administration the villages were divided into khels and each khel had an *ariju* or male dormitory and every man belonging to the khel was responsible for the building, upkeep and repairing of the *ariju* as well as other duties which would be too unwieldy for the whole village. Smith observed that in matters of the duties towards the village and khel the individual will was subservient to the good of the entire group. But in many things it seemed that the individual was more important than the village. He further elaborates by saying that the 'Ao villages are very democratic and one man is as good as another'. Although the headmen had some influence they did not have any authority. He noted that 'in a Naga village the will of the majority is not binding upon the minority.' But if 'something was all wrapped up in tradition and supported by magic,' there was no difficulty in compelling the individual to yield to the village.

James Phillip Mills, who served as the Sub Divisional Officer at the Sub Divisional Headquarters at Mokokchung from 1917 to 1924 with a break of one year's leave, wrote a detailed monograph *The Ao Nagas* published in 1926. This book gives a comprehensive account of the habitat and affinities of the tribe, their dress, ornaments and appearance, their villages, agricultural practices, methods of production and the technology of crude tools; their religious and social customs and ceremonies are also described in detail. 'As with all Nagas the real political unit of the tribe is the village. For most purposes however, the social unit is the khel'. The khels have separate administrative councils which oversee all matters pertaining to the khel but in trans-khel matters the village acts as a united entity. The villages are highly organised units in which everyman shoulders his burden of service and responsibility.

To the Aos the village is the most important aspect of his life; the cultural heritage is derived from the village and the village is where his roots are found and therefore his identity. The attachment to the village of birth is indeed very strong as Mills observed, 'it is very rarely that an Ao does not stick to the village where his ancestors lived before him. An immigrant finds he has little status in his new home.' To an Ao the village of birth gives him not only an identity but also a place in society. The newcomer thus finds that he is not included in the age-set grades for he did not enter the age-set system of the village along with others of his age; therefore he cannot do any community work assigned on the basis of the age-set grades, thus he is excluded from community related activities. In the village council too he has no standing and certainly no meat shares will be given to him. Clearly then, it is the village that gives an Ao his identity and sense of belonging, without which he is nothing. Thus the Ao villages do not break up easily as Smith observed for the villagers do not leave their birth place permanently.

Surendra Nath Majumdar who served as a medical officer in charge in Mokokchung wrote a short monograph on the Ao Nagas, which gives a faithful but sketchy account of the life, habits, customs and institutions of the Ao. While his work might not have generated as much academic interest as did Mills and Smith's works, it is the first monograph written by an Indian on the Ao Nagas.

About the Ao village Majumdar wrote, 'every Ao village is a well barricaded fortress.' He writes that 'every Naga village is divided into several khels or localities, and the young men of every khel have their *morung* (male dormitory), where they commence spending the night from the age of ten or twelve.'

Majumdar's work does not give much insight as to the sociological or anthropological implications of what he describes but it is of general interest, particularly since it is a first hand account of an Indian doctor, written in the early twentieth century. Apart from these three monographs some of the other studies on the Ao Nagas are as follows.

A case study of an Ao village was done on Waromung village, situated in the Changkikong range, under Mokokchung district by Roy-Burman published in the Census of India 1961, monograph series. A description of the village, its social and political organisation, food habits, agricultural practices, patterns of land ownership, religious and social customs and so on are given in detail and analysed. About the village, Roy Burman wrote that 'the village is no longer an isolated corner of humanity, that it was a few decades ago.' The improvement in the means of communication, spread of education, advent of Christianity and so on brought about far reaching changes and development in the village and connected the village to a wider network with the outside world. However, despite all these changes Roy Burman says that some aspects of the village remained intact such as the traditional Village Council, the clan organisation and age-set system, which constitute the core of Ao social structure.

Another essay on the Ao Naga is by Bhowmik (1971). A general description of the habitat, people, their customs, social and political organisation, agricultural practices, community activities, kinship and marriage and so on are given.

Ao (1980), an advocate, wrote in detail the customary laws that govern the Ao people. The customary laws are unwritten and have been passed down since time immemorial through the oral tradition. Ao wrote that the Ao village is a highly organized unit in which every man of the village renders his service for his village and welfare of his village.

For the Ao living in the village, his contribution towards the community is mandatory for without cooperation with fellow villagers his own survival comes into question. In the democratic system of government there is a council formed by representatives of clans. The participation of the people in the village government is reflected through the representatives who are the elder members of the clans. The representatives are jointly responsible for executive and judicial actions of the government but they have no inherent power for making laws. It rests on the direct participation of the people.

The political organisation of the Ao rests with the respective Village Council with a Council Chairman presiding and although the powers and authority of the Village Council and the Council Chairman is not binding, but the people usually abide by its ruling for such ruling is based on customary law for which the people have the greatest respect. Such time-honoured customary law is not issued by a ruler or by a ruling body but is part of the culture of the people and thus such law brings a measure of order and stability to the society.

Imchen (1993) wrote about the Ao Naga culture and religion, social organisation, customary laws and procedures, economy, land relation, institutions and the system of social control. In this book Imchen discussed the socio-political beliefs and practices of the Ao Nagas before the advent of Christianity, the arrival of Christianity and its impact on the Ao religion, the culture and society.

Describing the ancient Ao village, Imchen wrote that 'the ancient Ao village was thus a sovereign state, capable of internal administration and external diplomatic relations and welfare with a pure form of democracy where every citizen enjoyed his freedom of speech and was respected.' Imchen reiterated that customary law regulated individual and societal behaviour and as the social, political and religious life of the Ao was bound by customary law the activities of every man revolved around this value system which is community related.

Jamir (1997) wrote in detail the emergence and social evolution of the Aos, their learning institutions, laws, customs and rites and the traditional organisation of the Aos. He also compiled the Ao poetry and songs, which he had learned through the oral tradition.

From the literature reviewed on the Ao Naga tribe, we can see that village as an entity and the internal structure and the dynamics of the relationships within the village gave the people a distinct identity and sense of belonging. The traditional and customary way of village self-rule has also ensured a well-defined and independent village society. The autonomy of the village within its own jurisdiction is jealously guarded and the customary law enforces and ensures that it maintains the status quo.

It is interesting to note that customary law intrinsically binds up the Ao villages. The value system of the people revolves around the customary law, which has been handed down the ages through the oral tradition. Each village follows its own system of governance and social organisation based on such law and this makes the Ao village autonomous. The Ao villages are composed of multiple clans, which ensure that clan exogamy is enforced.

An Ao village may be defined as having a distinct and well demarcated territory made up of khels, jhum lands, reserve forests, cultivable lands, and rivers and so on characterised by a simple agrarian technology. The Ao village is single-tribe and has its own indigenous political and social systems. The village administration and organisation is based on customary laws independent of outside influences or forces and the population is composed of various exogamous clans.

In the Ao society, the village is considered as the most important entity in the lives of the Ao people. If membership of a clan provides an Ao his identity, the village provides him another source of identity particularly vis-à-vis members of other villages. The customary laws and usages as well as the oral tradition are the repository of Ao history.

Objectives of the study

Keeping the above discussion in mind an empirical study of Changki village in the Ao Naga territory was carried out in order to understand its structure. Changki was chosen for the simple reason that as such no studies have been carried out in this village although Changki is well known for its high literacy rate and its people have been pioneers in various fields such as in the administrative and academic fields as well as in sports and politics in Nagaland. Another motivation was that the traditions and cultural traits of Changki village are fast being forgotten and as no records are available of such, it was felt that whatever has been preserved and is being practised, need to be recorded and hence this study is a humble endeavor in that direction. This study attempts to highlight the village as the most important entity in the lives of the people and to show the continuity of traditions through various institutions as found in the village despite the forces of changes.

The present study was designed as an exploratory and descriptive one. The focus is on the system of institutions and the functional interdependence between different aspects of life which gives rise to the multifaceted interrelationship among the institutions: kinship and marriage, political, economic and religious.

Methodology

The methodology adopted in this study was primarily empirical and it was based on primary sources of data. As there are practically no records or documents on Changki, the interview guide technique was used to collect information as the people's sense of history, perception and understanding are of great value for such a study. The primary data were collected from the village elders from whom information regarding kinship and marriage was gathered. The Village Council Chairman and council members, Gaon Buras as well as ex-Gaon Buras provided the information on the political aspects of the village. The Pastor, associate Pastor (women), Youth Director, Child Director and other church workers supplied the information on religion and the functions and activities of the church. The findings on the economy of the village as well as on kinship and marriage were collected from village elders and residents of the village. The demographic and general information on the village were collected from the VDB (Village Development board) list, school enrolment lists, church registers, clan registers and informal interviews with a cross section of the village people. The non-participant observation method supplemented by interviews with a cross section of the village people were utilised to collect the data.

Field Work

The study was conducted intermittently over a course of almost three years from 2001 - 2004. The researcher found that the knowledge and information with regard to the tradition and culture of Changki village is confined to a handful of old people. With the advent of Christianity and education many Changki people abandoned the traditional aspects of life such as celebrations of traditional festivals, observances of '*genna*' (taboos), the giving of feasts of merit, the art of story telling through the oral tradition and of songs; in fact since Christianity first took root in 1901, in the hundred intervening years, so much has been lost that is traditional and essentially the cultural fabric of the village. On the other hand the traditional aspect of village governance and the acceptance and application of customary laws as also the importance of clan and kinship makes an interesting contrast. This will be further illustrated in the body of the book.

The researcher having been brought up in Shillong, did not have much contact with her own people and being a casual visitor to her own village, she had the advantage of having a degree of objectivity while studying her own people. It did help though that the researcher knew the language and both parents being Changki she was accepted and did not have to establish her credentials.

The oral tradition has been the only source of knowledge handed down from generation to generation but this has often led to disputes, the outcome being heavy fines imposed when such disputes arises. This is particularly true with regard to the foundation of the village and the history of the clans. One of the respondents who had written the story of the village foundation and had given me the documents that he had painstakingly written was summoned by his clan and roundly chastised. This came about because being mindful of how sensitive the people are with regard to such matters, the researcher sought clarification on the authenticity of the story and also since it was written in the Chungli Ao dialect and not being proficient in the Ao dialect, the researcher had to get someone to translate. It was found that some of the stories with regard to other clans were not accurate and so a formal complaint was lodged with his clan. He was summoned by his clan elders and asked for an explanation as to how he could touch upon the stories of other clans without their consent and since the other clans viewed the case seriously, his clansmen not wanting to make it into an inter-clan issue gave him a stern warning and confiscated the documents. The major problem the researcher faced in the field was that the people were wary about giving information particularly about the origin of the clans and so on, the reason given for this was that such stories are handed down to the males only. However it was also found in the course of the field work, the people themselves were rather vague about the origin of the clans. The Oral tradition was the only source of information but when the people embraced Christianity such practices were rejected and so much of the information died out with the old people who were the repositories of history, information and traditional knowledge.

In the course of the fieldwork the researcher was fortunate to get the cooperation, help and hospitality of the villagers. The villagers were at first puzzled by the researchers frequent visits; and was mistaken for a photographer and member of the census team, but when it was explained as to the nature of the work, the people gave all the encouragement and assistance and acceptance into their fold. However there were certain areas that the researcher could not gain access to such as the Village Council meetings and the clan meetings. Changki society is patriarchal and women have no right to be represented or even to be present in such meetings. However, on the visit to the field in January, 2004, after almost three years of frequent visits to the village, the researcher was granted permission to take photographs of the *Samen Menchen* of one of their informal discussions at Alingtemen, which is the community hall for small gatherings.

2

LAND AND PEOPLE

Nagaland became the sixteenth state of India in 1963. It is situated in Northeast India and lies between $25^0 60'$ and $27^0 40'$ latitude north of the equator and between the longitudinal lines $93^0 20'$E and $95^0 15'$E, with an area covering 16,579 sq. km. It is bounded by Assam in the North and West, by Myanmar and Arunachal Pradesh in the East and Manipur in the South and runs more or less parallel to the left bank of the Brahmaputra (Statistical Handbook of Nagaland, 2003:2).

Nagaland comprises a part of the hill ranges, which separate the basins of three major rivers – the Brahmaputra, the Chindwin and the Barak. There are 1,278 inhabited villages in Nagaland. About 150 of these are located in the foothills, along the state's boundary with Assam in the west. The remaining villages are located on the top of ridges or on slopes, at latitudes of 500 to 2,500 metres above sea level. Nagaland has a total land area of 1,657,900 hectares of which about 1,450,000 is owned by the people in the villages (Gokhale, 1995:151-152). There are at present eleven districts in the state namely, Kohima, Mokokchung, Wokha, Zunheboto, Phek, Tuensang, Mon, Dimapur, Longleng, Kiphiri and Peren. However the last three districts were upgraded only in 2003 and the data shown in Tables I and 2 does not reflect the data for these three districts.

The population of Nagaland is almost entirely tribal. There are fifteen recognised major tribes in Nagaland each occupying a distinct area. These major tribes are the following:

1. Angami
2. Ao
3. Lotha
4. Sema
5. Konyak
6. Chakhesang
7. Sangtam
8. Chang
9. Khiemungam
10. Yimchunger
11. Phom
12. Zeliang
13. Rengma
14. Pochury
15. Kuki

Each tribe is distinguished by its language, traditions and customs. A tribe consists of sub-divisions called clans, which are strictly exogamous. The Angami, Zeliang, Rengma and some other minor tribes inhabit Kohima district. Phek district is the home of the Chakhesang and Pochury tribes. Mokokchung district is inhabited by the Ao tribe, Wokha district by the Lotha tribe and Zunheboto district by the Sema tribe. Tuensang district is the home of the Chang, Sangtam, Khiemungam and Yimchunger, Longleng district is inhabited by the Phom and some minor tribes, while Mon district is the home of the Konyak tribe.

The Naga society is traditionally agrarian and rice is the main agricultural crop. There are four rice farming systems practiced namely: jhum cultivation, rain fed terrace rice cultivation, wet rice cultivation and alder based jhum system. Jhum cultivation is most widely practiced due to the topography of the land.

The state of Nagaland, which was inaugurated on 1st December 1963, does not have any appreciable industry or manufacturing activity in the state. The state government has been the main employer and it is only recently that the unemployed youths are venturing into private businesses and enterprises.

Table I shows the district wise distribution of area, population and density of Nagaland. The total population of Nagaland is 19, 88,636 with a decennial growth of 64.41 per cent between 1991 – 2001. The female-male ratio is 909:1000 and the density per sq. km is 120 persons (Census 2001)

Table 1
District Wise Area/Population/Density of Nagaland

Sl. No	State/ District	Area in sq. km	Population	Density per sq. km
1	Nagaland	16579	1988636	120
2	Mon	1786	259604	145
3	Tuensang	4228	414801	98
4	Mokokchung	1615	227230	141
5	Zunheboto	1255	154909	123
6	Wokha	1628	161098	99
7	Dimapur	927	308382	333
8	Kohima	3114	314366	101
9	Phek	2026	148246	73

Source: Nagaland Basic Facts 2003

The literacy rate of Nagaland is 67.11 per cent and among the districts Mokokchung district which is inhabited by the Ao tribe has the highest rate with 84.27 per cent (see Table 2).

Table 2
District Wise Literacy Rate of Nagaland

Sl. No	State/ District	Population	Persons	Per centage
1	Nagaland	1988636	1146523	67.11
2	Mon	259604	93859	42.25
3	Tuensang	414801	183513	51.30
4	Mokokchung	227230	172208	84.27
5	Zunheboto	154909	90864	69.73
6	Wokha	161098	113704	81.28
7	Dimapur	308382	205230	78.15
8	Kohima	314366	200137	74.28
9	Phek	148246	87008	71.35

Source: Nagaland Basic Facts 2003

The Nagas are a Mongoloid people and speak dialects of the Tibeto-Burmese language. The origin of the word 'Naga' is obscure. Verrier Elwin (1962:4) wrote that the most likely derivation of the term 'Naga' is from the word '*nok*' meaning 'people' in the Tibeto-Burman languages such as in Garo, Nocte and Ao. Captain Butler and J.H. Hutton were of the opinion that the word was derived from the Hindi word *Nanga* meaning naked while others such as Owen and Rowney held the theory that the word is closely related to the Sanskrit word Nag meaning snake or snake worshipper but this idea has been rejected as there has been no evidence of the Nagas ever being snake worshippers. A.Z. Phizo the legendary Naga leader maintained that the term Naga was derived from the Burmese word *Naka*. In Burmese, '*na*', means ear and '*ka*' means pierced for both Naga men and women pierce their ears (Imchen,1993:17)

Naga themselves never had a common term for the different tribes occupying the hilly tracts. The nomenclature Naga, popularized by the British colonial rulers, is used as a suffix to the individual name of the tribe, for example, Ao Naga, Angami Naga, Lotha Naga, to assert both the individual identity as well as their collective identity. The recorded history of the Nagas began with the advent of the British military forces in the early nineteenth century, although some accounts of the Naga tribes are found in the *Buranjis*, the chronicles of the Assam court from the thirteenth century onwards when the Ahoms came to Assam. The tribal ethnographic reports produced during the colonial period were meant to serve the colonial demand to gather information about the native for effective governance (Das,1993:24). The British assumed active administration of the Naga Hills from 1866, when the Government declared the Naga Hills a District of British India, a newly established District of the earlier occupied Assam state (Ganguli,1984:14).

Along with the colonial rule, the advent of Christianity also made inroads into the tribal areas and after initial resistance the majority of the Nagas were converted to Christianity. Reverend Dr. E. W. Clarke an American Baptist missionary was the pioneer who along with an Assamese convert Godhula went to Molungkimong village in the Ao Naga territory and began to preach Christianity. In 1872 some Ao converts were baptized by Dr. Clarke and thus the mission began to expand and Christianity spread from thereon in the Naga Hills. Christianity brought in its wake education and it was through education that the tremendous social changes came about in Naga society. Most notable of these changes was in employment opportunities, mode of dress, living standards and so on.

Yang (1959:80) analyzing the pre-communist Chinese village of Nanching postulated that the 'lack of occupational diversification in the agricultural economy and the insulating character of subsistence farming fostered a uniform mode of life, enhanced intimate economic and social co-operation, restricted population mobility, and furthered the internal cohesion of the lineage group, the kinship organisation.' Following this line of argument we may also state that the Naga villages were isolated and insulated within the confines of their village settlements mainly due to the practice of headhunting and the rugged terrain. The Naga villages were independent and had to depend on their own resident villagers for defense as well as for looking after the village works. Thus in the process a strong cohesive social structure was developed based on inter-dependence and co-operation and to ensure that this social order did not become disorganised or break up easily, customary laws were enforced. Through the generations people living in the same place and following the same mode of life organised themselves into a traditional social order 'which derived much of its high degree of stability from successful institutionalization of group practises in various aspects of social life' (ibid:261).

Thus despite the changes that Christianity and education brought about, certain aspects of the Naga culture remained embedded in the psyche of the people. Customary laws remained very much a part of the Nagas despite Christianity and this could be so because the Naga system of governance, especially in the administrative and judicial aspects of village government was well formulated and organised, with a deep understanding and respect of human psychology and behaviour thus providing for adequate social control mechanisms. The mechanisms of social control as per the customary law were in the form of 'fines' for any wrong doing which was extracted in the form of pigs, cows and paddy. However the 'shame' associated with the fines were felt much more because for generations, the story of being fined was kept alive and a person's lineage was 'marred' by having an ancestor/elder who was 'fined'. This form of penalty for wrongdoing is still prevalent although in most cases cash is the usual mode of payment. However among the Ao tribe pigs are still extracted as 'fines', the number and size of which are according to the severity of the crime or wrongdoing. Along with customary laws, traditional festivals and costumes also survived although much of the folklore and so on was lost as it was based on Oral tradition and were not recorded. The loyalty, affinity and adherence to the native village by all Naga tribes which continue to be the most important factor have remained unchanged. This is so because it is only through membership to a village that a person gets an identity and social recognition. An individual is identified vis-à-vis other people through membership to a particular village.

The Naga villages are single tribe, multi-clan, divided into *khels*, and have their own indigenous social, political and religious systems and they are also characterised by simple agrarian technology. Before the advent of Christianity the Naga villages had the institution of *morung* or male dormitories; however the institution of *morung* was abolished by the missionaries who regarded it as a place of heathen practices and immoral activities.

To a Naga, his village is the most important entity for his identity; the cultural and traditional heritage is derived from the village and the village is where his roots are found. The village is the real political and social unit for all Nagas and even today the village plays an important part in the lives of the Nagas for it is the membership to a particular village that distinguishes one Naga from another. Most of the educated Nagas live in the urban areas but their links and ties with the native village remain as strong as ever. The links are maintained through the Village Unions in the urban areas where members of the particular village are enrolled.

In times of celebrations, emergencies and deaths the Village Unions are the first to give support, help and assistance.

The Ao Nagas

The Ao Nagas are one of the fourteen major tribes of Nagaland. They were the first people to accept Christianity and subsequently education. The literacy rate among the Ao is 84.27 per cent while that of the state is 67.11 per cent (*Provisional census 2001*). The Ao territory falls under Mokokchung district covering an area of 1,615 sq.km and it is bounded by Wokha district in the south-west, Zunheboto district in the south-east, Tuensang district in the east, Mon district in the north-east and Assam in the west. There are 102 Ao villages under Mokokchung district.

The Ao area is divided into six administrative ranges: Ongpangkong, Asetkong, Langpangkong, Changkikong, Japukong and Tzürangkong. The Ao believe that that their ancestors emerged out of the earth at *Lungterok* (literally, six stones). These stones are located above a village called Chungliyimti on the South bank of the river Dikhu, in the Sangtam area. Chungliyimti is situated east of Mokokchung town and it is 34 km away from Mokokchung town. At present it is now one of the villages in the Sangtam area of Tuensang district (Jamir, 1997:1). The Ao myths records that of the six stones, three were males and the other three females, making three pairs of siblings. According to Ao legend *Tongpok* and his sister *Lendina* emerged first and they were called the Pongener clan, then *Longpok* and his sister *Yongmenala* emerged and they were called the Longkumer clan. Lastly *Longjakrep* and his sister *Elongshe* emerged and they were called the Jamir clan. Thus, three distinct clans emerged who could intermarry (ibid:1). The Ao practice clan exogamy where marriage within the same clan is considered to be incestuous and is strictly taboo.

There is no common language among the Nagas. Each tribe has a language of its own which is mutually unintelligible. The Ao too have a distinct language simply known as Ao-O (Ao language). Unlike the other Naga tribes the Ao language has three distinct dialects, **Chungli, Mongsen** and **Changki**. The **Chungli** dialect has now become the standard Ao dialect, due to the fact that the first American missionaries settled in a Chungli-speaking village and naturally that dialect was learnt and adopted for all subsequent communication and translation. On the other hand, all the folk songs and traditions are preserved and transmitted through the **Mongsen** dialect (Ao,2000:2). Why this is so is not very clear but it could be that the **Mongsen** group was the first settlers in the Ao area and this became the standard dialect through which the oral tradition was transmitted. The **Changki** dialect is very similar to the **Mongsen** dialect but as Mills pointed out it differs markedly from the **Mongsen** and **Chungli** dialects in many respects. The Changki dialect is spoken only in Changki village with slight variations in the Changki area, but for all other purposes the Changki group uses Chungli, which is the standard Ao language.

According to legend, the **Mongsen** group came out of the earth first and settled at **Kubok** while the **Chungli** group emerged next and settled at **Chungliyimti**. The Chungli people were constantly being killed but by whom they could not fathom. One day *Shiluti*, a great Chungli warrior and hero, discovered a narrow path while out hunting and curious to see where it led, he pushed his way along it and soon found that it was blocked with living cane. However he found that forked sticks were used to prop up the cane so as to be able to pass through but again allowed to fall to block the way. *Shiluti* crept through propping up the cane as he went and came upon the huge village of *Kubok* of which his people had no knowledge. He knew then that raiders from this village were constantly making forays into his village and killing his people. When he got home he told only his wife but someone overheard the conversation and reported to the village elders who summoned him. *Shiluti* told them what he had seen and a raid was decided on, and *Shiluti* wanting only the bravest of the brave put the warriors through a test to make sure that they were as warlike as their words. A very large pig was killed and a large fire lighted. When the fire died down *Shiluti* threw thirty pieces of fat on to the embers and took one piece bubbling with heat and put in his mouth. Twenty-nine other warriors followed suit and so the thirty men from Chungliyimti raided *Kubok* and defeated it and the Mongsen were forced to come to Chungliyimti and form a khel side by side with the Chungli. Thus The Mongsen and Chungli groups came to live together and learn to speak each other's language (Mills,1926:8)

The etymology of the word Ao, according to local tradition means 'those who went away'. This is in direct reference to the migration of the people from the village established by the Ao tribe called **Chungliyimti**. Legend has it that the present day Ao migrated from the original village, crossing the river Dikhu and dispersing to the various villages where they are living today. The term '*Aor*' (Ao) was coined by those who stayed back, distinguishing the migrants as 'those who went away' (across the river). Those who did not cross the river were called '*mirir*', the term used for Sangtam, Chang, Phom and Konyak (ibid:1)

The Ao society is divided into the Chungli and Mongsen groups based on the dialects and this has had far reaching implications in Ao society. The Chungli and Mongsen groups follow different norms in observing the festivals, rites and customary laws and in the formulation of Village Councils. In the case of inter-marriage, say for example, between a Chungli speaking woman and a Mongsen speaking man, the wife will communicate with her husband only in her own dialect but will speak her husband's dialect with her son, as he, by tradition must be taught his father's dialect. The Ao are a patrilineal society and males are sole inheritors of land and other property (Ao, op. cit.:3).

Tradition claims that it was at Chungliyimti that the village organization that is prevalent to this day was initiated and formulated. Both the Chungli and Mongsen system of village organization originated from Chungliyimti. The institution of *Putu Menden* (Chungli)/*Samen Menchen* (Mongsen) or the Village Government was established here and all the conditions and rules of this body were also laid down here, as also the '*Ariju*' or dormitory system, which have been handed down to each successive generation through the oral tradition. By the time the general migration of the Ao began, the tradition that began at Chungliyimti were already bred in a well defined, well articulated culture and thus the people carried with them the tradition and culture that originated from Chungliyimti to their new settlements (ibid:30).

The Ao dispersed from Chungliyimti and formed various villages on the hilltops located on the ranges running parallel to each other. The Ao call the ranges by various names such as Ongpangkong range which means the higher hill tops, Langpangkong range (*langpang* meaning bed and *kong* meaning hilltop) because the topography of this area resemble a bed, Asetkong range meaning island because it lies between the two rivers Melak and Menung, Changkikong after the name of Changki village, Japukong after the name of the village Japu and Tzürangkong after the name of the river Tzürang.

Changkikong range comprises of nine villages namely Changki, Chungliyimsen, Waromong, Mongchen, Dibuai, Khar, Molungyimchen, Molungkimong and Molung. All these villages have political ties in the form of the Range Council represented by each village as well as kinship ties through inter marriage. The people of this range have an emotional affinity to each other simply because they belong to the same range. In the Changki village formation it is believed that the Changki people passed through the range before finally settling in Changki.

Changki Village Formation

According to Sanyu, (1996:5) 'the migration of people and tribes has been an important aspect in history since the very inception of human society'. With regard to the history of Naga migration it is difficult to know where the original homes of the Nagas were before they came to the Naga Hills. However the founding of the individual Naga villages have been recorded and handed down from generation to generation through the oral tradition which has been the original mode of recording the history of the people before the advent of the British, Christianity and education.

Sanyu surmises that crude agricultural practices based on shifting cultivation being the basic activity for survival meant that the people moved from place to place in search of more land as shifting cultivation meant the shifting of fields rather than a shifting of crops. He states that 'keeping in view the claims of the clan, the kinship obligations, particularly at a time when everything was to be made from the produce of the land and in view of the primitive agrarian technology and the means of irrigation, there clearly was a low land to man ratio (ibid:10). This meant that due to the pressure of population on limited resources, mainly land, the people had to migrate in search of more favourable conditions.

The formation of the Naga village may then be taken to mean the settlement of a group of people, belonging to various clans, in virgin forests or land where the first settlers claim the choicest sites and where the people demarcated their territory by marking various natural phenomena such as rivers, cliffs or hills as the boundary. It may be put forth that ecological factors dominated the formation of a village. The founding clans were also not averse to other groups settling in the village, for the more people there were the better it was for defense and community work purposes. The Nagas practiced headhunting and so each village had to be well defended against raids and when they were the aggressors too it became imperative that they had a sizeable number of able-bodied men to carry out the raids. But the founding clans reserved certain rights and privileges that were denied to the later settlers.

Based on this premise it may be said that the Changki group also began its migration and passed through various routes and places in search of land and resources that were favourable and in abundance. Mills (op.cit.1926:11) surmised that the Changki group was the first settlers in the Ao territory and makes the connection between the Nokrangr, one of the early Konyak inhabitants of the Ao territory, and the Changki group by pointing out that Nemchem, one of the Changki group of villages, was definitely said to have been founded by Nokrangr. He also pointed out that pot making which the Konyaks and the Changki villagers practise is definitely taboo with the rest of the Ao. The history of the migration of the Changki group is based on the oral tradition that has been handed through the generations and one which has been documented by the elders of the founding clans.

In the beginning it is said that the Changki group comprised of seven clans namely, Longchari, Amri, Changkiri, Chao, Koto, Kizakiti and Tsüngmi. These clans began their migration from *Pangsang* located presently in Tuensang district to *Tsütsüng*, which is at present in the Longsa village area in Mokokchung district. In course of time their wanderings took them to *Lilongjok*, in Longmisa village area then to *Longzakyimjok* in Mongsenyimti village area and to *Pupopang* in the Mongchen village area, which are all located in Mokokchung district.

At *Pupopang* the Longchari, Amri, Changkiri and Koto clans separated from the other three clans Chao, Kizakiti and Tsüngmi and went to Jangpetkong while the other three clans went towards Alongtaki. Jangpetkong is the highest summit in the Changkikong range and it is told that the Longchari, Amri, Changkiri and Koto clans who had settled there found it damp and cold. The paddy would not dry properly and the rice beer would not ferment quickly and due to the dampness, the people fell ill often. As the location was not good, scouts were sent out to find a better place. One of the places that were investigated was *Ongchen*. (*Ongchen* in Changki dialect means 'that which can be seen'). From the high summit, the Changki people could see this place where different types of birds were seen perched on the trees and eating the fruits and berries and where the sun shone brightly. On investigation this place was found to be ideal for habitation so the group decided to settle there. *Ongchen* is now one of the '*kiong*' or locality in the upper *khel*. After the Longchari, Amri, Changkiri and Koto clans had settled at *Ongchen*, the Alingri clan came from Nemchem and settled there. It is said that from the very beginning of the migration, the group was known as the Changki group. Therefore the village was named Changki.

It is also told that at one time Changki village was abandoned due to the fear of reprisal by other Ao villages. Apparently the Changki people had invaded and annihilated *Ritu* village and exhibited not only the heads but also the severed limbs of *Ritu* villagers at the gates of Changki village. This was in contravention to the accepted norms of warfare.

Therefore in order to escape being annihilated one group of villagers led by **Imchatsüng** of the Longchari clan, Amri clan led by **Melipong**, Changkiri clan led by **Yangrusangba** and Alingri clan led by **Kübzasu** and Koto clan led by **Thong** left the village and took shelter in Nemchem village.

Another group led by **Imlisangba** of Changkiri clan, **Atsüngden** of Longchari clan and **Alangri** of Amri clan took shelter in Yimpang village, located in the present Wokha district. The village was thus completely deserted.

After lying low for some time the two Changki groups met somewhere in Assam and they decided to go back to Changki village and in accordance with the prevailing custom agreed to return to their village on the seventh day of the meeting. However while the Nemchem group arrived at the village on the appointed day, the Yimpang group was late by three days.

As per the custom, on their return to Changki village, the group that reached the village first, namely the Nemchem group cleared the sites, which in effect declared their ownership. However **Yangrusangba** of the Changkiri clan did not demarcated or lay claim to any site for his brother **Imlisangba** who had led the Yimpang group. **Imlisangba** was not happy with his brother for while others who had come late had sites demarcated by their brothers, his own brother did not demarcate any sites for him. **Imlisangba** asked his brother where he should build his house, to which his brother replied that the rest of the land below the established village site was his for the taking.

Therefore **Imlisangba** decided to set up the lower *khel* in the village and called it **Imlisangba Yimkem** meaning 'village established by Imlisangba'. Thus the lower *khel* was established. When Imlisangba set up the lower *khel* there was no *Tsüngba* or priest to perform the religious rites and as the priests were considered to be essential for conducting religious ceremonies, he brought a group led by **Mejonger** and **Apangsen** of Pongen phratry from another village where they were reported to be of the *Yimpuri* (founder) clan. In Changki they were given the title **Medemtsüngba**, (*'medem'* meaning of one accord, *'tsüngba'* meaning priest) as the Changki people of both the upper and lower *khels* in one accord made them the *Tsüngba* or priest of the village. To this day they are known as Pongenri although the title Medemtsüngba is also used.

Much later the Changki villagers spotted some people led by **Imchaba** at a place called *Changki Longpok* within the Changki area and they were brought to the village. When asked by the Changki villagers where they would like to settle, they opted for the lower *khel*, and thus they settled there and attached themselves to Imlisangba of Changkiri clan for which they were given the name Emrem **Changki**. *'Emrem'* in the Changki dialect means 'to be attached'.

Another group led by **Yalemchang** was found at a place called *Alulangba* in the Changki village area by the Changki villagers. This group merged with the **Emrem Changki** clan.

Later on a group migrated to Changki village led by **Imtsüdangba** of Longkumer clan who came from *Mangla* village, located in the present Wokha district.

Another group of people belonging to Alingri (elder), Metsüri, Losangri and Nokzari clans came and settled in Changki village.

There is a very interesting story about how a group of Chungli speaking Ao people from *Changpang area*, located in the present Wokha district, comprising of the Longkumer, Tzüdiri, Moliri, Ningdangri and Akhori clans migrated to Changki and were allowed to settle in the lower *khel* of Changki village with their own *kiong* (locality) called *'Tsüngli kiong'*.

In those days warfare with other villages and tribes were frequent. The Changki warriors conducted headhunting raids frequently against the Lotha tribe who were their neighbours, for successful collection of heads was one way of ensuring renown in a man's lifetime and a glorious memory after his death. The Changki warriors used *Changpang* village as a transit and resting place in times of warfare with the other villagers as the two villages were on friendly terms.

It was on one such expedition that a warrior **Imdongdangba** of the Changkiri clan came upon **Takuyangrula** of the Longkumer clan, who was weaving outside on the 'kilangmi', an open bamboo platform. It is said Imdongdangba fell in love with her and in course of time Takuyangrula also reciprocated. Imdongdangba frequented her place whenever the Changki villagers raided other villagers. Soon she became pregnant and when her father, **Sentimongba**, came to know of it, he refused to let her go to another village, as she was the only child. Imdongdangba was so enamoured by Takuyangrula that he was willing to do anything to take her with him to his village. Her father too was adamant that his only child should not go to another village. Imdongdangba then devised a plot, which would be irresistible to not only Sentimongba, his lover's father but also to the rest of the villagers.

He put forward the following suggestions to the Changpang *Yimten* (Changpang village government): To compare the '*Yimten Ozüng*' (rules and regulations of the village government) of the two villages that is Changki and Changpang. The deal was that if the Changpang system of village governance were found to be better then Imdongdangba would leave his village and settle there. If the Changki system of village governance were found to be better then Changpang people would move to Changki and settle there. The following customs were compared to find out which were better.

1. **Lumelen** (Tax levied for cultivation)

   (a) Changpang *Yimten* (Changpang Government): No body could cultivate on land claimed by the original settlers. Tax of three jugs of beer was levied if anyone cultivated the area demarcated by the original settlers.

   (b) Changki *Yimten* (Changki Government): One measure of special rice beer was levied for the land cultivated on the *Achep* (western) part of the village. There was no tax levied on the *Ajen* (eastern) part of the village if this part of the land was cultivated.

2. **Kilamet** (Adultery Cases)

   a) Changpang *Yimten*: Any man who committed adultery with another man's wife was fined seven pigs.

   b) Changki *Yimten*: Any man who committed adultery was fined one cock and one measure of special rice beer.

From the above comparison it was agreed that Changki had better sense of governance, as it did not impoverish the wrongdoers too much. Thus abiding by the agreement made, the Chungli speaking Changpang villagers came to Changki to settle there permanently. Altogether five clans, namely, Longkumer, Ningdangri, Akhori, Tzüdiri and Molir came from Changpang to Changki and settled in the area called *Tsüngli kiong* on account of the fact that they were Chungli speaking people.

The people from Changpang were allowed to settle in the area of their choice and allotted land for cultivation. This group had their own *Yimten* (government) and it was recognised by the Changki people. On reaching Changki they joined the village government of the lower khel as Imdongdangba who had brought them was from the lower *khel*. They maintained their own separate *Ariju* (dormitory for males) and in every other aspect such as in language, customs and wearing of ornaments they were separate from that of the Changki people. Thus the lower *khel* came to be known as **'Ayim Anet changri'** (people of two villages). But now the Tsüngli (Chungli) people have been assimilated into the Changki fold and speak only Changki, as they have forgotten their language and have adopted the Changki customs although in certain aspects such as in inheritance rules they differ from the other clans. This will be explained in the chapter dealing with Kinship and Marriage. It was after the Tsüngli group, that one **Lalok** from Nemchem came and merged with 'Emrem Changki' clan (*Source: The Changki Emkumri Kin Asem Otsü Committee).*

At present there are thirteen clans in Changki namely:

1. Longchari
2. Amri
3. Changkiri
4. Alingri
5. Metsuri
6. Losangri
7. Pongenri
8. Akhori
9. Molir
10. Longkumer
11. Ningdangri
12. Tzüdiri
13. Emrem Changki

Changki *lusa* (territory)

As the Changki *lusa* or territory was vast, in the olden days, the British Government decreed that a Sema group would be relocated to the **Satsükba** area and settled there.

When the Changki villagers protested, they were told that unless a settlement with no less than 30 households was established there, the British would carry out the order. Therefore in order to protect their land, the Changki villagers built 30 small houses and on the appointed day when the British SDO was supposed to come for inspection some villagers were taken down to Satsükba and pretended to be residents of that settlement. The British Government recognised Satsükba as an established village for all intends and purpose there and then. Some of the people who had gone down to Satsükba decided to stay on there and in this way the village was established. In the beginning the village was under direct control of Changki village but as more people settled there not only from Changki village but those who also migrated from other villages, Satsükba village became independent and established their own village government.

At present there are about a hundred households and by Ao standards it is considered to be a small village. The people have right to the land for their own use but cannot sell to outsiders and as the land that they cultivate fall under "***emlu***" of Changki village that is, Changki community land, they do not have to pay any tax but should the Changki Village Council decide that the land is required by the village, they will have to surrender the land. For example, the land under ***Tzürang Külemkong*** was utilised by the Satsükba villagers for jhum cultivation, but in 2003 the Changki Village Council decided to take the land for development under the Department of Horticulture, Nagaland Government under the Excellence Scheme. Thus the Satsükba villagers handed over the land to Changki village to be utilised by the Changki villagers. The people of Satsükba speak the Changki language and in every aspect they are similar to the Changki people and till date there is close relationship between the two villages.

The village of **Chungliyimsen** was also established on Changki *lusa* (territory) but now it is an independent village with its own customary laws and traditions. However in appreciation of the land given to them Chungliyimsen village and in acknowledgement of this Chungliyimsen pays tribute by extending the service of *ayamelen* to Changki village. This means that Chungliyimsen village acts as a special messenger of Changki village in times of emergency and trouble. They also act as *utongdari* or special envoys and negotiators for Changki village whenever the need arises. However if the Chungliyimsen villagers want to cultivate on Changki jhum land, they can do with proper permission and on payment of Rs.2/- as *lumelen* or land tax for every *athi* or rest house-cum- granary that they construct in the jhum area.

In the days when headhunting was practiced, the villagers of **Aliba** took shelter in Changki when Longkhum village attacked them. The place that they took shelter is to this day called Aliba *kiong* (locality) which is located in the upper *khel*.

The Changki *lusa* (territory), which stretched down to Tzürang valley, was left uninhabited for ages till some settlers came and established their villages. A group of people approached Changki Yimten (Changki village government) and after getting permission established **Moayimti** village, approximately 25 km away from Changki village. Till date Moayimti village calls Changki village 'father' in acknowledgement of the latter's munificence. Other villages, which were established in the Tzürang area, are Chungtia Yimsen, Watiyim, Longphayimsen, Aokum, Medemyimti and Ao-Sungkum.

Atophumi and **Sahaphumi,** which are Sema villages, established themselves in Changki territory with direct intervention of the then British Government with permission from Changki *Yimten* (government). Under Sahaphumi,

Puniphuto compound was established, adjacent to Sahaphumi village. Earlier Lemjem village and Changki had no boundaries between the villages as they were of the same group that migrated to Changki area. In the process of migration some people settled in Lemjem while others settled in Changki. However in the intervening years due to population pressures and other factors, Lemjem and Changki became distinct villages with clearly demarcated boundaries.

In 1960 some Changki villagers went down to **Longnak** valley which is 16 km from Changki village and established a locality or *kiong* there called **Merakiong** and in due time three other *kiong* grew, namely, Noken, Chechet and Naronikùm. These four *kiong* are under the jurisdiction of the traditional government of Changki village. There are 73 households in the Longnak area with a population of approximately 350. The Fruit Canning Factory under Horticulture Department, Government of Nagaland was established in 1965 in Longnak followed by the establishment of the Electrical Department and through these establishments, Longnak developed and the settlement grew in population.

Longtho which is about 27 km away from Changki village also falls under the category of "**emlu**" (Changki village community land). There is a privately run sawmill which has been established here by a Changki entrepreneur. There is also a sub-police station there, as well as a Forest Check gate. The population of Longnak valley as well as Longtho is Changki and both Longnak and Longtho are under the jurisdiction of the Changki Village Council.

Changki Village: The Study Area

Changki village is located at $26^{0}20 – 26^{0}31'$ latitude and $94^{0}18' - 94^{0}27'$ east longitude and has an altitude of 979 meters on the Changkikong range of hills. The village is part of Mangolemba Circle and is 40 km from the district headquarter, Mokokchung. It is bounded by Tzüeit River in the east, Upper Assam in the west, the Lotha village of Mekokla in the south and Mejangchut River in the north. The neighbouring villages surrounding Changki are the Ao village of Chungliyimsen in the north, which is 5 km away, Mekokla, a Lotha village, 22 km to the south, Sahaphumi, a Sema village, 19 km to the west and Aliba, an Ao village, 15 km away to the east. The state border road from Mariani in Assam (which is also a rail link for the area) to Mokokchung runs through the village area making the approach to the village easy and communicable. Mariani is also the closest market town.

Changki village is referred to as "***Ayim Asem Changri***" by the villagers which means people of three villages. This is in reference to the first settlement of the village where ***Süngdakba*** or the upper *khel* was first established and in the course of time the lower *khel* was established. At a much later time, the Tsüngli people came to settle in the village from Changpang in Lotha area and established a separate *kiong* or locality called *Tsüngli kiong*, and as they had come with a recognized "*Yimten*" or village government and with their own dialect and customs, they were treated as a separate village. The lower *khel* was thus referred to as '***Ayim Anet Changri'*** meaning 'people of two villages'. However the Tsüngli people merged with the lower *khel* as far as village governance and organization was concerned. Thus Changki is referred to as **Ayim Asem Changri**, meaning People of Three Villages.

Officially the upper *khel* is known as **Süngdakba** and the lower *khel* is known as **Ayim Anet**. But the upper *khel* is commonly called **Luko** (which in Changki dialect literally means 'up') and the lower *khel* **Lulang** (literally meaning 'down').

The people of Changki belong to the Mongoloid race and they speak the Changki dialect which belongs to the Tibeto-

Burman language group. The Changki dialect is a derivation of the Mongsen language. The Changki people are composed of two different Ao groups, that is, the Mongsen and Chungli groups. The earliest settlers of Changki village belonged to the Mongsen group, while the last major group that settled in Changki belonged to the Chungli group, called *Tsüngli* in the Changki dialect.

Physically the people are strong, muscular and of medium height who have been endowed with the ability to endure hard physical labour. The average height of the men is around 5 feet 8 inches while the women are shorter than the males. The people are fair complexioned in general. The Changki women were known for their good looks in the past and many songs comparing them to angels were composed in tribute to their beauty. The people are hard working, hospitable and have a very good sense of humour. Most of the villagers are literate and education is taken seriously and most parents who can afford send their children out of the village for school and college education. The village is clean and every Changki woman takes pride in keeping her home and surrounding areas clean and tidy. The traditional Changki *ani* (skirt) worn by the women is called *awhani* (blue with red rectangular design) and *Yangnakni* (black with red rectangular design) and the shawl is called *khel taktepsü* (white background with blue stripes). The shawl worn by the males is the traditional Ao shawl called *sübangsü.*

Topographically the village is situated on a five km narrow ridge but it is endowed with a fertile valley eleven km below the village called the *Tzüong Tsupak* and it is here that the paddy fields are located wherein there is a perennial source of water from various streams making wet rice cultivation an economically viable practice. The highest peak is *Jangpetkong* and the main rivers are *Tzüeit, Tzüong* and *Tzürang.*

The village has 422 households and the number of permanent residents of the village are1673; including students from the village studying outside numbering 105. We find that there are 9 uninhabited houses in the upper *khel* and 7 uninhabited houses in the lower *khel*. The owners of these houses live ordinarily outside the village and the houses are kept uninhabited so that should these people visit the village, they will have their own homes to stay in.

The total number of Changki people within the village is 1673. Of the 1673 people, 829 are females and 844 are males. The students studying outside consisted of 47 college students and 59 school students who are in various places. The population of the lower *khel* was found to be 681 with 146 households while that of the upper *khel* was found to be 992 with 276 households.

Table 3
Sex-wise distribution of population in Changki

Sl.No	Population	Frequency	Per centage
1	Male	844	50.45
2	Female	829	49.55
	Total	**1673**	**100**

The sex-wise distribution of population in the village is shown in Table 3. There are 844 males or 50.45per cent of the total population of 1673 and 829 females constitutes 49.55 per cent of the total population.

Süngdakba (Upper *Khel*)

The village settlement area starts from Wachen *kiong* (*kiong* means locality in the Changki language) in the upper *khel* popularly known as X junction. This is the intersection of the state highway leading towards Mokokchung and to the other villages in the Changkikong Range, and towards Mariani and to Changki village. This is a very busy intersection because it is the halting point for the various buses, trucks and small vehicles plying the highway. The Changki people particularly the upper *khel* people have opened up small restaurants and tea stalls as well as petty shops. The people also sell various indigenous vegetables, fruits and the Changki clay pots, which is the traditional trademark of the village.

From this junction the single tarred road climbs up about a kilometer or so towards Aliban *kiong* which is situated on a hillock. There are thirty-four households in these two *kiong* (localities) that is Wachen and Aliban.

As one follows the road we pass the Tekongkülem Government Primary School in Nasenongti *kiong*. There are forty households spread out from the single main road and up over a high hill. A steep flight of steps leads upto the houses on the right. In this *kiong* (locality) the telephone exchange is located.

As we carry on towards Ongti *kiong* and Aliba *kiong* we find that the houses are sparsely spread out on either side of the road. There are only twenty-one households in these two *kiong*. The Baptist church granaries (three in all) are located at Ongti on the left side of the road and directly after the granaries on the right side of the road on the slope of a hill the upper khel graveyard is maintained.

Immediately after crossing the graveyard, the road curves and at the turn on the left side of the road the upper *khel* Community Hall (also referred to as Panchayat Hall) called ***Orija Salang*** is located on the top of a hillock. Opposite to this is the Students Union office cum library and adjacent to it is the Atsüngjuma Government Primary School. Here too we find the only bakery cum grocery store in the village. In this shop we get almost everything from the locally made cakes, biscuits, bread, wild vegetables to camera roll films.

As we approach Alongtepok *kiong* we see the Baptist church looming over with the Mission School tucked away on the right side of the road. There are thirty-one houses on either side of the road. The houses are connected by footpaths starting from the main road. From this *kiong* the road proceeds downhill and we pass Alongtema *kiong* which is the last *kiong* in the upper khel which has twenty houses.

From the description of ***Süngdakba*** or the upper khel we find that there are seven *kiong* or localities, the upper *khel* has its own Community Hall also called Panchayat Hall with the local name *Orija Salang*, two Government Primary Schools where the students are from the upper *khel* only, the church run Mission School is also located in the upper *khel* but the students comprises of both the upper and lower *khel*, there is an upper *khel* student's union office-cum-library and there are nine petty shops catering to the needs of the upper khel population.

In Table 4 the distribution of household-wise population of the upper *khel* by size is shown. Household population shows a variation from a single member to ten members in a household. In the upper *khel* it was found that the number of single member households was 37 or 25.34 per cent out of a total of 146 households. The number of households with 2 members was found to be 17.80 per cent or 26 households out of the total of 146 in the upper *khel*. Households with 3 member was found to be 12.33 per cent or 18 households, 4 member households was 16.44 per cent or 24 households, 5 member households was 12.33 per cent or 18 households, 6 member households was 6.85 per cent or 10 households, 7 member households was 5.48 per cent or 8 households, 8 member households was 2.74 per cent or 4 households and 10 member households was 0.68 per cent or 1 household out of the total of 146 households in the upper *khel*. From the statistics we find that big family norm usually associated with the village folk is not the standard in the upper *khel* in

Changki village. In fact the per centage of single member households was found to be the highest in the upper k*hel* with 25.34 per cent or 37 out of 146 households. The reason for the high number of households having only a single member is because of the fact that most of the single member households comprise of elderly people who are widowers or widows whose children have left the village and settled elsewhere. Despite the entreaties of their children these elderly people refuse to leave the village preferring to live alone as their desire is to die in their own homes in the village.

Table 4
Distribution of households by size: Süngdakba (Upper *Khel*)

Sl.No	No. of members	No. of houscholds	Percentage
1	1	37	25.34
2	2	26	17.80
3	3	18	12.33
4	4	24	16.44
5	5	18	12.33
6	6	10	6.85
7	7	8	5.48
8	8	4	2.74
9	9	-	0.00
10	10	1	0.68
Total		**146**	**100**

In Table 5 the distribution of population between the ages of 0-10 and 11 – 20 in the upper *khel* was found to be 109 and 124 or 16.00 per cent and 18.21per cent respectively. The break up of population according to the age group of 21-30 was 88 (12.92 per cent); the age group of 31-40 was 80 (11.74 per cent); the age group of 40-51 was 82 (12.04 per cent); the age group of 51-60 was 70 (10.28per cent); the age group of 61-70 was 60 (8.81 per cent); the age group of 71-80 was 46 (6.75 per cent); the age group of 81-90 was 20 (2.94 per cent) and 91-100 was found to be 2 (0.29 per cent) of the total population in the upper *khel.*

Table 5

Age-wise distribution of population according to locality in Süngdakba (Upper *khel)*

Age Categories	Alongte-pok	Aliban & Wachen	Nase-nongti	Along-tema	Aliba & Ongti	Total	Per-centage
0 – 10	22	27	41	6	13	109	16.00
11 - 20	21	35	46	6	16	124	18.21
21 – 30	12	19	33	12	12	88	12.92
31 – 40	20	25	18	5	12	80	11.74
41 – 50	7	32	26	5	12	82	12.04
51 – 60	9	26	27	2	6	70	10.28
61 – 70	2	20	23	5	10	60	8.81
71 - 80	8	5	16	8	9	46	6.75
81 – 90	4	-	6	5	5	20	2.94
91 – 100	-	1	-	-	1	2	0.29
Total						**681**	**100**

Ayim Anet (Lower *khel*)

The lower *khel* starts with Longma *kiong* (locality) where the Alingtemen community hall cum primary health dispensary is located. There are two small monoliths erected here on the right side of the road besides the steps, which is a short cut to the church and the Baptist church women department's guesthouse cum office. In this *kiong* there are twenty-four houses.

Just after Longma *kiong*, which is the first *kiong* (locality) of the lower *khel,* there is an electrical transformer on the left side of the road. Below this transformer is the Sangpangmen Government Primary School and a footpath leads to Lemjen *kiong* which is spread out down on the eastern side and the only way to reach this *kiong* is by the footpath. There are thirty-six houses here.

From the transformer the road goes downhill very steeply towards Tsüngli *kiong*. This is the *kiong* where the last group of migrants settled. The houses are distributed on either side of the road but as the eastern side slopes down gently there are more houses on this side. Altogether there are seventy-eight houses in this *kiong*, which makes it the most populated *kiong* in Changki. The five Tsüngli (Chungli) clans are settled here.

At the end of this road we come to the Aodang hillock, which was considered to be one of the sacred sites in the ancient days. The lower *khel* graveyard is maintained on the right side of the road here. Opposite to the graveyard we have the library maintained by the *Changki Lanuri Kaketsüri Telongjem* (students union), which is a RCC building, and it doubles up as the office of the student's union. One room in this building has been rented out as a shop. On the right the Changki Yimlang Baptist church is located adjacent to the graveyard. The Aodang Primary School is located next to the church.

Opposite to the church is the lower *khel* Panchayat Hall, called the ***Ayim Anet Salang*** and in between the church and the Panchayat Hall right on the road we find the basketball court cum volley ball court and this recreational area is called the Aodang ground, which also serves as the public ground for meetings and variety shows and so on.

To the left of the Aodang ground is Longtsüen *kiong* where there are only fifteen houses making it the least populated *kiong* in the lower khel. The houses decrease towards the forested area where people maintain kitchen gardens.

From the Aodang ground as we follow the main road there is a slight climb leading into Litsüng *kiong*. Just as we enter this *kiong* (locality) on the right side we find the Changki Yimlang Baptist church's granary next to the primary school. There are houses on either side of the road totaling to seventy-one houses which is just a few houses less than Tsüngli *kiong*.

The gradual climb of the road levels out when we enter Tsünglaong *kiong* which is mostly located on a steep hill opposite to the road as we follow it. Here the indoor stadium cum library started by the *Changki Lanuri Kaketsüri Telongjem* (students union) lies half finished. We also reach the second village gate here. From here we have a panoramic view of the rice fields as there are no house built on the right side of the road as it is very steep.

Just a minute's walk from this gate is a junction. The road to the right leads to the Government High School as well as the army camp. The proposed telephone exchange plot also lies here which is an open ground. The road to the left leads to Narisobo *kiong* comprising of fifty-two houses. This is the last *kiong* (locality) in the village and the road continues towards the state highway from this *kiong*.

In the lower *khel* we find that there are seven *kiong* (localities), 12 petty shops and one office-cum-library of the lower *khel* student's union. There are more households and number of people in the lower *khel*.

Table 6
Distribution of households by size: Ayim Anet (Lower *Khel*)

Sl. No	No. of members	No. Households	Per centage
1	1	51	18.48
2	2	42	15.22
3	3	54	19.57
4	4	55	19.93
5	5	29	10.51
6	6	16	5.80
7	7	15	5.43
8	8	10	3.62
9	9	2	0.72
10	10	1	0.36
11	11	-	0.00
12	12	-	0.00
13	13	1	0.36
Total		**276**	**100**

Table 6 shows household-wise population in the lower *khel* where the single member household was found to be 51 (18.48 per cent) out of 276 households. Those with 2 members was 42 households (15.22 per cent), while 3 member households was 54 (19.57 per cent), the 4 member households was 55 households (19.93 per cent), while 5 member households was 29 households (10.51 per cent). 16 households (5.80 per cent) had 6 members, 15 households (5.43 per cent) had 7 members, 10 households (3.62 per cent) had 8 members,

2 households (0.72 per cent) had 9 members while 1 household each had 10 and 13 members respectively (0.36 per cent) of the total number of 276 households in the lower *khel*. In the lower *khel* we find that 4 member households are the highest with 55 households (19.93 per cent) of the total number of households.

In table 7 the distribution of population according to the age group of 0-10 in the lower k*hel* was found to be 142 (19.33 per cent) of the total population while that of those between the age group of 11-20 was found to be 151 (19.64 per cent) of the total population. The number of young people was found to be higher than that of those within the age groups of 21-30 and 31 – 40, which were respectively 134 (10.17 per cent) and 133 (13.69 per cent) of the total population. Those between the age groups of 41-50 were found to be 103 (9.26 per cent) of the total population while those between the age group of 51-60 were found to be 101 (8.69 per cent) of the total population and those between the age groups of 61-70 and 71-80 were 82 (7.28 per cent) and 51 (3.99 per cent) of the total population. Those between the age groups of 81-90 and 91-100 were found to be 62 (5.01 per cent) and 33 (2.58 per cent) respectively of the total population in the lower *khel*.

From the statistics regarding the population of both the upper and lower *khel* we find that in the village there are more children between the ages of 0-10 and youngsters between the ages of 11-20 with an average of 526 (31.44 per cent) of the entire village population. Those between the ages of 21-60 were found to be at an average of 791 (47.28 per cent) of the total population of the entire village. It follows then that 47.28 per cent of the entire village population is at its productive stage. Those above the age of 60 number 356 (21.28 per cent) of the entire village population.

Table 7
Age-wise distribution of population according to locality in Ayim Anet (Lower *Khel*)

Age Categories	Longma	Longtsüen	Tsüngli	Litsung& Tsünglaong	Lemjem	Narisobo	Total	Percentage
0 – 10	16	18	21	46	21	20	142	19.33
11 – 20	7	10	35	47	27	25	151	19.64
21 – 30	17	13	29	44	14	17	134	10.17
31 – 40	10	14	28	31	23	27	133	13.66
41 – 50	4	11	24	30	9	25	103	9.62
51 – 60	3	5	10	38	6	39	101	8.69
61 – 70	4	6	22	23	10	17	82	7.28
71 – 80	2	6	13	13	7	10	51	3.99
81 90	2	4	7	11	8	30	62	5.01
91 – 100	-	-	3	16	13	1	33	2.58
Total							**992**	**100**

With regard to education we find that the Changki people consider education as a very important factor and there is almost cent per cent literacy rate because almost everyone has had some level of schooling and can read and write. The Village Council too monitors the functioning of the schools very closely especially with regard to the teachers as they are penalized very heavily for dereliction of duties. If teachers are found neglecting their duties, the Village Council can summon them for explanation calls. If the Village Council is not satisfied with the teachers' explanations, fines are imposed. For a teacher who is regarded very highly in the village, the imposition of such fines would be the ultimate social disgrace.

After school hours, which end at 12 pm for the primary schools and 2 pm for the Mission School and High School, there is also study hour in the late afternoons where each school assigns teachers for such duties on rotational basis. Every morning the first bell for school is rung so that the children and the teachers will get ready after which the second bell will be rung for the start of the school. Punctuality for both students and teachers is strictly maintained. The school buildings were constructed by the people themselves with collections from the villagers and donations from well-wishers and with some financial aid from the Nagaland Government. Each school is responsible for the maintenance and upkeep of its premises.

There are four Government primary schools, two each in the upper and lower *khels*, one high School and one private School run by the Baptist The educational qualification of the people in Changki shows that there are 52 matriculates, 48 pre-university passed, 22 graduates and 2 Post graduates. Altogether there are 628 school going children within the village itself which (53.81 per cent) while the under graduates who have studied from pre primary to Class I to any Class below the 10th Class number 415 (35.56 per cent). We find that in the village 4.45 per cent are matriculates, 4.11 per cent pre-university degree holders, 1.89 per cent are graduates and 0.17 per cent is post graduates. There are 105 students studying outside the village out of which 86 are college students and 92 are school students. The literacy rate of the village is 69.75 per cent.

Table 8
Educational Qualification of Changki people living in the village

Level of Education	No.	Per centage
Under Matriculates	415	35.56
School going children	628	53.81
Matriculate	52	4.45
Pre University	48	4.11
Graduates	22	1.89
Post Graduate	2	0.17
Total	**1167**	**100**

It was found that a total of 247 children were studying in the four Government primary Schools, with 129 or 52.22 per cent (of 247) being boys while 118 were girls (47.77 per cent of 247) while a total number of 104 children studying in the church sponsored Mission School were 62 boys (59.61 per cent of 104) and 42 girls (40.38 per cent of 104). At the high school level, those studying in the Government High School were found to be 192 out of which 79 or 41.14 per cent were boys and 113 or 58.85 per cent were girls. Those studying in the church sponsored Mission School was 85 out of which 36 (42.35 per cent) were boys and 49 (57.64 per cent) were girls.

Altogether 77 teachers are employed in the 6 schools in Changki, of which 45 were males and 28 females. Out of the 77 teachers 8 were non-locals; 5 in the Mission school and 3 in the Government High School.

The infrastructure of the schools were found to be in very good condition as all the school buildings are RCC buildings and except for the Mission School and Atsüngjuma Primary School in the upper Khel, all the other schools have playgrounds/fields. The Government High School has a basketball court and also space for badminton. In the year 2003, the Mission School Changki took some of the students from class VII above to Kolkata on a sight seeing-cum-study tour.

From the description of the village in general we find that although Changki represent a compact unit as a village, within the village there is a sharp social division between the upper and lower khel. Each khel is a distinct unit, having its own locality/*kiong* and each khel has its own administrative set-up and Primary schools as well as graveyards. Mills (1926) had written about the Ao tribe in general and stated that the '*khels* are run with separate organizations, but the village usually united for wars and keeps at least the important *amung* in common... For most purposes, however, the social unit is the *khel*.' The *khels* in Changki have its own organisations and in a sense the two *khels* exists almost like two separate villages within a village.

Each *khel* has its own Primary schools, Students Unions, libraries and recreational/public grounds. The Primary schools in the upper *khel* are the Government Primary Schools Tekongkülem and the Government Primary School Atsüngjuma. The lower *khel* primary schools are Government Primary School Sangpangmen and Government Primary School Aodang. The students' were enrolled according to the *khels* in which they resided. That is students from the upper *khel* enrolled in one of the upper *khel* primary schools closest to their residential location. The same was found in the lower *khel*. The privately run Mission School is maintained by the Baptist church, Changki located in the upper *khel*. The enrolments of the students were not based on *khel* but rather on the ability of the parents to pay the higher school fees. The Government High School, which is the only Government run high school, caters to students from both the *khels*. The Changki Baptist church runs one library, while three other small libraries are maintained by the three students unions in the village.

There are three students unions; one is from the upper *khel* called the *Changki Süngdakba Kaketsüri Longjem* (Süngdakba Students Union). The other two students unions are from the lower *khel* called the *Changki Yimlang Students Union* and *Changki Lanuri kaketsüri Longjem* (Sangpangmen students Union) respectively. In the lower *khel* the two students' unions came about due to the split in the mother church. When the church split in 1947, the breakaway church established its own school which was later taken over by the Government and came to be known as Aodang Government Primary School. Earlier the school students were mature youths as they started school late and it was felt that the youths should have their own separate students' union and thus *Changki Yimlang Students' Union* was started.

There is one common student's union comprising of all the other three students unions called the Changki Kaketsuri Longjem (Changki Student's Union), which is affiliated to the Ao Kaketshir Mungdang (Ao Student's Conference) the apex body of all the Ao student's unions in Nagaland. The Ao students' union hold a genral body meeting every three years in different villages of the Ao area. The Changki Students Union is also affiliated to the Changkikong Range

Students' Union, which is the student union for the range comprising of all nine villages in Changkikong range. In this way the Changki students are linked to the Changkikong range students' body as well as to the apex body of the Ao students' union.

The student unions organises sports and games during the winter holidays as well as put up variety shows. Fund raising events are also organised. The Changkikong Students' Union organises general body meetings every two years and the meetings are held in the villages of the range on a rotational basis. Changki village hosted the last general body meeting in 2003. In such meets apart from the usual agenda, cultural competitions such as traditional songs and dance are held so that the students do not forget their culture and also reinforce pride in one's own traditions. In such meets which is usually held over three days, prominent speakers are invited and the students interact through discussions and debates. Sports and games competitions are also organised during such meets. The host village arranges for the food and lodging of the student delegates from the various villages, by allotting two to three students in each household. The host family then looks after the delegates but meat is given by the students' union, to help ease the burden of feeding the guests. Through such exchange programmes organised at the grassroots level, the students get to know more about their neighbouring villages. In such big events, the Village Council and the various clubs of the village also pitch in to help with the arrangements and so on.

For recreational activities such as games and other activities, an indoor badminton stadium-cum-library is under construction in Tsünglaong kiong, which is an undertaking of the Changki Lanuri Katetsüri Longjem (Sangpangmen Student's Union). The village had one football field in the lower *khel* but it was taken over by the Army in 1996 as their camp area. The basketball courts at Aodang and the Government High School in the lower *khel* and the football ground at Jungmaba in the upper *khel* provide for recreational activities.

There are four youth clubs in the village, which are Young Club, Rising Sporting Club in the lower *khel* and Ossana Club and All Round Seeker Club in the upper *khel*. These clubs organises inter-club volleyball and basketball tournaments and they take active part in the church programmes. They also organise variety shows during Christmas etc. There is another club, which represent the village as a whole called the Orija Club. In sports and other competitive activities organised at the range and district levels, Orija Club represents the village.

There are no women's societies or clubs except for the Changki Arogolari, which is the women's department of the two churches in Changki. Their activities are solely church oriented.

The Changki Baptist Church situated in Ongchen *kiong* (locality) in the upper *khel* was the first church established in 1901 and the congregation comprised of all the Changki villagers from both the upper and lower *khel*. However in 1947 there was a split in the congregation due to some misunderstanding between members of the congregation belonging to the lower *khel*. The Changki Yimlang Baptist church situated in Aodang sector in the lower *khel* was established in 1947. The split was primarily between the people of the lower *khel* and as such the congregation of the break away church comprises of only the lower *khel* people, whose number is very small. The mother church comprises of all the upper *khel* people and the majority of the lower *khel* people.

All the Changki villagers are Baptist Christians and do not celebrate any other Ao traditional festivals like *Moatsu* or *Tsungremmong*, which are celebrated in other Ao villages. Easter and Christmas are the main Christian festivals observed and celebrated by the villagers. The people observe Easter starting from Passion Thursday where the people hold a special evening church service. On Good Friday the people abstain from eating meat and hold evening prayers and service in the church. On Saturday the people clean the graveyards and the church premises and on Easter Sunday, Sunrise Service is conducted at the crack of dawn followed by a special Easter Sunday church service in the afternoon and another service at night.

During Christmas the mood is more geared towards feasting where pigs are killed and distributed among family, relatives and friends. Family members living outside the village come for holidays and spend Christmas with their families. The Christmas festival is marked by family reunions and family feastings and variety shows put up by the students' unions or the various clubs. Memorable events of the year are presented in the form of skits and play with much exaggeration and hilarity and such entertainments are held on the 23rd of December. On Christmas Eve there are two special church programmes one in the afternoon and one in the evening. On Christmas day a special service is held in the church and sometimes a community Christmas feast is given to the congregation, by a family or individual who reside outside the village but have come to spend Christmas with relatives.

With regard to the physical aspects of the village we find that the village is situated on a high ridge with a single narrow road going through the village dividing it into the *Ajen* (east) and *Achep* (west). The houses are built close to each other on either sides of the road and gradually tapering down the slopes on the *Ajen* and *Achep* sides. The houses closest to the road are built on high stilts due to the lay of the land.

Originally the traditional houses in the village were made of woven bamboo walls with thatched roofs, having a *kima akumbok* which was a small verandah leading to a small room called a *thiong*, where the firewood, pigs and chickens etc were kept. The next room was called *atepdang*, which was the main room in the house. This was a large room where the fireplace was built in the middle and where the people slept on bamboo or wooden slats next to the fireplace. This was the room where the people cooked, ate, entertained and slept. A small partition was made out of this room into a small room-like cubicle where personal belongings were kept, called the *kieo*. Sometimes it was also used as a guest room.

The *atepdang* opened out directly into the *kilangmi*, which was an open platform made of bamboo bound together by strips of bamboo called *aling* and supported by long bamboo stilts that served as a place for washing clothes, utensils, and for drying paddy and clothes as well as for storing water. In a corner of the *kilangmi* a small cubicle was partitioned which served as the latrine. Earlier the excrement was eaten by the pigs which roamed around the village freely. In the olden days the villagers also built granaries away from their houses called *athi*. These were one room structures like a miniature house built of bamboo and on stilts. The reason why it was built away from the house was that the threat of fire engulfing the houses packed closely together was very real and so to safeguard their annual stock of paddy the granaries were built away from the houses.

Nowadays traditional houses are not found in the village as the majority of the houses have tin roofs and instead of woven bamboo walls the people use wood or concrete and the layout of the houses is different from the traditional houses. But even today the kitchen has the traditional fireplace and it serves as the main room where the people cook, eat and entertain, and the *kilangmi* is still an important utility space that is very much a part of Changki houses. In Changki we find that the houses are built on either side of the single main road and as the village is situated on a narrow ridge with steep slopes on either side the houses are constructed in an elongated manner, that is, the rooms are built one after the other with a corridor running along so that the rooms open out to the corridor. In many cases the first room is the kitchen, followed by the rooms with the *kilangmi* built at the back. The granaries are also built next to the houses or under the houses as the houses are built on stilts, although a few individuals have the traditional granaries built away from their houses. Three such granaries are also in the Upper *khel* belonging to the Changki Baptist church and one in the lower Khel belonging to the Changki Yimlang Baptist church.

Along with the change in the pattern of houses, proper sanitation in the village has also been strictly enforced by way of pit latrines or septic tanks, which is mandatory for each household. No pigs or cows are allowed to roam freely in the village and if such are found the owner is penalized by the imposition of fines by the Village Council.

The village is fully electrified and water supply is connected through pipes. The main source of water from where it is piped to the village is the river *Chempongtsu*, north to the village, near Chungliyimsen village. The village also has telephone connection since 2001. At present there are around a hundred households with telephone connections. The villagers also have such electronic goods like television sets, refrigerators, generators, CD players and so on. From the early part of 2004, a Changki entrepreneur has brought cable TV to the village and quite a number of houses have cable connection.

There are two privately run village buses, one each from the upper and lower *khels*. The buses run services to

Mokokchung and to Mariani and Dimapur. The roster for the services has been worked out on a weekly basis. That is if the lower *khel* bus go to Mokokchung, the upper *khel* bus will run its Mariani and Dimapur services and in the following week the lower *khel* bus will run its Mariani and Dimapur service and the upper *khel* bus will run the Mokokchung service.

As the village is on the highway and due to the improved transport and communication system the villagers can also subscribe and have daily local newspapers in English and the Ao dialect brought directly to their houses. The popular newspapers in English are *Nagaland Post* and *Eastern Mirror* (published in Dimapur) while the *Ao Milen* (published in Mokokchung) is the popular vernacular newspaper.

The Changki people are primarily agriculturists who practise both jhum and wet rice cultivation. The agricultural season for *tukong lu* or jhum cultivation is from January to August while the *Tsülu* or wet rice cultivation is from May to November-December. In recent times with the permission of the Village Council, private entrepreneurs have taken up horticulture as well as tea cultivation in the fertile *Tzürang* valley.

As mentioned earlier the village is situated on a 5 km narrow ridge but it has been endowed with a fertile valley 11 km below the village and it is here that the paddy fields are located wherein there is perennial source of water from various streams making wet rice cultivation an economically feasible and viable practice.

There is a clear demarcation of rice fields between the upper and lower *khel* too. The rice fields belonging to the upper *khel* are *Tsümerem, Lutiba, Tsürongrong, Longnak, Longnakchuie, Chechet, Mangkosüng* and *Tsüsasa* while the names of the rice fields belonging to the lower khel are *Chembi, Mangkosünglulangba, Ingtzü, Nakaola,*

Alongkaba, Langpaliokba, Chiengba, Chaniti, Otsüngpong, Aotzü, Imtsüngchang, Jungjen and *Nokzaba*.

In the earlier days there was a system of mutual help called '*Yangtep*' where close friends and relatives of an age-set grade would work in each others fields on a rotational basis. (The '*Yangtep*' system will be explained further in chapter V dealing with the economy of the village.) Therefore it may be surmised that the reason for the rice fields being demarcated between the upper and lower *khel* could be based on the fact that that earlier when much of the agricultural activity was dependent on manual labour it was important to have rice fields close to friends, relatives and neighbours so that mutual help through the '*Yangtep*' system could be organised. As explained earlier the village is clearly divided into two khels having its own social organisation and administration.

The main peaks are *Changkitenum, Aliban, Nasenongti, Ongti, Atsüngjuma, Tekongkülem, Tsünglaong, Tsüngmeli, Milongmenchen, Alitongtong, Charemtasüba, Charemtepetipa, Ongkomen, Teplongkong, Tesumetkong, Süongjang, Alikorang, Ongtenba, Kümbalani, Aimejang, Samesa* and *Merongkongba*.

The main river towards the southern part of the village is *Tzüeit* and the tributaries are *Kuromen, Chemongtzü, Tzümet, Chalem, Chanaing, Heni, Longlangba* and *Aitzü*. Towards the north the main rivers are *Tzürang* and *Tzüong* and the tributaries are *Mejangjuet, Zaong, Longpen, Chechet, Longnak, Kotakolemba, Tzümeremba, Ovinak, Aotzü*, and *Jungjen*.

Ala Chela – Community Fishing

Community fishing is an important aspect in the lives of the Changki men where correct courtesies are observed. In the traditional community fishing expedition the youngsters learn the art of statesmanship from their seniors by observing them and through the training imparted to them by their seniors in the ways of conducting themselves in formal occasions. The age-set grades are also properly instructed about their role, duty and obligation pertaining to their grades. In a sense the community fishing is a training course where through actual participation; the villagers learn discipline, the distribution of work according to their age-set grades and the *Yimten* or village government procedures. Most importantly it is also an expedition where the villagers learn about their village boundaries and territorial rights. The community fishing is undertaken by the upper and lower khels alternately. If the upper khel goes for community fishing this year, the lower khel will go the next year. However whenever a khel goes on such an expedition, the catch is shared with the other khel where token fish is given to each of the oldest member of each clan. In such community fishing expeditions, the Changki men learn about how the rivers and streams have always been boundary markers between villages, and even within village boundaries such as khels, between individual landholdings as they are permanent natural phenomena.

Community fishing is a serious affair and is preceded by elaborate arrangements. From time immemorial, the Changki community fishing or *Ala Chela* has been taking place in *Tzürang*, which is the biggest river in the area. In this annual event, the Assamese villages that pay '*khat*' or tax to Changki village are also invited. The Assamese villagers, as they come up the river, spear tortoises, which they share with the Changki villages. The Changki villagers share the fish that they catch, with the Assamese villagers. There are some Assamese villages like Bosagaon, Kankhua, and Beherie etc that take part in this annual event. This relationship has been maintained through the ages and exists to this day.

There are certain rules that are followed as per tradition –

1. When the date for the annual fishing is announced, each clan collect their rations for the trip and material needed for setting up camps.

2. The villagers sleep overnight in the jungle, half way from the Tzürang river so as to ensure that they abstain from sleeping with their wives. It was believed that abstinence brought luck and ensured a good catch.

3. On reaching the river, each clan set up their camps and kitchens.

4. As per customary law, the age-set grades led by the junior Council members (Samen Nuzabari) downwards set to work and going up to the farthest side of the Changki boundary, they use the traditional method of putting poison weeds in the river so as to stun the fish and waded down stream towards the camps and the *kilang* or the traditional trap set up for the purpose of catching the fish. The Azüakang group (the 3rd and 4th grades of the age-sets) are the last to come down stream for their duty is to check on the other age-sets grades and to ensure that no fish is left to float away from the path to the '*kilang*'.

5. After the fish is caught or driven downstream to the traditional trap, the elders decide the share that each member may receive by assessing the catch. The Azüakang age-set grade then calls out the decision made. The biggest fish is set aside for giving as thanksgiving, then the next biggest fish is set aside for the one selected to seek the blessings of the river.

6. The one selected to seek the traditional blessings from the river holds a strip of cane and striking the river

invokes the river to yield more fish for the coming year. After this everyone strikes the river with cane strips repeating the prayer.

7. The rest of the fish is then divided among the clans according to seniority.

8. This community fishing is considered very important for it is during this time that all the male members of the village come together in one place and can discuss village matters. In this way confidentiality is ensured and as no children or women are present, all matters relating to sensitive village issues are discussed openly.

9. This meeting and discussions are always held in the Changkiri clan camp when the lower *khel* organises the fishing expedition. When it is the turn of the upper *khel* the same are held in the Longchari camp. Each clan lights huge bamboo torches and bring it to the Changkiri or the Longchari camp.

10. A unique feature of this fishing trip is that if a male has asked for the hand of a girl, he brings all his rations from the girl's house and he camps in the future father-in-law's clan camp. When he comes up to the village at the end of the fishing expedition, he goes straight to the father-in-law's house and gives his share of the fish. In this way, he declares his intentions and thus the proposal is approved and blessed (*as told by Tajenyuba Changkiri*).

'Khat'

During the Ahom–Kachari contest of supremacy over Assam, the Ahoms approached the Nagas including the Ao to assist them in defeating the Kachari. The Ahom kings recruited the Nagas into their regiments who fought against the Kachari. The Ahom kings too took refuge in the hills and saved themselves from the enemy. In gratitude the Ahom kings gave not only valuable presents but also granted arable plots of land called khels and fishing rights over the waters known as *Bhils* on an understanding that they would desist from making any predatory raids into the plains. These lands were called *Naga-Khat* and were managed by the Assamese agents known as *Naga-Kotoki*. Their duty was to communicate between the Ahom and Nagas. The Ao on reaching the Ahom territory had to deposit their spears and dao with the *Kotoki* and reclaim them on their way back home. This practice prevailed as a symbol of peace in those days. Changki was called *Bordobia* by the Ahom and in recognition of the friendship and services by the Changki villagers to the Ahom kings, Changki was also granted *Khats*. Till date the Changki villagers maintain friendly relations with the villages that pay token tax as being a *Khat* belonging to the Changki village.

3 KINSHIP AND MARRIAGE

The Changki society follows unilineal principle based on patrilineal descent. The largest divisions in the society based on this principle are in terms of clan, which in Changki dialect is called *kin*. A *kin* (clan) is an exogamous unit where each of the members is believed to be agnatically related. All the members of a *kin* (clan) refer to each other as *pacha* (among males) and *pachalari* (among females) and this forms the basis of identification between members of a clan even if they happen to be strangers. In Changki we find that the information with regard to the origin of the clans is vague and the people are reticent of their origins. We surmised that this could be because the oral tradition which was the only way to record legends, stories and history of the people have long been forgotten. With the advent of Christianity and education the people gave up such cultural traits with the belief that all these were heathen practices and in the intervening years much of the information was lost.

In Changki *Tenik* refers to the forefathers who had settled in the village, got married and had children and in the same manner their sons perpetuated the lineage thus establishing different branches of the lineage, called *kidong*. The notion of clan, which in Changki dialect is called *Kin,* is very much ingrained in the psyche of the Changki people. The individual clans are identified by a distinct name which is adopted as the surname of an individual. The clan distinctions are one of the most important social arrangements that define and govern the society.

The social recognition of a person is through membership to a clan. The clan in general is called *Kin* but when a person refers to his own clan the possessive term used is *Pacha.* The number of *Tenik* (which is a combination of two words: *Teni,* meaning 'of a group' and *Sanik,* meaning of 'same blood') or branches of lineages of a clan grouped together is referred to as *Kidong* (which literally means 'of one tree').

Thus in Changki, descent is reckoned through the unilineal principle of agnatic lineage. The agnatic lineage of several generations in depth, tracing back to a common forefather is called *Tenik.* The *Tenik* of the clans may be one or more, for the person/s who led the clan to the village are considered to be the first settler/s and thus established lineage or *Tenik.* The arrangements of blood relations by degrees of nearness are based on the several branches of lineages that sprung from the *Tenik,* and these branches are referred to as *Kidong.* The group having agnatic descent in which all the members regard one another as in some specific sense kinsfolk is called in Changki dialect *Kin* or clan.

Table 9
***Tenik* of each clan in Changki**

Sl No	Clan	Tenik
1	Longchari	Koba
2	Amri	Melipong, Jempangjang, Imtisungkum
3	Changkiri	Yangrusangba & Imlisangba
4	Alingri	Noksang & Ingkuba
5	Metsüri	Apongtuba

Sl No	Clan	Tenik
6	Longkumer	Imtsüdangba, Sentimongba & Takushilu
7	Tzüdiri	Sabangjungba
8	Molir	Bendangnokcha, Mayangjungba & Ningtiba
9	Akhori	Imlenjungba & Nokdang
10	Ningdangri	Tebusangba
11	Pongenri	Mejongri, Imnanokchaba, Chalupong & Tinumeri
12	Losangri	Akitsüng
13	Emrem Changki	Longrimeren, Imtisuja & Lanukaba

In Table 9 the names of the *Tenik/s* of each clan are given. *Tenik* in the context of Changki refers to the first settler/s who led the clan to Changki and thereafter settled in the village and is thus regarded as the forefather/s of the clan.

The founding clans namely, **Longchari, Amri** and **Changkiri** say that they were together from the very beginning and moved to Changki from Jangpetkong where they had settled for a brief period. The different clans and their forefather/s or *Tenik* and the chronological order of their settlement in Changki village are given below:

The three founding clans **Longchari**, **Amri** and **Changkiri** established the village. The **Longchari** clan was led by **Koba**, the **Amri** clan was led by **Melipong**, **Jempangjang** and **Imtisüngküm** while the **Changkiri** clan was led by the descendents of Changkiba; **Yangrusangba** and **Imlisangba**.

The **Alingri** clan has two *Tenik*, that is, one group led by **Noksang** came from Nemchem while the other group led by **Ingkuba** came from Mangla. In the course of migration they had separated and were living in these two different places.

The **Metsüri** clan led by **Apongtuba** came from Mangla which is now in the Lotha area of Wokha district.

The **Longkumer** clan came in three waves. The first group led by **Imtsüdangba** came from Mangla, the second group led by **Sentimongba** came with four other clans from Changpang, which is in the Lotha area of Wokha district, while **Takushilu**, came from Longkhüm village (Ao village in the Ongpangkong range).

The **Tzüdiri** clan led by **Sabangjungba**; the **Akhori** clan led by **Imlenjungba** and **Nokdang**; the **Moliri** clan led by **Bendangnokcha**, **Mayangjungba** and **Ningtiba**; and the **Ningdangri** clan led by **Tebusangba** came along with the **Longkumer** clan from Changpang, now in the Lotha area of Wokha district.

The **Pongenri** clan led by **Mejongri**, the oldest *Tenik* and the third *Tenik* **Chalupong,** came from Aitepong which is now in the Lotha area of Wokha district, the second *Tenik* led by **Imnanokchaba** came from Lemjen which is close to Changki village and the fourth and youngest **Tinumeri** came from Longjang village (Ao village in the Asetkong range).

The **Losangri** clan led by **Akitsüng** came from Mangla which is now in the Lotha area of Wokha district.

With regard to the **Emrem Changki** clan, the respondent Anoktiba (78 yrs) could not give the information regarding the first settler or the place from where the clan came and instead gave the present living *Tenik*, namely that of **Longrimeren** (Elia) **Imtisüja** and **Lanukaba**.

The researcher has taken only the names or the *Tenik* of the first settler/founder because to trace the genealogy of each clan and the various branches of the *Tenik* would require a complete study of its own. Therefore the respondents of all the clans were asked to give the name of the first *Tenik* from whom the various branches sprang forth.

In Changki clan exogamy is practiced and Changki is a multi-clan village having thirteen clans each distinctly different from the other in its history, lineage and the distinction is emphasized by the clan name which is used as a surname by the members.

Clan exogamy is strictly enforced and any union within the same clan is considered to be incestuous. Although such strictures are imposed, there have been cases when young people of the same clan fall in love, which have resulted in premarital pregnancy. Traditionally the unacceptable same clan union and the pregnancy brought about by such a union was punished by tying the couple together and throwing them off the highest cliff killing the couple as well as the unborn child. Nowadays such cases of same clan unions are punished by imposing fines and ultimately expulsion from the village if the couple decides to marry. In Changki the fine imposed is Rs.100 /- and the couple will have to take an oath that they will not stay together but if they go ahead and live together, they are fined Rs.500/- and expelled from the village. The sum paid as a fine might be considered light but any fine even if it is just 50p carries social implications. The loss of face is felt greatly by the one who is fined and the shame associated with the fining and the ill repute it carries is passed on for generations.

The most important aspect of Changki kinship is the affective as well as jural weight attached to the recognition of paternity. The patrilineal norms, as well as the importance of clan exogamy and the sanctity of marriage are reinforced thus, for a child is born not only into a family but also into a clan. The establishment and recognition of paternity gives legitimacy to the child and ensures that the child belongs to a clan and has an identity as well as certain privileges, rights and responsibilities as a member of the clan. It is only through clan membership that an individual's social standing is established in society.

To understand how clan membership influences every aspect of life, especially for a male, will be difficult unless one belongs to the society but it might be useful to illustrate this point with a story of a woman who in her teens got involved with a boy of her own clan and gave birth to a son. Although the shame associated with premarital pregnancy and eventual birth of a son out of wedlock was painful and distressing, her ordeal became worse when her son began to grow into adolescence and soon became a young man. The young man had no one to call father, for the progenitor did not acknowledge him as his son, or to take on a clan name for he had no such claims. He was part of the age-set system but although he could take active part and be involved in all the work connected with his age-set grade, he had no right to assume leadership for he did not have any right to hold high office within the traditional village political set-up. Even if he reached the grade where he would automatically become a member of the village government, he would never be given any opportunity to be the Village Council Chairman or *Gaon Bura*. Men of high individual caliber and most importantly of good lineage held such responsible offices. Moreover he would have no right to own clan lands although he might be permitted to make use of it.

If this was not bad enough, his lack of identity deprived him of maternal uncles who play a very important role in a person's life. The maternal uncles cannot be of the same clan as the father's. The *Tiuo Tukori* (meaning maternal uncles in Changki dialect) are the brothers of a woman and also includes all her clansmen. The role of the *Tiuo Tukori* is to protect, support and give assistance to the sister as well as to the nephews and nieces. Technically the young man had maternal uncles but in social terms he had no one to call as his *Tiuo Tukori*. His parents were of the same clan; therefore he had relations belonging to one clan only. In this situation he could call both his parents' brother's *abazemba* (elder father) and *asa* (younger father) only. He could not call anyone *ako* (term used to call maternal uncle) to signify that he had *Tiuo Tukori*. The suffering in this case was as much for the mother as well as the son. The son had no place in the society as far as social status was concerned and the mother was held responsible for the young man's predicament.

The son also does not have a future either because should he want to marry, the question of paternity and lineage would crop up and he would have no reply. Being of 'polluted' stock he would not be able to make a good alliance through marriage at least within his own community.

To have no membership to a clan in one's own community renders this young man rudderless for he has no identity. And to have no identity means there will be no one to claim him as his own. If he gets into trouble or requires assistance he will not have the support base that the clan or the *Tiuo Tukori* would have provided in his defense for the simple reason that he does not have anyone in those two categories of relatives.

As the story exemplifies, the clan membership forms the basis of the kinship system in Changki. A person's life is ruled by this all pervasive aspect of clan in the society. The people identify and recognise the relationships between each other by the usage of classificatory terms which is an important feature of the kinship system. The breach of the law of exogamy is regarded as a very serious social offence because it affects the very social structure of the kinship groups. It affects the accepted pattern of kinship terminology as there are separate sets of specific terminology to address relatives and members of clan from the father's side as well as from the mother's side. Social relations of individuals are very largely regulated on the basis of kinship, where patterns of behaviour for each of the recognised relationships are formed between the paternal and maternal kindred. The social roles and categorization of individuals into particular social groups are based on kinship as it is the major organisation principle for the social structure, therefore a child born out of the same clan union cannot find a place and has no role, status or identity.

In cases where a child is born out of wedlock to parents belonging to different clans, should the man decide not to marry the woman but acknowledges the child by giving it a name on the sixth day as is the norm, the child for all intends and purposes, becomes his child and belongs to the father's clan. The child will be given rights to clan lands and will even have a share in the father's property.

Kinship Terminology in Changki

Cognates:

English Changki

1. Father's father ---------------------- *Aowo*
2. Father's mother -------------------- *Azü*
3. Father -------------------------------- *Aba*
4. Father's elder brother ------------ *Abazemba*
5. Father's younger brother -------- *Asa*
6. Father's brother's wife ----------- If of speaker's mother's clan *azümo* if older, and *anuzai* if younger than speaker's mother.

		Otherwise *aya* with name.
7.	Father's sister	*Ata*
8.	Father's sister's husband	If descended from the speaker's mother's clan *Ako*. Otherwise *aba* with name.
9.	Mother's father	*Aowo*
10.	Mother's mother	*Azü*
12.	Mother	*Aya*
13.	Mother's brother	*Ako*
14.	Mother's brother's wife	If of speaker's clan *Ata*. If not so related but of speaker's grandmother's clan *Azü*.
15.	Mother's elder sister	*Azümo*
16.	Mother's younger sister	*Anuzai*
17.	Mother's sister's husband	If of speaker's clan *abazemba* or ***asa*** according to age. Otherwise *aowo* with name, *aba* with name or *anga* with name.
18.	Elder brother	*Anga*
19.	Younger brother	*Künu* or name
20.	Elder sister	*Ata*
21.	Younger sister	*Künu* or name

22.	Father's brother's son	*Anga, Künu, Keti* or name depending on age
23.	Father's brother's daughters	*Ata, Künu* or name depending on age
24.	Father's sister's son	*Kümnak*
25.	Father's sister's daughter	*Kümi*
26.	Mother's sister's son	If of speaker's clan *anga* if older, and *Künu* if younger than speaker, and *Küti* if of the same age. If not of speaker's clan *Tiyachem*.
27.	Mother's sister's daughter	If of speaker's clan *Ata* if older, and *Künu* if younger than speaker, and *Atinu* if of the same age. If not of speaker's clan *Tiyachem*.
28.	Mother's brother's son	*Ako*
29.	Mother's brother's daughter	*Azuzai* with name, *Aya* with name or *Ata* with name according to age.
30.	Son	*Aki* or *Küchaba* or name.
31.	Daughter	*Küchala* or name.
32.	Son's wife	*Kümi.*
33.	Daughter's husband	*Kuchanakba.*

34.	Son's son	*Semtsüri*
35.	Son's daughter	*Semtsüri*
36.	Daughter's son	*Semtsüri*
37.	Daughter's daughter	*Semtsüri*

Affines:

1.	Husband	Name. When speaking of him to a third person *Kübaza.*
2.	Wife	Name. When speaking of her to a third person *Küno.*
3.	Wife's father	If of speaker's mother's clan *Ako.* Otherwise *Aowo* with name or *Aba* with name according to age.
4.	Wife's mother	If of speaker's clan *Ata.* If of speaker's mother's clan *Aya.* If not of speaker's clan but of his grandmother's clan *Azü.* If no such relation traceable *Azümo* with name, or *Anuzai* with name according to age.
5.	Husband's father	As for wife's father.
6.	Husband's mother	As for wife's mother.
7.	Wife's brother	If his mother is of speaker's clan *Kümnak.* Otherwise *Ako* or name.

	Relationship	Term
8.	Wife's elder sister	If her mother is of speaker's clan *Kümi*. Otherwise *Ata*.
9.	Husband's elder brother	*Kürham*. Name forbidden.
10.	Husband's younger brother	*Kürham*. Name not forbidden.
11.	Husband's elder sister	*Ithung*.
12.	Husband's younger sister	*Ithung*.
13.	Wife's elder sister's husband	*Kuzaba*
14.	Wife's younger sister husband	*Kuzaba*
15.	Husband's elder brother's wife	If of speaker's clan *Ata*. Otherwise *Ithung*.
16.	Husband's younger brother's wife	If of speaker's clan *Künu*. Otherwise *Ithung*.
17.	Wife's brother's wife	If of speaker's clan *Ata* or *Künu*. Otherwise name used.
18.	Husband's sister's husband	If of speaker's clan *Anga* or *Künu* according to age. Otherwise name used.

In the kinship terminology we observe that the terms used to address the various relatives are based on clan membership. Apart from a man's immediate relatives from his father and mother's side we also find that clan members play an important role. A man regards all the clansmen who are his father's age as his father or *aba*, his father's older brothers and those belonging to his age grade as *abazemba* or older father, his father's younger brothers and their age grade as *asa* or younger father, his older brother's age grade as *anga* or older brother, his younger brother's age grade as *kenu* or younger brother and his age grade as *keti* or brother. His father's sisters are called *ata* or sister by the Mongsen speaking group while among the Tsüngli group the father's sisters are called '*oni*'.

Both his paternal and maternal grandmothers are called *azzü* or grandmother, and both his paternal and maternal grandfathers are called *aow*. The women belonging to his grandmother's clan, regardless of their age, even those who are younger to him will be called *azzü*. In the same way, his grandfathers' clansmen are called *aow* or grandfather regardless of their age. All grandchildren whether male or female is called by the same term - *semtsüri*. An ego's older sister is called *azzümo* or older mother; his mother's younger sister is called *anuzai* or younger mother. All his mother's clanswomen are called either *azzümo* or *anuzai* depending on their age, in effect all his mother's clanswomen are his 'mothers'. His mother's brothers are called *ako* and this term is used for all his mother's clansmen.

The most important kinship relations of a man are evidently those with the members of his own agnatic lineage. But the man's maternal brothers are also persons with whom kinship is important and in the same token so are the children of his sister, especially the sons of his sister. In the kinship relationship between the man and the sons of his sister, there is reciprocal exchange of rights and duties. There are various categories of kinship relationships in Changki which are given in the following:

Relationship with agnates

We find that in the Changki kinship system the father's brothers constitute one category and the mother's brothers and sister's sons another. A man's agnates are all regarded as father, brother and son depending on their age. All clansmen are regarded as '*abazemba*' (older father), '*asa*' (younger father), '*anga*' (older brother), '*kenu*' (younger brother) and '*keti*' (brother).

The father's brothers are regarded as the man's 'older' ('*abazemba*') or 'younger' ('*asa*') fathers. A man's relationship to his father's brothers is significantly closer for he calls them father and in the event that his father's brothers die without leaving any heirs, he becomes their heir and inherits all immovable property. The father-eldest son relationship is usually one where the father is an authoritarian figure when the boy is growing up. The belief is that the son must respect and defer to the father and through strict discipline, learn to be a 'man'. As the boy matures into early adulthood, the relationship becomes closer with the father consulting the son on every matter, such as building or repairing a house, looking after the rice fields, concerning family matters such as education of the younger siblings and so on. As the son becomes an adult, much of the responsibilities with regard to property (house sites, rice fields, and forests), family welfare, and clan matters and so on are put on him and his father begins to rely on his judgment and advice. In the same token if the father's brothers do not have any sons, the father's brothers' also look upon their brother's eldest son as their own and take him into confidence and consult him on all matters relating to property, family matters and other sundry matters. As the heir the son is expected to know every detail for he will soon be the head of the family. The man is also is also rendered every possible assistance by his father's brothers but his filial duty towards them is greater and often he has to obey them and carry out whatever responsibilities he has been assigned.

Among the parallel cousins the oldest male is regarded as the eldest brother and thus he become the guardian and protector among them and he is given respect and deference by his cousins. The relationship of the man with his paternal kin is based on obedience and respect and he has legal as well as social obligations to perform according to customary usages.

Tiuo Tukori

In Changki society a great deal of importance is attached to the relationship of mother's brother and sister's son. The mother's brothers are called *Tiuo Tukori*, which translated means maternal uncles. However when the children address him, he is called *'ako'*. The *Tiuo Tukori* (maternal uncles) is regarded as the guardians of their sister and her children and their role is to safe-guard their interest. They are expected to support and protect their sister and her children in everything. If the sister is mistreated or abandoned by her husband, her brothers will be the first person she turns to for help and redress. The nephews and nieces also look to their maternal uncles for material help and moral support. For example, if there is a case against a person, it is not only the paternal uncles and clansmen who will be there to defend him. His maternal uncles will be there too and if the need arises they can also speak on his behalf.

The term *Tiuo Tukori* also applies to all the mother's agnates and the elders of the mother's clan also play an important role especially in times of crisis or celebrations. The *Tiuo Tukori* gives security to the sister as well as to her children. In a sense, for the woman, her position in the natal home as well as in her clan is maintained and the continuity is through the relationship with the *Tiuo Tukori* who acts as her guardian and protector. The *Tiuo Tukori* will never allow any slight or harm to be inflicted on her and on her children and they will always be on call should she need them. This does not mean that the *Tiuo Tukori* can arbitrarily interfere in their sister's affairs. If any crisis should arise between husband and wife they are the one's to act as the mediators and try to patch up things.

The personal relationship between the husband and his wife's brothers is also an important factor but in any event, the *Tiuo Tukori* does not have the right to interfere in their sister's internal domestic affairs. But should the sister misbehave or does not perform her duties, the brothers have the right to upbraid and 'straighten' her out for her behaviour reflects on their standing with her in-laws. The relationship between the *Tiuo Tukori* and their sister's in-laws in general are rather formal and distant and hence each tries to maintain equidistance and decorum. However, the relationship between the children and the mother's brothers is more intimate and friendly and there is more indulgence and affection between the *Tiuo Tuko* and their nephews and nieces. The nephews are called *Kumnak* and the nieces *Kuomo* by the *Tiuo Tukori*.

Tiuo Tukori and Temnakja

Temnakja are male offspring's born to a man's sisters or clanswomen. However the sons born to a man's sister is called the *Temnak Temen*, meaning 'closest by blood'. A man becomes the *Temnak Temen* of his mother's brothers and his sister's sons are his *Temnak Temen*. However the sister's sons are commonly called *Temnakja*.

The term *Temnakja* roughly translated means 'to guard'. The duty of the nephew is thus to guard his maternal uncle and to be on hand to give support, both physical and material, throughout his lifetime. In the same token, the grandson born to a daughter is also his 'guard' and 'protector'. However it is the relationship between the maternal uncle and nephew that is more specific and important for it is one of dependence and exchange, which in the traditional custom, is an indispensable part of a man's life.

In the same token, the son's of all his clanswomen are his *Temnakja* but his closest *Temnakja* are his nephews born to his real sisters. All *Temnakja* are addressed as *Kumnak*. The call of duty for the *Temnakja* is confined not only to big events like weddings, funerals or for emergencies. He is the one who is on hand for his uncle for every little thing that might be required. The *Temankja* will stand as witness when demarcation of land is carried out through sale or purchase or when other disputes arises; the *Temnakja* will accompany the maternal uncle on certain occasions such as when going outside the village for medical treatment and so on. The maternal uncle relies and depends on his *Temnakja* not only for physical support but the obedience and duty that he can command from his *Temnakja* also enhances his social standing and respectability in the village. *Tiuo Tukori* and *Temnakja* share a reciprocal relationship.

Chanakri – Relationship with affines

The sister's husbands (brother-in-law) and daughter's husbands are called *Chanakri* and they have certain duties and obligations towards their in-laws. The *Chanakri* are the male affines through marriage. The *Chanakri* is the caretaker of the sister and daughter and he is the progenitor of the man's *Temnakja* and thus he is accorded due respect and privilege. In times of celebrations, accidents or tragedies etc. the *Chanakri* works in close tandem with the *Temnakja* and undertakes responsibilities according to the situation. A man can call for his *Chanakri's* services anytime and they will be duty bound to carry out whatever tasks have been assigned to them. In the same token, a man is obliged to give support and help whenever his *Chanakri* requires.

The difference between the *Temnakja* and *Chanakri* used to be emphasised in the meat share, for the share of the *Temnakja* was bigger than that of the *Chanakri*. In Changki it is said that the *Temnakja* is related by blood while the *Chanakri* are like the '*nokpang*', which means the handle of the *dao* (Naga version of the machete), which can be broken anytime. The relationship with the *Temnakja* is for life and they are an integral part of a man's life while that of the *Chanakri* could change either due to death or divorce and the *Chanakri* could become the in-law of another family. Thus the meat share of the *Temnakja* was always bigger. However such differentiation is not prevalent nowadays.

Temnakri – Relationship with Temnakja and Chanakri

Both the *Temnakja* and *Chanakri* of a man are called *Temnakri*. These will include the sons of a man's sister and the sons of his clanswomen, who are his *Temnakja* and brothers-in-law and sons-in-law who are called *Chanakri*. The *Temnakri* are the ones to whom a man will turn to whenever the need arises. In times of emergencies, tragedies, celebrations etc the *Temnakri* work together. The *Temnakja* and *Chanakri* are addressed as *Teza Temnak*.

At the empirical level we find that although each household is independent and follows the neolocal pattern of residence, the linkages with the clan, the *Tiuo Tukori* and the *Temnakja* is one of interdependence. The family affairs are conducted independently and privately but there are certain spheres where the clan, *Tiuo Tukori* and *Temnakja* can intervene such as during marriage, funerals and divorce as well as inheritance should there be any dispute regarding the distribution of shares of the inheritance.

The various categories of relatives, described so far, form the various network of kinship relationship in Changki society but the foundation of the kinship relations is based on membership to a clan. The clan is the most important factor in a man's life and citizenship in the village is determined by membership to a clan which is by birth.

Clan system

Mandelbaum (1972:576) speaking of the tribal wrote "in tribal life the principal links for the whole society are based on kinship. Individual equality as kinsman is assumed; dependency and subordination among men are minimized. Agnatic bonds form the fundamental web, affinal ties are of lesser significance. Lineages or clans tend to be the chief corporate units; they are often the principal units for land ownership, for defense, for economic production and consumption. Each man considers himself entitled to equal rights with every other"...and..."most tribesmen have larger corporate groups than the family and wider social cooperation." According to Radcliffe-Brown (*op.cit.*:41) the term 'clan' has been used without any clear definition but that it should be used only for a group having unilineal descent in which all the members regard one another as in some specific sense kinfolk. Membership to a clan is normally determined by birth and the structure of clans from the point of view of an individual appears to be a grouping of his relatives. 'A clan system, however, also provides a division of a tribe into a number of distinct separate groups, each having its own identity. The clan may then, as groups, play an important part in the social, political or religious life of the tribe' (ibid:40). Malinowski (1971:103) stated that 'the functions of the clan are mostly legal and ceremonial, at times also magical and economic.' He went on to say that 'the clan, by the very nature of its formation, is a dependent and correlated unit' (ibid:103). The clan is not only a corporate unit in the legal or jural sense but is also the primary political association. The clan system, in the context of Changki society, first of all provides the individual with citizenship, and thus identity, in the village with its attendant legal rights and duties. Secondly the clan forms the principal unit for land ownership and lastly the political association is based on the founding clans who control the majority of land holdings in the village and who are accepted as traditional leaders by virtue of being the founding clans.

The hierarchical order of the clans is governed by the migration of the clans to the village. The first settlers in the village are called the *Emkümri* or founding clans. Occupation of land for cultivation and settlement as well as reserved forests distinguishes the founding clans from the clans who settled in the village later and are called *Emjenri* or latecomers. The founding of a village usually comprised of many clans so that clan exogamy was maintained. Thus in Changki we find that there are three founding clans, namely the Longchari, Amri and Changkiri clans. Originally there were seven clans, but three clans went their separate ways, while one clan died out. In the intervening years after the village was established if any other clans wanted to settle in the village, they were welcomed for the status of the village as a 'big' village in relation to other villages was enhanced by the increase in the population.

In the earlier days when migration took place, those coming in groups kept their own clan names, for example, the Alingri, Metsüri, Süngalosang, Ongtsüri/ Longkumer, Akhori, Tz?diri and Ningdangri clans and maintained their clan identity. In the case of the Pongenri clan, although it was an individual who migrated to Changki, as he was brought to the village to be the *Tsüngba* or priest, he was given due respect by being allowed to maintain his clan name.

When other groups of people migrated to the village at a later stage, it was also an accepted custom for these groups to attach themselves to the founding clans which is known as '*kin emba*' (literal translation is to cultivate a clan, but it also means to acknowledge or be adopted by a clan) or '*teba emba*' (literally it means to call father) or '*tinu emba*' (which translated means to attach to a clan) but although they were given lands and treated as the sons/brothers of the clan to which they had attached themselves, their origins were not forgotten even after they got assimilated and became a part of the clan with rights and duties. Thus the people who migrated and settled in the village as a group, family or individual were granted citizenship in the village through this system of adoption. The people who were adopted in the past when the village was established and was strengthening its numerical power have been assimilated and through the ages have become members of the clan that adopted them but even today there are whispers of their origins though such thoughts are not expressed openly. The oral tradition has ensured that the lore and history of the people are preserved and handed down.

Earlier non-Naga individuals were also allowed to attach themselves to a clan elder and call him 'father' and were adopted as his son/s. There are a number of such cases of non-Nagas in the village who got married to Changki women and settled in the village and they are accepted as Changki villagers but nowadays the Village Council does not allow the adoption of non-Nagas. The following tables show the groups and individuals who migrated to Changki, attached themselves to the Changki clans and settled in the village.

Table 10

Group/Individuals that migrated from other Ao villages and settled in Changki

Sl. No	Village of origin	Adopting Clan in Changki
1.	Khensa Masü (from Khensa terrirtory)	Pongenri clan
2.	Khensa Masü	Amri clan

(Contd...)

Sl. No	Village of origin	Adopting Clan in Changki
3.	Khensa village	Metsüri clan
4.	Longsa village	Emrem Changki clan
5.	Unger village	Metsüri clan
6.	Waromong village	Longchari clan
7.	Khangtsung village	Metsüri clan
8.	Aonokpu village	Longkumer clan
9.	Mangmetong village	Longkumer clan
10.	Nemchem village	Pongenri clan
11.	Japfu	Longkumer clan
12	Ungma	Emrem Changki clan

Table 10 shows the individuals who migrated from various Ao villages and attached themselves to various clans in Changki and settled in Changki. These settlers are those who came to the village circa 1960-1980. As per legend, Changki village was established about eight to nine hundred years ago.

In Table 11 we find that eighteen individuals who belong to other Naga tribes and non-Nagas have attached themselves to various clans. They have been adopted by members of these clans and have been given plots of land for residential sites and for cultivation. But the land will never become their private property nor will it be inherited by their children. The clan will make the final decision regarding the land upon the demise of the adopted man.

Table 11

Other Naga tribes/Non-Nagas that migrated and settled in Changki village

Sl.No	Origin	Adopting Clan in Changki
1	Bengali	Metsüri
2	Bengali	Metsüri
3	Nepali	Changkiri
4	Nepali	Changkiri
5	Nepali	Changkiri
6	Nepali	Changkiri
7	Nepali	Changkiri
8	Malayali	Changkiri
9	Assamese	Amri
10	Adivasi	Changkiri
11	Anglo Indian	Tzüdiri
12	Manipuri	Longchari
13	Chang Naga tribe	Changkiri
14	Yimchunger Naga tribe	Longchari
15	Chakesang Naga tribe	Alingri
16	Manipuri	Amri
17	Yimchunger Naga tribe	Amri
18	Nepali	Longkumer

The adoption process whereby a group/individual will attach themselves to a clan by calling them father and who will in turn be given land and other rights and duties as per the norm proves the importance of clan membership and how much of a role it plays in the lives of the people. As a rule it is mandatory that a person attaches himself to a clan in order to be a member of the village community. The adoption process was confined to the clan alone. When an adoption takes place, the person who wants to call a clan elder 'father' will find out the possibilities and will send feelers through friends and relatives of the man. If the request is in the affirmative, the 'son' will give a gift of the clan's shawl or take a pig and kill in the 'father's' house, the pig's head will be given to the 'father' and the rest of the meat cooked and the whole family will have a meal together. In this the *Temnakri* (sister/clanswomen's sons and brother-in-laws/son-in-law) will be present too and the man who has allowed another person to call him 'father' will declare to all the news. In this way, the adoption is finalized. There are no hard and fast rules that a pig must be killed but in the event of a pig being killed by the 'adopted' son at a later date for whatever purpose, he will present the pig's head to his 'father' as a sign of respect. However when it comes to adoption of small children, the people have a belief that should a couple adopt a child, even if they are childless; the adopted child would 'eat' up all the family fortune and bring bad luck. The adoption of children of unknown lineage is discouraged, but the couple can adopt children of their own relatives who are orphaned. However the parentage of the children remains unchanged and they will belong to the clan into which they were born. The question of adopting a child, in addition to a couple's children does not arise at all, because it is believed that the adopted child would take away all the luck, fortune and even life of the couple's own children. Therefore the adoption process remains restricted to the clan only.

The clan is the source from where a man derives his identity, his rights, along with its attendant duties and obligations, and social standing in the village. The people assert that there are no sharp divisions based on clan membership in the village for each man is regarded as good as the other but we find that there is a differentiation between that of the founding clans and the clans who came later. This is most evident with regard to land and its usage.

With each successive wave of migration into Changki village, the founding clans namely the Longchari, Amri and Changkiri gave land for cultivation and settlement to the clans who settled in Changki later. The Longchari and Amri clans hold the majority of land holdings in the upper *khel* while in the lower *khel* vast land holdings are held by the Changkiri clan.

The settlement patterns by clans in the village show that in the upper *khel* the following clans have settled there namely, the Longchari, Amri, Changkiri, Alingri, Pongenri and Metsüri. In the lower *khel* we find that the clans who have settled there are Changkiri, Metsüri, Emrem Changki, Losangri, Longkumer, Tzüdiri, Molir, Ningdangri and Akhori. The settlement patterns also indicate the migration of the clans to the village.

Table 12
Population and households based on clan in Süngdakba (upper khel)

Sl No	Clan	Males	Females	No. of households
1	Longchari	103	101	64
2	Amri	107	133	60
3	Alingri	105	92	38
4	Metsüri	52	47	15
5	Ningdangri	8	12	9
6	Pongenri	11	9	9
Total		**386**	**394**	**195**

In Table 12 we find that there are six clans settled in Süngdakba or the upper *khel* and the number of households is 195. The total population stands at 780 out of which 386 are males and 394 are females.

Table 13
Population and households based on clan in Ayim Anet (lower khel)

Sl No	Clan	Males	Females	No. of Households
1	Changkiri	138	150	53
2	Longkumer	49	63	56
3	Metsüri	97	115	51
4	Tzüdiri	20	12	14
5	Moliri	15	4	10
6	Akhori	12	4	6
7	Ningdangri	9	11	10
8	Pongenri	28	22	15
9	Losangri	30	20	12
10	Emrem Changki	62	25	34
	Total	**460**	**426**	**261**

The table above shows that in Ayim Anet or the lower *khel*, there are ten clans and there are 261 households comprising a total population of 886 out of which 460 are males and 426 are females. It may be noted that the **Metsüri**, **Pongenri** and **Ningdangri** clans are settled in both the khels. Earlier the Changkiri clan also lived in the upper *khel* but they have all died out and as such the Changkiri clan is found only in the lower *khel* at present.

One of the distinctions that differentiate the founding clans from the other clans who settled in the village later is land ownership. When the first settlers established the village, the first ritual was to demarcate a separate site for worship where religious ceremonies would be performed. After this sites were selected for the *Arju* or male dormitories and for the village meeting/recreational place. Then the founding clans would choose locations for residential sites as well as for jhum cultivation. In this way we find that majority of the land holdings would be in the hands of the founding clans. However when other clans came and settled in the village at a later stage they were allocated land for cultivation and settlement, and these become their lands and the clans have exclusive rights to the land allocated to them.

The founding clans have certain rights and privileges and even though each Changki man is regarded as equal to the other, the concept of *Emkümri* (or founding clan) has certain prestige attached. Their status as *Emkümri* (founding clan) commands respect and in subtle ways they are accorded deference. For example, when they founded the village, the founding clans established their own system of government called '*emli*'. Accordingly the village government was run and when the other clans migrated and settled in the village, they became incorporated into the existing system. Thus '*emli*' (system of village government) was the established system by the founding clans but in the execution of the administrative work, the later clans also had rights and duties and could be part of the government. The *Emkümri* use the phrase '*i emli teraksa*' which translated mean 'don't break our *emli*'. In other words they are laying claim to the privilege of having been the ones to establish the village '*emli*' (system of village government) and thereby proclaim their position as founding clans. Sometimes when disputes arises and the other clans express their opinions which is unacceptable to the *Emkümri* (founding) clans they use the phrase '*yasü ra zangairi ningla nü ta metekü*', which translated mean 'you all came only yesterday, what do you know.' In this way, they effectively assert their dominant position in the village.

With regard to land and its allocation the *Emkümri* (founding clans) has the major land holdings such as residential sites, cultivation and jhum lands and forests in the immediate vicinity of the village site. The other clan members who might want to utilise these lands or the products from it such as bamboo, wood, etc owned by the founding clans will have to take permission from them. In this way the relationship between that of the founding clans and the other clans was one where there was reciprocity, based on land and its usage. The founding clans dispensed the land and the receiver of the land was obliged to perform certain favours in return, although this is not tacitly stated. In this form of exchange we find an informal system of patron-client relationship although it is not rigidly followed.

We find that in Changki the founding clans are called '*kin asem*' which translated simply mean 'the three clans' while the other clans are called '*kin tebenja*' meaning the 'rest of the clans'. In this way the people themselves differentiate between the founding clans and the other clans who settled in the village later.

It has been mentioned that other clans who migrated to the village at a later stage can attach themselves to the clans already settled in the village by calling the oldest clan member or other clan elders 'father'. However the origin of the adopted clan/group is never forgotten although they are given land for cultivation and residential sites. Should any clan member migrate to another village, he forfeits all rights to the land and if he has private property he can sell or give only to his clan members. In this way, land never gets fragmented and the stability and continuity of land ownership by the villagers alone has contributed to the traditional land ownership patterns.

According to Radcliffe Brown,(ed, 1953.:41) a clan may be spoken of as 'corporate' when it possesses any one of a certain number of characters: if its members, or its adult male members, or a considerable of them, come together occasionally to carry out some collective action – for example, the performance of rites; if it has a chief or council who are regarded as the representatives of the group as a whole; if it possesses or controls property which is collective, as when a clan or lineage is a land-owning group. Following this assertion we may say that the clans in Changki are corporate groups with land holdings that are exclusively meant for the use of members of the particular clan. Mandelbaum (op.cit.:587) also wrote that "tribal lands tend to be vested in clans; the kinsmen of a clan together share a productive territory." Any other clan members taking out even a twig from the land/forest are fined not only by the clans whose property he encroached but also by his own clan for breaching the code of conduct and bringing shame to his clan. The rules of exclusive rights where land is concerned are so deeply ingrained that violation of the rules is not tolerated. But in Changki nowadays some portions of the forests belonging to the clans are put in the category of reserved forests and are considered protected areas. In such forests the clan members themselves cannot take anything from it unless the '*Yimten*' or village government grants permission although the forest and its produce may belong to the clan.

Just as land holdings are exclusive to the clan, personal or the first names are also the exclusive property of a clan and within the clan there can be no duplication of a name (Ao,2000:21). It is believed that if the same name of a clan member is given to another child born to the clan, the minor does not survive for long. Each name has meanings and lore attached that commemorate certain events or achievements, which could be personal or pertaining to the clan. Such names were the means through which the history and legends of the clan were passed on from one generation to the other through the oral tradition.

Certain names also signify the special relationship between clans. For example, the name *Poktenba* belongs to the Changkiri clan. Legend has it that at one point of time this clan was about to end with *Kharibong* (only son of *Achusangba*) as no woman was willing to marry him because he was blind. There was a girl called *Tsünangsangla* of the Alingri clan, whose parents wanted her to marry *Kharibong*, telling her that though he was blind, she could become the mistress of vast landholdings and large cultivated fields and could live a life of comfort for *Kharibong* belonged to the founding clan. But she refused saying she did not want to marry a blind man.

It so happened that *Kharibong* was *Tsünangsangla's* neighbour and being blind he could not do any work except sit in the *kilangmi*, which is an open platform built with bamboos, keeping guard over the paddy being dried in the sun. He was given a long stick with which to drive away the chickens when they came to eat the paddy. From the adjoining *kilangmi*, *Tsünangsangla* used to tease *Kharibong* by imitating the chickens eating paddy and he would swing the stick in the direction of the sound. When *Kharibong's* parents became aware of this, they tied a charm (*awalong*) at the end of the stick and when *Tsünangsangla* teased him the next day, he hit her with the stick that had the charm tied to the end, legend says that she became enamoured of him. That very night, she informed her parents that she would marry only *Kharibong* and soon they got married. A son was born and he was called *Poktenba*, which means 'begins to burst forth' because the clan which was on the verge of extinction began to 'burst forth' with *Kharibong*. Two more sons *Yangrusangba* and *Imlisangba* were born, augmenting the great hope expressed through the name of the first born (ibid:18). Thus through this name and the lore attached to it the special affinal relationship between the two clans are kept alive.

Another example is the name *Imtinochet* belonging to the Changkiri clan. The name means 'one who brought a whole clan/group/people' (ibid:20). It refers to the lore where *Imdongdangba* fell in love with *Takuyangrula* and in his bid to bring her to the village the whole group from *Changpang* was brought to Changki village. The historical migration of the group is thus preserved and handed down through generations with the lore attached to this name.

In Table 14 some of the personal names of each clan in Changki are given. These names are unique to the particular clan and the other clans cannot use these personal names. Most of the names are gender neutral. However in a few cases they are gender specific, for example the name *Naro* (flower) is for females only and the name *Anok* (*Dao*-Naga machete) is for males only.

The clans in Changki have no affinity to other Ao clans in the numerous Ao villages in general, except for the Longkumer clan (who were one of the last settlers in Changki) for they can trace their origin to Longkhum village in the Ongbangkong range and still maintain relationships with their clansmen there. It is said that after coming from Koridang to Longkhum and after many generations, *Longpok's* eldest son *Mosamsa's* grandson *Imfuba* (*Imsuba)* was careless in setting fire to the jhum field and accidentally killed an old woman in the fire and also nearly burnt down the whole village. This was one of the greatest offences a man could commit and the penalty of such an offence imposed by the Village Government was five *Mithun* which was too heavy for the family to bear. On the urging of the family members, *Imfuba* along with his *Waisangla* and their five children *Imsensenba*, *Longlang*, *Ningsioba*, *Risendong* and *Peremchiba* went to Pangti village and settled in the Ao khel so as to escape the fine and the ruination of his extended family.

After a while his brother, *Risendong* and his family went back to Longkhum village, while *Peremchiba* and his family left Pangti and went to Mangla where they stayed with the *Anichar* clan. *Longlang* stayed back in Pangti and became very rich and gave many feasts of merit. This spawned a rivalry especially from *Pur* and *Abangjungba* which led to unrest and disharmony in the village. On account of the campaign against him by his rivals, *Longlang* left the village and went to Changpang and established a village there. From Changpang the Longkumer, Ningdangri, Akhori, Molir and Tzüdir clans migrated to Changki, the story of which is narrated in the Changki village formation section in the previous chapter

Table 14
Personal names belonging exclusively to clans in Changki

Sl. No	Clan	Personal names
1	Longchari	Tinuniken, Tekachang, Talimethong, Kungrola, Taliwabangla, Aorepla etc
2	Amri	Thaitsüng, Nisoba, Jungmisa, Mesuden, Relipangla, Angtsüng, Melipong, Jempangjang, Yangpichang etc
3	Changkiri	Lolentsüngba, Poktenba, Yangrusangba. Tasüngba, Karibong, Sangkai, Tsübongniken,Yangpinok, Yarangnaro, Changkikaba etc
4	Alingri	Ningsükaba, Noksang, Longendi, Semsa, Ponen, Kupzasü, Lodonga, Mongyang, Rangpo etc
5	Metsüri	Senpirong, Imsenpirong,

		Kilangzulu, Imtisensen, Watisang, Imsenkilepla, Katinangba etc
6	Longkumer	Mosemsa, Risendong, Okipong, Yangpir, Imtsüdangba, Imnasosang, Nikenmiri, Supisula, Chungminaro, Jungmayangla, etc
7	Tzüdiri	Pangjunglemba, Nangshikaba, Sangli, Sabangjungba, etc
8	Moliri	Kümsangdong,Tsüdongtzüba, Ningtiba,Tekalemla etc
9	Akhori	Imrongzulu, Nokdang, Imlenjungba, Sübongtemjen etc
10	Ningdangri	Pangerlemba, Tsüpokyimla, Limasungba, Jungkotemba, Nokzenketba, Tebusangba etc
11	Pongenri	Chalupong, Abangsen, Mejongri, Yimtsülaba, Tiangsen, Odangba etc
12	Losangri	Tsünangkümpon, Semoba. Aibanganaro, Sübongsangla, Menekchachemia etc.
13	Emrem Changki	Anoktiba, Tekangba, Sakuniken, Lanudangti etc

The names of the clans of Changki are also distinctly different from the other Ao clans. Mills (1926:26) puts forward the theory that 'the Changki, Mongsen and Chungli groups represent three waves of invasion of which the Changki group was the first and the Chungli the last.' However the Metsüri clan of Changki claims that they belong to the Jamir clan (Ao clan) and collaborates this by the personal names given to their clansmen such as *Imsenpirong* who belonged to the Jamir clan and was the one who discovered water according to Ao legend. From this we also see how personal names of particular clans can support claims of identification and membership. There is also a story as to why the Metsüri are called by this name. It appears that in the ancient past this clan refused to contribute towards the village fund and so the other Changki villagers called them Metsüri or 'those who did not participate/contribute' and the name stuck on. The Alingri clan also claims to have affinity with the Longchar clan, another Ao clan found in various villages. However the Changki *Senso* (Changki General Assembly) has declared that all Changki clans should retain their original names and do not attach much importance to such claims

But although the clan as a unit forms a close knit group, we also find that intra-clan rivalry exists and the members compete with each other especially in matters of seniority of *Tenik* or lineage. Being the 'oldest' has certain prestige attached, for he becomes the guardian of the clan and his advice and opinions are sought and his decision becomes final. In the distribution of meat too, the oldest member gets the head of the animal, signifying his position as well as the respect that it brings. As mentioned earlier the clan's history begins with its migration to the village for this establishes the position of the clan in the village society. The history of lineages of the clans in the village is somewhat vague for many of the old people who knew the genealogical order of the lineages are dead and those who may have some idea prefer not to talk about it because this is another sensitive issue, given that they have to rely on the oral tradition and that certain sections of the people are quick to take offence about the chronological order of the lineages and this has led to misunderstandings and even the taking of fines.

The researcher had a first hand experience of this in the village in the course of the fieldwork. One of the clansmen had given me a chart of the Longkumer clan's genealogical lineage. When I showed this to the clan's elders in the village so as to confirm that what I had got was true, it stirred up a hornet's nest with many of the elders disputing the chronological order and claiming that their lineage was older than the other. I was also warned not to venture into the issue of other clans' genealogical lineages for I would be fined pigs. Such issues are very sensitive and most people tend to keep to themselves any knowledge, if they have, of such issues to themselves.

The relationship between kinsmen depends on the chronological seniority of clan members and this is acknowledged by way of the respect shown and in the distribution of meat on certain occasions. On the occasion of a marriage the oldest clan member will receive the head of a pig and in this way respect is shown. The presence of clan elders also gives respectability to the people concerned. For example, on the occasion of a funeral it is the oldest clan member who will represent the clan by giving a eulogy, in his absence the next oldest member will do the honour and so on. It is believed that the clan elders give '*akum*' which roughly translated means to give honour, grace and the acknowledgement of kinship. The presence of clan elders on such occasion gives respectability and importance to one's standing in society and lends a certain aura emphasizing the seriousness of the occasion.

We find that age and generation play an important role in the network of kinship relationships. Status is ascribed on the basis of age and generational levels and a kinship member's form of behaviour and allocation of material benefits in relation to those of another member are partly determined by age and generational factors. Within the same generation, older members took precedence over younger members;

members of a senior generation took precedence over those of a younger generation. Older persons are accorded due respect and younger persons are expected to obey the older ones. With other clan members age and generational factors also play an important role.

In the interaction between the elders and younger members of a clan we find that they are formal and circumspect. The younger people cannot joke or even speak unless they are asked to in front of their elders and they cannot afford to show disrespect under any circumstances. Any verbal exchange that has sexual connotations is taboo between a man and a woman belonging to the same clan; it is strongly felt that it may be considered as incestuous.

The clan as we find in Changki is an exclusive and corporate body and in order to keep the traditions of the clan active and to ensure that the bonds of clan members are not severed, all the clans in Changki congregate once every two to three years in Changki *lusa* or territory. Each clan will organise its own *'Kübok Waba'* (which translated literally means to go camping) every once in a while. For example, in January 2004 we observed that the Metsüri clan held their camp in the Tzürang area.

The members who are residing outside the village are also informed and are expected to come to the village. The clan elders decide on a place within Changki *lusa* (territory) and the clan male members set up camp there for about two days and night. In this camp the members get to know each other and the elders tell stories of the clan history, heroes and legends. The younger generations are told about the clan territory, rights, responsibilities and traditions. In this way the bonding between clan members are forged and reinforced and the clan as a tight knit group is strengthened. The youngsters learn the intricacies of clan *ningja kuja* meaning terminologies, *awasü* meaning manners, *sala sana* meaning discussions of the clan *nungtak* meaning needs and agenda. Other confidential matters with regard to the clan are also discussed during such camps. At such times a live pig as well as other ration is taken to the camp that has been bought with the money collected for the clan fund, through membership fees from the clansmen annually. Such money is kept with a treasurer and utilized for purposes pertaining to the clan.

Among the women such camps are not held but the women too have their *pachalari* (clanswomen) fund which is collected from the members either in cash or kind. For example, the Longkumer clanswomen collected one tin of paddy (a tin holds approximately 10 kg of paddy) from each member and the paddy collected was sold. The money collected from the sale of the paddy was kept with the treasurer of the clanswomen fund. This money is lent out to clanswomen from time to time on an interest of Rs.3 for every Rs.100. The money is utilized for various purposes such as when a clanswoman falls ill then with the money from the fund either cash or kind is given in the name of the clanswomen. Again should a clanswoman get married then a small present is bought from this fund in the name of the clanswomen.

We have stated that the clan as a group forms a close knit and exclusive group and every member is expected to act in cooperation, collaboration and even self-sacrifice for the good of the clan. The clan as a group is very conscious and careful about keeping a good name and image, as it were, and the elders takes pains to ensure that the younger clan members do not bring a 'bad name' to the clan and in this way the elders can be authoritarian in their dealings with the younger generation. The phrase '*ning menok*' meaning 'defaming the name of the clan and throwing it into the gutter' is often repeated and told to those who are in the habit of getting into trouble. No matter where a person is settled, the clan elders in the village can summon him to the village if he brings shame to the clan. No one can ignore this summon for even if the person concerned may try to escape, his family and relatives will make sure that he obeys the dictates of the clan elders. In the village the clan elders will roundly chastise, berate and even fine him. But no matter what a person does or how badly he conducts himself, his clansmen will never abandon him. He may be treated with disdain and contempt but when it comes to the crunch in any circumstances the clan will be there for him, not so much as for the love of that particular person, but for the sake of the name of the clan.

The relationship of the clanswomen with that of the younger generation is more relaxed and intimate but here too, the women often act as the teacher often lecturing the youngsters on how to behave, how to speak and conduct themselves so that the name of the clan will not be tarnished. Obedience and duty towards parents, family and clan elders are emphasised. '*Tening Tebong enerirong*' this is the usual phrase used by the clanswomen which translated it means 'bring good name to the clan'. The prestige, good name and reputation of the clan is zealously guarded and all clansmen and clanswomen are keenly conscious of this and accordingly try to preserve and maintain it. It is this obsessive and passionate need to preserve the name of the clan that anything remotely thought of as a slur on the clan exacts an immediate fine and thus other clans are very careful and circumspect when it comes to other clans, as this is a very sensitive issue.

The possessive right that the clan has over the clan members can be best illustrated by the examples of certain clan members who make a name for themselves and reach great heights of achievement in their lifetime. Even if he has settled elsewhere and dies outside the village the clan has the right to demand that the body be brought and interred in the village. In this way the clan's prestige and reputation is kept for perpetuity and the lore associated with the clan member's accomplishments is never forgotten thus serving as an example. There is also the belief that should a man of such high stature be buried in an alien soil, the soul would be unhappy and the village will not receive the blessings such as that bestowed on the deceased who brought such glory for the clan and the village.

There have been cases when the body of the deceased could not be brought to the village but after a certain period of time, the bones has been brought to the village and interred in the graveyard of the village. Even if it is only the bones that are brought, the clan ensures that the burial ceremony is conducted with due solemnity and respect befitting someone who has brought laurels to the clan. This is the ultimate respect and recognition that the clan can give to a clan member. It may also be mentioned that even if a clan member does not achieve anything outstanding, the clan has possessive rights over his dead body and ensures that he is interred in the village even if he had settled outside the village.

The personal name of the deceased clansman will be given to any boy born to the clan thereafter and often it is believed that if the name of a clansman who had accomplished much is given to a newborn, this boy might grow up to bring the same kind of laurels to the clan. But more than that the lore of the glory brought to the clan through the clan member is preserved with the perpetuation of the name.

With regard to the clanswomen, the clan may not exercise such rights over her body although when she dies the clan ensures that their duties and obligations towards her are not neglected at any cost. However the clan has possessive right over her personal name. When a clanswoman marries her father declares to all present when she is about to leave the house, 'from this day onwards, this daughter of ours is yours. Her duty, her devotion, and even her physical being will be yours. But on the day her soul leaves her body, please bring her *name* back to us' (Ao, *op.cit*:25). 'Giving back the name' is prevalent even today. When a woman dies her husband or her sons will go to her father's house along with some of her personal effects, symbolizing the ritual of giving back the name, and in all solemnity formally hand back her personal name. In the event of a girl being born into the clan thereafter, her name will be given the name to the newborn thus perpetuating the name, which belongs to the clan only.

The clan is for all purposes the pivot in which a person's life revolves. From the day a person is born his every word, deed, and achievement reflects upon his clan. Socialization and social control is exercised through the influence that the clan has on its member. In many ways it is the clan that gives security and stability to the members and these factors contribute towards maintaining the cohesive and strong ties that bind the members of the clan and for the fact that even today the importance of the clan has not diminished. The notion of clan as has been stated is very much ingrained in the psyche of the Changki villagers and even today this is felt just as strongly, even among the educated young people. The continuity of the traditional social structure is maintained through the clan system and the various roles and relationships forged through it. The function of the clan is the enforcement of social and moral order among the members. Conflicts between individuals or families are normally arbitrated by the committee. As a close-knit group, the clan performs the functions of protecting kinsmen against injustice from outsiders. Inter-clan conflicts are also handled by the committee. The clans dominate collective life of the village that without clan membership a person is socially isolated and without it a person cannot be a citizen of the village.

Position of women in Changki society

The position of women in Changki society is secondary to

that of the men. The Changki society follows the unilineal principle of patrilineal descent which means that it is the father-son-brother constellation that dominates; while the women's only role is that of being daughter/sister/wife/mother. The man has complete control over property rights and also over his children. The women are debarred from participating in the Village Council, which is the highest decision making body at the grassroots level. In fact they cannot even enter the hall when such meetings take place. The women cannot inherit immovable properties like house sites, rice fields, and so on, either from her father or her husband. She may be allowed to live in the house where she lived with her husband or in her father's house and to use certain portions of the agricultural land during her lifetime but she has no control over such properties. Should the male heirs decide to take back the house or land, she will have no choice but to hand those properties back.

The women perform the role of a wife, mother, child bearer, food producer and household manager. The women have a greater range of responsibilities, ranging from household maintenance to various agricultural activities, and they have greater work burden in both as well. The women are held responsible for the proper management of the family; should the family prosper and the children do well, she earns the respect of the people but should the family fall on hard times due to mismanagement of domestic affairs, it is the women who bear the brunt of ill repute. Clearly the onus of domestic management falls on the shoulder of the women.

The women participate in all agricultural activities and are the main workers in the agricultural sector. Except for ploughing, the women are involved in all the agriculture work such as transplantation, weeding, reaping, threshing and winnowing. The women do most of the drudgery prone and monotonous work. For example, the drudgery of household work like cooking is carried over to the rice fields too because the women usually cook there in the noon. However when it comes to decision making within the family, it is the husband who makes the final decision. At the community level, women are debarred from clan committees as well as from the Village Council.

The girl child is given every opportunity to get an education but we find that if the parents are not well to do, they will inevitably put the sons in a better school, such as the Mission School, while the daughter will be put in the government primary schools. The sons will also get the first chance to study outside of the village. Even if a girl does well and finds a good job, her social status is enhanced only when she gets married. Marriage with a man outside the community is discouraged, especially with a non-tribal, the reason cited being that once a woman goes away, and the relatives will not be able to protect her interests. We find that with regard to children, although all children are regarded as God's gifts, sons are preferred. The woman who has a son finds herself in a better position with regard to her husband's clan, for her son being the heir provides the link through which she can extract certain benefits such as produce from the clan lands and house and agricultural sites to live and work on. A spinster will have the right to live in her father's house (even if he has expired) during her lifetime and live off the rice field belonging to her father, with the express consent of her brother. If a man leaves behind only daughters then his brothers and their sons will have the right to take all his immoveable property. But in many such cases the brothers and their sons allow the woman and her daughters to live in the house and cultivate the rice fields during the woman's lifetime and till such time as the daughters get married. All women who are spinsters, widows or divorcees are called '*Milari*'. We find that the status of the woman is invariably associated with her father, brother, husband and son and the husband's agnates.

The women are protected by the men - father, brothers, *Tiuo Tukori* (maternal uncles) husband and son and by the clansmen. Mills (op.cit:211-212) wrote 'An Ao woman is far from being a slave and a drudge. Her position is no whit inferior to that of a man. She always has her clan behind her, and were a bad-tempered husband to bully his wife he would soon have a swarm of angry in-laws buzzing around his ears...' It is interesting to note that the women themselves expressed the insecurity they feel if there are no male relatives to help, support and protect them in myriad ways. For example, in the case of a divorce, the woman will have by her side the presence of her father, brother, *Tiuo Tukori* and clansmen throughout the proceedings and if the need arises they will argue in favour of her case and if she is abandoned she will find a place in her paternal home. In the event of a calamity it will be to her father, brother, *Tiuo Tukori* and clansmen that she will turn to and seek help. For example, in the village when an old lady's house needed repairs it was her clansmen who collected the funds among themselves and took a day off from their personal works to repair her house for she had no one to help as her husband was dead and her children had left the village. In such ways, the women are under the protection of the men and from an early age the men are taught to protect and defend their women.

Marriage

Marriage in Changki society is not only about a couple uniting in matrimony but also two families and two clans strengthening kinship ties. Clan exogamy is strictly followed and this is the most important factor in the marriage negotiations. The family background and personal character of the couple in question are also taken into consideration. A person who is of unknown lineage, whose family has a history of insanity, thievery, violence and so on is obviously not the right choice as a partner. Sometimes clan distinctions also have a major role to play. People would definitely prefer alliance with a founding clan member for obvious reasons (Ao, *op.cit.*:44). The position and status of a woman married to a founding clan would be enhanced and if she gives birth to a son. Her access to land and its produce would be ensured through her son.

Marriage also signifies the union of two families, therefore the brothers and sisters of the married couple cannot marry one another for they all become the in-laws and hence, relatives. Marriage between parallel and cross cousins up to the third generation is forbidden for it is believed such cousins have too much 'blood closeness'. Marriage with very close relatives, it is believed, sometimes creates tension and upsets relationships, thereby breaking up the solidarity of the family. Another reason given is that the union of close cousins begets abnormal children, therefore marriage between such cousins are restricted. There have been cases where first cousins marry but they are considered to be in an incestuous relationship and therefore are looked down upon. Marriage with one's own people is encouraged, that is, a Changki man marrying a Changki woman is the accepted norm because it is believed that marrying into one's own culture and tradition strengthens the village, for in doing so the ties with the village remain strong through the children. Most importantly, for the family of the woman this will ensure her security and safety as they can keep an eye on her. If a woman marries outside the village she is considered 'lost' to the family and village as she will have to follow her husband. After marriage the wife will not assume the clan name of her husband and thus she maintains her identity as a member of her father's clan. But the children will belong to the husband's clan and will take on the father's name.

In Changki the clans are exogamous groups but however we find that inter-marriage between the Metsüri and

Losangri clans are not allowed. It is said that Losangri being too few in numbers attached themselves to the Metsüri clan as a constituent clan. Therefore as Metsüri and Losangri are said to be *'mulok emtepba'*, which literally translated means 'joining of two baskets', they are considered to be close relatives and thereby not allowed to marry each other. To elucidate further, *'mülok emtepba'* meaning 'joining of two baskets' came about because in the olden days, *mülok* (basket) was the measure used for collection of clan funds which was in terms of paddy. Therefore when two clans merged, it also signified the joining of two clan funds. Although each of the clans keeps its own clan identity, sometimes they are commonly referred to as Metsülosang.

'Mülok emtepba' is a socially accepted system whereby a clan can attach itself to another. Thus *'mülok emtepba'* is a system whereby the numerically stronger clan gives protection to a numerically weaker clan. By accepting the numerically weaker clan as a relative requiring protection, the numerically stronger clan accepts responsibility for the adopted clan. Thus the relationship established is that of an older brother taking care of a younger brother, therefore inter-marriage between these two clans is not allowed. In this system, personal clan names cannot be interchangeably used by these two clans. Inheritance and succession are also confined to the particular clan only; that is, a Metsüri cannot inherit from a Losangri and vice versa.

Inter-marriage between the Changkiri and Emrem Changki clans are also not allowed. This is so because the Emrem Changki attached itself to the Changkiri clan in a process called *'tinu emba'* which translated means to adopt as father/brother. The Emrem Changki clan when it came to Changki was adopted by the Changkiri clan as its relative and these two clans lived as brothers, therefore inter-marriage is not allowed between these two clans. In this system, the two clans cannot use the personal clan name interchangeably and they have different '*charu mülok*' which literally translated mean 'collection basket', meaning that each clan has separate clan funds. The inheritance and succession also remain within the clan, that is a Changkiri cannot inherit from an Emrem Changki and vice versa. But they are considered to be brothers and therefore as close relatives they cannot inter-marry.

The respondents could not give any accounts of the marriage ceremonies that took place before the advent of Christianity, however some details of the early Christian marriage ceremonies was told. In the earlier days when a marriage took place, the family and relatives of the bride and groom would feast in the day time in their respective houses. Then at night the marriage ceremony would be conducted in the church after which the bridal couple, their families, relatives and guests would go over to the newly constructed house built by the groom and his family. There in the reception the guests would be given a ball of cooked sticky rice, a betel nut and two betel leaves with some lime. The people were also given black tea while those who could afford it gave tea with milk and sugar. The wedding ceremony was always performed in the night as the other people would be back from the rice fields only then and would be free to attend the wedding.

Since the 1980's the marriage agreement is sealed with a formal engagement. There are no exchange of gifts between the prospective groom and bride. But in recent times, following the western style, an engagement ring is given by the groom to-be to the woman he intends to marry, although this is not mandatory. The manner of getting married is simple and in Changki the western style of getting married in the church wearing a white wedding gown is in fashion. Wedding cards are printed and distributed and a reception where lunch is served is the normal practice. The wedding usually takes place on a weekday and in the daytime.

Although the wedding ceremony is based on the Christian and western mode, some of the traditional customs are still followed. For instance when a couple decide to get married, the boy will formally go to the girl's parents house with his parents, mother's brothers (*Tiuo Tukori*) and his brother-in-law (*Chanakri*), should he have one. The boy's father will then inform the girl's parents about the couple's intention and make a formal proposal. In this way, an agreement is made between the two families and discussions follow for the arrangement of the wedding. Usually it is the groom's family that meets the bulk of the expenses and the groom's family takes care of the major portion of the arrangements for the wedding.

A very important ritual of the wedding ceremony is the *sala sana* or meeting between the groom's and bride's family and clan elders as well as the *Temnakri* that usually takes place after the wedding reception. The ceremony takes place after the reception and the meeting is arranged by the groom's family and clansmen. The meeting is formal which begins with a prayer followed by speeches made by the clan elders of both the groom and bride. Here the clan history is told and the importance of the alliance between the two clans through the marriage is emphasized. In this ceremony the groom's family and clan members formally accept and welcome the new daughter into their fold. The father of the bride too formally gives away his daughter and he makes an important declaration to all present that should his daughter die, her personal name should be handed back to the clan. In a sense, the father is declaring that even if his daughter is physically given away, her membership to his clan is inalienable and in this symbolic gesture, he lays claim to this right over his daughter. Most of the traditional rituals connected with the marriage day and the ceremonies associated with it have long been forgotten but this meeting of the families and clans is still prevalent and forms the most important ritual in the present day marriage day and ceremony. Through this ceremony the clan elders acknowledge the union of their members and give their blessings.

Another traditional feature of wedding preparations that is an integral part of the Changki marriage celebrations is the role that the *Temnakri* take perform. For example, if a Changkiri man marries, his sister's sons, as well as the sons of the other Changkiri women and the husbands of the Changkiri women will have the responsibility of making the necessary arrangements and preparation for the marriage for they are the *Temnakri* to the Changkiri man. The brothers-in-law and sons-in-law play a very important role during such times.

The eldest among the *Temnakri* is selected as the leader by the other *Temnakri* based on chronological age, and he is given overall charge of the preparations. He will then assign specific jobs to the rest. The pigs are killed, cut and the meat cooked and distributed by the *Temnakri*. Whenever a pig is presented as a wedding gift, it is the duty of the *Temnakri* to ensure that the head of the pig is returned to the one who presented the pig. This is a traditional way of acknowledging the gift.

The preparations start a day or two before the wedding and end a day after the wedding. A separate kitchen is built by the *Temnakri* and this space is meant only for the *Temnakri*. The *Temnakri* are given overall charge and they are the one's who cook and distribute the meat of the pigs killed. They can demand from the house owners whatever they need and they will dispense with the things, as they like. The researcher had attended a wedding in the village in the course of the fieldwork, where the lady of the house went to the *Temnakri* to voice her disapproval of some of the things that the *Temnakri* were doing. She was roundly scolded and told in no uncertain terms that she had no right to interfere and was told to stay away from *their* territory.

The distribution of meat at the time of marriage is a serious task and the *Temnakri* carry out this by seeing that the clan elders are given the appropriate portions of meat according to seniority and that the immediate family members are also given a token piece of the meat. Even if the marriage takes place outside of the village in other towns, the *Temnakri* from the village as well as from the particular town are duty bound to take charge of the preparations and distribution of the meat. The success of the marriage feast and celebrations depends on the *Temnakri* and no matter where the marriage takes place, whether in the village or in other towns, the role of the *Temnakri* is the most important part of the celebrations.

Remarriages are allowed; here too clan exogamy is strictly adhered to. In Changki society the sororate form of marriage wherein the man marries the deceased wife's sister is permitted. Normally the younger sister is taken as the wife although there is no bar on the man taking the older sister as his wife. A man can marry his deceased wife's youngest sister, if she is unmarried and the reason for approval of such a marriage is that the new wife will not be a step-mother but a younger mother, being the sister of the deceased, and will therefore take better care of the children. If a couple co-habit, without taking any vows in the church, if they are together for many years and whether they have children or not they are considered to be legally married.

Once a couple gets married it is the custom for the newly weds to set up their own independent household. The neolocal nuclear family is the prescribed norm and the reasoning is that, it is only when the newly weds establish their own independent household, they will become responsible and know the hardships faced in starting and running a family. It is believed that only then will they learn and appreciate and experience the intricacies of family life. When a child is born certain norms are still observed especially with regard to the naming of the child. The child, if male, is named on the sixth day after birth and if female, on the fifth day by the paternal grandfather, if still alive or by the father. The name is chosen with care and after much consultation with other clan members. With all solemnity the name is made known and the family celebrates it by having a feast. A cock is killed on this day and a little bit of the cooked liver is rubbed on the child's mouth so as to signify that the child has also been included in the feast and that he has been given his share. After naming the child, if the child does not keep well and frets abnormally, it is believed that the name given is not suitable or agreeable with the child. Even today when such a thing happens, the parents after consultation with the grandparents and elders change the name of the child and thereafter a new name is given to the child.

Within the elementary family or *kibong* the father is the head of the family. His children call him '*aba*', while the mother is called '*aya*'. The father's authority in the family is respected and the final decision with regard to family matters rests with him. The father is responsible for the conduct and liabilities of his children and he expects unfailing obedience and respect from them. The mother also expects the same considerations from her children but she is more openly affectionate and lenient than the father and is usually the medium through whom he is approached. The husband and wife do not address each other by their personal names, especially in public. For example, if they have children, and the eldest child's name is *Yala*, the man will refer to his wife as *Yala tiuo*, meaning *Yala's* mother. And the wife refers to him as *Yala teba*, meaning *Yala's* father.

The socialization process of the children starts within the family on ways of behaviour expected of them. The older children from an early age learn to be responsible for their siblings and to help their parents. The youngest child, whether male or female, is regarded, as the 'baby' and the parents as well as the siblings will look after, protect and indulge the youngest child. *Telakba,* if male, or *Telakla,* if female, is the affectionate name given to the youngest, meaning the 'tail end'. It is believed that the youngest is the unluckiest because his/her share of the family property and sometimes even of the features such as brains, looks, talents, even luck and so on is the smallest and hence the tendency for everyone to spoil the youngest.

In Changki there are cases when the parents have spoilt their children and in most cases it is the son who is spoilt thoroughly. The sons are the one's who get most of the attention and for those who are sent out to study in other places get the maximum amount of pocket money. Some of these boys who were given too much freedom and money have got trapped in drug related problems. Drug abuse is beginning to be a problem in the village but in many cases the families try to hide or deny that such problems exist. The Village Council has tackled this menace by the simple method of putting the drug abusers into cages made out of a wood which makes the skin itch even at the slightest touch.

In one such case due to excessive abuse of drugs the young man who is now in his twenties has become mentally challenged. The problem was becoming so bad that his family called on the clansmen, *Tiuo Tukori* and *Temnakri* (six in all) and hired one of the vehicles in the village and literally dragged the young man to Tezpur to be institutionalized in the mental hospital there. The relatives simply dropped whatever they were doing and accompanied the young man and his older brother. This case has been mentioned to show the kind of assistance that clansmen, *Tiuo Tukori* and *Temnakri* render in times of need.

We also observe that when it comes to cases of delinquency, the handling of it involves not only the family but also the clan, *Tiuo Tukori*, *Temnakri* and sometimes the Village Council. There was a case when some Changki youths beat up a person belonging to another village in Longnak which is in Changki territory. This incident became a matter of grave concern because the victim reported to his clansmen as well as his Village Council and the culprits were summoned to the victim's village.

The culprits were given a thorough tongue lashing by the older family members as well as the clansmen. But they were accompanied to the victim's village by the older brothers, a representative from the respective clans, a *Tiou Tukori*, *Temnakri* and a representative of the Village Council. The matter ended with a fine as is customary in such cases. The support of the different categories of relatives represents a network of relationships that is obligatory and based on interdependence.

In the management of the household we observed that it is the women who shoulder most of the burden. The women look after the children, the house and the finances. This is so because the men folk are kept busy with village works, clan duties and church activities. All Changki men are part of the age-set system and as per tradition are bound by customary rule to participate in the village administration. The details of this will be given in the next chapter on Political Institution.

Each household is independent and the people are very attached to their homes. We find that of the in the upper khel of the 146 households, 37 households are single member households, which means that 25.34 percent of the total households have only a single person living in the house. In the lower khel of the total of 276 households, 51 or 18.48 percent of the total number of households have only a single member living in the house. A closer observance revealed that these households are composed of old people living on their own. The majority was above the age of 70 but they were adamant not to move out of the house where they had lived most of their adult lives. Their children had moved out of the village and settled elsewhere and despite their entreaties they continued to live alone in their homes determined to die there. The old people have hired help staying with them, usually Konyak (a Naga tribe from Mon district) boys who come to the village to work in the homes in exchange for education as well as upkeep.

We find that household compositions are uniform with nuclear family living in neolocal pattern of residence. There are no married couples living with the parents after marriage as it is considered a shame. Even if they should live with the parents it is just as a stop gap arrangement till they can find a rented place or build their own houses.

When marriage between a man from the upper khel and a woman form the lower khel takes place and vice versa, the woman will leave not only her parent's home but also the khel where she was born and brought up. We find at present there are 21 women from the lower khel who has settled in the upper khel after marriage and 30 upper khel women have settled in the lower khel after marriage. These numbers pertain to only the Changki women who are permanent residents of the village.

We observed that the relation of the wife is always closer to her own parents than her in-laws. But we also observed that should there be any marital discord, the parents urge the daughter to first talk with the husband and in-laws so that there is no escalation of the discord. The wife is expected to bear whatever problem she may be having with her husband with fortitude and patience and these qualities are looked on as virtues. The daughter is not only a wife but also a mother and her responsibilities are serious so she cannot sacrifice her duty and responsibilities for personal happiness. The societal pressures on a married woman to conform to what is considered the 'ideal' wife and mother is greatly felt and some women expressed the opinion that sometimes all of it gets too much and regretted getting married.

The husband on the other hand is expected to provide for his own family but at the same his responsibilities towards his parents, sisters, brothers and clansmen will always be a lifetime duty. In addition he is also the *Tiuo Tukori* (maternal uncle) to his sister's and clanswomen's children so his obligation towards them is also important.

Young children are looked after by neighbours, grand parents or relatives when the parents have urgent work to do. We observe that the people are indulgent, caring and careful with children. In fact children are loved and we see that the young fathers try to take active part in the upbringing of their children and take care of their children such as babysitting when the mothers are busy and so on. There appear to be a trend where the young fathers try to be friends with their children rather than authoritarian figures as their fathers may have been with them.

We find that the marital relations are fairly durable in the village and although divorce is not unknown we find that these are exceptions rather than the rule. Divorce in Changki is discouraged through sanctions from the church as well as societal disapproval in general. Divorce may take place on account of adultery cases, incompatibility, barrenness, and abusive treatment of a spouse or desertion.

Divorce

The divorce proceedings always take place in the traditional manner. When a case for divorce comes up, the concerned parties will inform the families who will try their best to make the couple come to an understanding. If this does not work and the parties are adamant, the concerned families will inform the *Temnakri* and *Tiuo Tukori*. The *Temnakri* will then have the responsibility of informing the clan elders and act as go-betweens for the concerned parties and their families. A date will be fixed and the two families with their *Temnakri*, *Tiuo Tukori, Chanakri* and clan elders will sit together for a meeting and the eldest clan member of the two parties will preside over the proceedings.

If the husband is the one who wants a divorce he will be asked to speak and give the reasons for calling the meeting. If it is the wife she will be asked to speak first. The relatives and elders will then listen to both the sides. After hearing them out the clan elders and *Tiuo Tukori* will speak and try to reason with the couple. If their entreaties and argument do not bring about a reconciliation the husband and wife will asked if they wish to continue being married. The one who answers in the negative is considered the guilty party and will forfeit all property that the couple might have acquired when married. The one who does not wish to remain married will walk away with only the bare minimum personal effects. Sometimes divorce may take place with both partners mutually wanting to part ways. In such cases, the family and clansmen allow the couple to divide the property according to their wishes except for the house site and rice fields which will remain with the man. In case there are children, the daughters will stay with the mother and the sons with the father.

In the case of adultery, the guilty party will be fined three pigs and will forfeit all rights to property, should the spouse demand divorce. Sometimes after the fining, the couple does come to a compromise, and after the guilty party has taken an oath and his/her spouse forgives him/her, the couple can be reconciled. In the case of abuse, the guilty party will forfeit all rights to property and the victim is justified in separating from the spouse. However it may be noted that immoveable property will not be given to the woman although she may be allowed to use it. If she has sons, such property will be in her care till her sons takes over.

In a divorce case there will always be a meeting and each party will argue their case in their own interest. In this way the divorce proceedings can be long winded with the family affairs being aired in public, although decorum is maintained at all time so that the proceedings does not degenerate to mud slinging and become offensive. The clan elders and other relatives ensure that all formalities are observed. But whatever the outcome maybe, the man's right to his children is inalienable and although the woman may have the custody of the children, she cannot deny access to the children for the children belong to the man and through him to his clan. If the woman is at fault she forfeits all rights to property and children. If the children are too small or if she is still nursing the child, she will have custody till such time that they are manageable without a mother. In many cases, the women lose the most in the event of divorce, especially that of the custody of her children and also social standing. This is more so if the woman is not financially independent, therefore we find that often the women will not resort to divorce too easily.

Inheritance

In Changki inheritance is through the males where the eldest son is the heir and gets the majority of the family property. Among the Mongsen group such as the Changkiri, Amri, Longchari clans and so on, the youngest son will inherit the parental house, but the rest of the property, immovable as well as moveable, will be inherited by the eldest son. The eldest son can then distribute the paddy fields and settlement sites among the other brothers, if any. The immovable property always goes from the eldest son to *his* eldest son and so on. If there are no sons, the ancestral property will go to the next brother and *his* eldest son will inherit the property and so on. With regard to the parents house the youngest son inherits the parental house and can live there but the land does not belong to him and he cannot sell it.

However among the Tsüngli group such as the Longkumer, Tzüdiri, Ningdangri, Moliri and Akhori clans, the eldest son inherits not only the major share but also the parental home and consequently *his* eldest son will inherit and so on. The house as well as the land belongs to the eldest son but he cannot sell it for it is considered the ancestral property. The other property such as agricultural implements, household things, paddy and so on is shared equally among the brothers.

If the father is of considerable wealth and means and if he so wishes he can give landed property to his daughters, provided that the property has been acquired by him and does not belong to the clan or is ancestral family property. Such land is usually outside of the village in other towns. But he can give his daughter only during his lifetime and in acknowledgement the daughter will have to make a token payment to the father to seal the deal. Any amount from Re. 1/- to Rs. 100/- is given to the father for the land in front of witnesses. With this payment, the property is considered to be hers to do as she wishes.

A woman who has accumulated wealth or property on her own can dispose of it as she wishes. If she has children of her own she can leave equal shares to them. But there have been rare cases when her clansmen have laid claim to her property on the grounds that she belongs to their clan and as such her property rightly belongs to the clan and cannot go to another clan through her children. In case a woman is a spinster and if she has acquired property on her own, the immoveable property goes to the eldest brother and even if he had died before her death, the eldest son of the eldest brother is the rightful heir. In this case the younger brothers cannot inherit her property, unless it is distributed by the rightful heir.

For example, when Miss X died, the brother next to her could not inherit her immovable property for he had only daughters and therefore no heir. The brother next had died earlier, but he had a son, so he became the rightful heir, even though Miss X had other younger brothers. Thus according to customary law her nephew, that is the son of her second brother, inherited the bulk of the property she left behind, for accordingly in the traditional way, the nephew was considered older than his uncles for in the line of succession he came first. With regard to other property, for example, jewelry, ornaments and household items, her sisters would inherit these items and if they so wish they can distribute some of the personal items such as *ani* (traditional skirts) and *asü* (shawls) among the nieces, grand daughters and close relatives belonging to the same clan.

Just as property is inherited, debts are also inherited and this burden is borne by the eldest son, however if the debt is considerably high, the other brothers will also help in settling the debt. Even if the father is dead the debtors will demand repayment of debts from the son and the son is bound to repay the debt. However, if the person, to whom debt is owed, forgives and waives off the debt then the case is settled on the grounds of *taochi* (mercy).

In case a man dies leaving no heirs, if he has any debts, his clansmen will then settle the debt. In the same token if a clanswoman dies leaving behind no heirs, if she had accrued any debts, her clansmen would be duty bound to settle the debts. In case a man dies, his wife would be allowed to stay in the house till she dies or till she marries, in which case she would move out to her new husband's house. An unmarried daughter would be allowed to live in her father's house till her death or till she get marries. In either case once the woman dies, the immoveable would revert back to the male heirs, whether it is her brothers or sons. If there are no male heirs, the house will belong to the clan so also the paddy fields.

We find that in Changki the relationships forged with both the male and female relatives play an important role.

The commonality is established after the birth of the child and through the child, the solidarity of the group is further strengthened through the network of relationships formed from the father's side as well as the mother's side. These relatives are put in distinct categories with well defined roles and responsibilities. But the most important feature of the kinship system is the clan and clan membership. From birth to death this aspect controls a person and through the clan and clan membership a person finds his identity, social standing and support base.

Friendship

Another very important relationship that forges strong ties and bonds is through friendship. Friends often become a part of the family and in this way the relationship forms a network outside of the clan but plays an important role within the families of the friends. The friendship ties are taken seriously not only by the friends themselves but also by the families involved. There are also certain terms to denote the friendship ties.

1) *Küriko*: Female friends who are very close call each other "*kuriko*' which is a term of affection reserved only for the best of friends belonging to any clan and any age group.

2) *Keti* : Close male and female friends belonging to the same clan and same age call each other '*keti*'.

3) *Attino*: Close female friends belonging to the same clan and same age call each other '*attino*'.

4) *Kuba*: Close male friends belonging to different clans but who are of the same age-set grade call each other '*kuba*'.

5) *Annala*: Close female friends belonging to different clans but who are of the same age call each other '*annala*'

From the terms cited above, we find that although friendship is an important part of life, the clan and age-set system plays a very important role and these factors are always kept in mind. The terms used for friends between older and younger persons are denoted by calling the older person '*ata*' (female) or *anga/ako* (males).

In Changki we find that the kinship ties and the network of relationships is established through the clan and marriage alliances; and the web of social relations within the village is such that it is said that invariably each and every Changki person is related to each other in one way or the other.

However at the empirical level we find that a group of people who had attached themselves to a clan in the village have been trying to claim the position of the clan which adopted them and in effect have caused problems that vitiated the village as a whole and created intra and inter-clan rivalries that have permeated not only the social but also the political realm as well as the religious institution.

Earlier we have mentioned that one clan that had attached itself to one of the founding clans and at some point of time began to assert itself as *the* original founding clan and has been trying to claim the position of the founding clan through various intrigues and means.

To elaborate further, we need to refer to the migration pattern of a particular group of people and the manner in which they settled in Changki. Changkiri is one of the founding clans of Changki. At one point of time, which was after the establishment of the lower khel by one *Imlisangba* of Changkiri clan, one *Imchaba* accompanied by some others was brought from Changki Longpok, in the northern part of Changki territory, to Changki village. He opted to settle in the lower khel with *Imlisangba* of the Changkiri clan because of which the villagers gave him the title 'Emrem Changki' meaning 'the one who sought and adopted *Imlisangba* of

Changkiri clan'. From that day onward *Imchaba* and his descendents came to be called Emrem Changki.

Later on one *Yalemchang* and some others arrived at Changki from *Alulangba* and attached themselves to *Imchaba* and also came to be known as Emrem Changki. Another group led by *Laluk* came from Nemchem and attached themselves to Emrem Changki. Thus the Emrem Changki clan comprising of these three groups arrived at Changki at different points of time from different places and lived as constituent clans attached to the Changkiri clan.

The two clans lived in harmony as brothers in the lower khel for ages till about eighty years ago, when some members of the Emrem Changki clan, started intrigues to lay claim as the original Changkiri clan. The subsequent history of relationship between these two clans was that of discord and rivalry that began to spill over to the social, political and religious aspects affecting the whole village.

This discord between the two clans resulted in the formation of two groups comprised of the Changkiri clan and their *Tiou Tukori, Temnakri,* friends and well wishers on the one hand and the Emrem Changki clan and their *Tiuo Tukori, Temnakri,* friends and well wishers on the other hand thus dividing the Changki society to the extent that the differences in opinion began to affect even the village administration. The intra and inter-clan relationships also began to be impinged upon by the differences between the two clans as some members of the other clans also started to align with either the Changkiri clan or the Emrem Changki clan and were divided among themselves. In this way the solidarity of the lower khel in particular and the village in general began to be affected.

For example, due to this discord and lack of solidarity among the Changki villagers, large portions of Changki territory have been encroached upon by some neighbouring villages and Changki village cannot take action to reclaim its territory. The fall out of this difference between the two clans is most evident in the religious realm, as the church was split with the Emrem Changki and their supporters forming a parallel church of the same denomination. Changki has the dubious distinction of being the only village with two churches of the same denomination. When the state electoral process of party politics was introduced in Nagaland after statehood, the internal groupings within Changki society were further compartmentalized with each group supporting different parties thus vitiating the already divided society. Thus we find that kinship patterns in Changki are deeply influenced by the schism created due to the rivalry and dispute between these two clans.

4

POLITICAL INSTITUTION

Elwin (1961:6-7)) stated that the Naga villages are characterised by a varied pattern of near-dictatorship and extreme democracy. There is a system of hereditary chieftainship among the Semas and Changs. The Konyaks have very powerful chiefs or *Angs* who are regarded as sacred and whose word is law. The Aos have bodies of elders based on clans and the Angami, Lothas and Rengma are democratic and independent.

Yonuo (1974:10) wrote that the Sema, Konyak and Mao Naga tribes have hereditary monarchy. The Konyak kings (*Angs*) have greater powers than the Sema or Mao chiefs, for the *Ang's* word is law. According to Yonuo the Sema chiefs have no arbitrary power, either secular or religious as he has to work in tandem with the village council and is bound to the web of ancient tribal customs and laws. He goes on to say that the Angami, Lotha and Rengma have chiefs who are chosen from the clans for their oratory skills, proficiency in diplomacy, bravery or wealth. These chiefs were assisted by the village council who exercised moderate authority. But the chiefs were more or less nominal heads with very little authority and the office of chief was not hereditary.

Mills (1937:140) noted that the office of chief was hereditary in the clan but not in the family. It did not necessarily pass on from father to son, but to the most suitable man in the leading families of the clan. However among the eastern Rengmas, Mills says that hereditary chieftaincy was not the norm, as influential men always ruled the village.

Hutton (1968, reprint:122) wrote that the basis of the Sema society is the village, or part of a village, which is under the control of a chief. He goes on to say that the 'real pivot of Sema society is the chief'. This is so because although a village may comprise of many clans but the predominant position of the chief and his agnates, leads to the rough classification of the whole group as of their clan. About the Angami tribe Hutton wrote that 'although the village may be regarded as the unit of the political and religious sides of Angami life, the real unit of the social side is the clan'. In the olden days each khel was founded by a clan and intense clan rivalries kept each khel separate and barricaded against the other, so much so that it was almost like each khel was a village itself within the village.

The norms and rules that govern each society differ in the way they are enforced and acknowledged. The political organization of a society is generally aimed at the maintenance of ordered relations between different categories and groups of people in a society within a particular territory. Beattie (1966:142) states that 'when we are discussing political phenomena in many small-scale societies, there is much to be said for speaking of the political *aspect* of certain social institutions rather than of specifically political institutions. For often institutions which have political importance are socially significant in a number of other contexts as well.' The political systems vary from those 'approximating to a centralized government and executive, of which western-states are extreme cases, while others possess no such institutions at any level, and so may be fairly described as segmentary or acephalous' (ibid:145).

The age-set system falls within the latter type of politically decentralized system. The age-set organization is combined with the allocation of authority on the basis of seniority. Citing the examples of the Masai and Nandi tribes in East Africa, Beattie says that 'in most societies in which age-sets are important, every man is not only a member of a particular set, but also at any given time he occupies, with his age-mates, a particular grade. These grades are clearly distinguished from one another, so that a man can only occupy one grade at a time. A typical series of grades (after childhood) is junior warriorhood, senior warriorhood, junior elderhood, and senior elderhood. Specific rules are associated with each grade; thus warriors fight and defend from attack, elders settle disputes, make important decisions and intercede with the ancestral ghosts. The essential thing about this system is that the sets move through the various grades as complete units' (ibid:146).

Mair (1965:117) wrote that in the age-set system 'it is important to note that what is significant is not chronological but *social* age. A man is recognised as an adult when he is formally admitted to adult status, not when he reaches a certain birthday; he is eligible for admission at puberty, but his admission may be delayed for one reason or another'. She goes on to say that 'it should not be supposed that kinship ceases to have any political importance whenever political functions are allocated on some other basis. If we contrast political systems based on age-sets with those based on descent groups alone, we see that in the former more aspects of public life are organized outside the descent groups, but it does not follow that the descent groups lose all their political functions' (ibid:120-121).

Evans-Pritchard (1956:254) in his study of the Nuer of Southern Sudan in Africa, noted that the age-set system is not a military organisation and that 'it is in more general social relations, chiefly of a domestic and kinship order, and not in political relations that behaviour is specifically determined by the positions in age-set structure'. He further stated that the age-set system among the Nuer differs from the territorial and lineage systems in one important aspect. 'Whereas the people of a territorial segment remain, in the same structural relation to other territorial segments for their whole lives, and whereas the members of a lineage have a fixed relationship to other lineages, an age-set group changes its position in relation to the whole system, passing through points of juniority and seniority. This mobility of age-set groups is peculiar to the system and is a necessary characteristic of it, for it is an institution based on the succession of generation' (ibid:256).

Evans-Pritchard noted that the relations between the sets are defined in the idiom of family relationships. The members of a man's father's age-set are his 'fathers' and the members of his father's brother's age-set are also his 'fathers'. The sons of a man's set are his 'sons', while the wives of his father's age-set are his 'mothers' and the wives of his sons' set are his 'daughters'. All members of a man's own set are likewise his 'brothers'. The age-set system thus influences persons through a kinship idiom and on the pattern of kinship. The sets never acts corporately, but they function locally between individuals and in ceremonial situations, between small aggregates of persons who live near to one another, for a man only has frequent contacts with those members of his set and of other sets who live in his district. The age-set patterns of behaviour are, except in specific rites, of so general a nature that they cannot be isolated in a community where everyone is related in a number of different ways to everybody else (ibid:258-259).

Mills (1926:176) wrote that 'as with all Nagas the real political unit of the tribe is the village.' He then described the organisation of the Ao villages as being based on two principles. 'First the whole village is divided into age grades, which the various communal duties are assigned. Secondly the control of affairs lies with a council, whose method of election and tenure of office vary in the different language groups' (ibid:177). The Ao Naga villages even today are organised on these two principles. Every three years a group of boys born within the same three years enter the *Zunga* (Chungli) or *Yanga* (Mongsen) age-set system and remains in the original age-set grade till he dies although every three years they will move on to the next senior age-set grade progressively. But his age mates will remain the same. The duties and roles of each age-set grade are well defined and articulated. Mills writing about the Ao stated that 'from the cradle to the grave, a man is part of a machine. Only on these lines could a village of perhaps two thousand souls, without king or chief, be run' (ibid:117).

The age-set system among the Ao have clearly demarcated duties and roles assigned to each grade whereby each grade carry out the responsibilities given as a group. In the social, economic and political set-up of the village, the age-set system plays an important role. The community work like repairing of village gates, clearing of village paths, community fishing and other developmental works in the village are divided among the age-set grades. In economic activities too such as agriculture, the age-set grades work in cooperation. In the village administrative work the age-set grades are allotted various duties. Thus the smooth functioning of the village depends on the work force supplied by the age-set system.

The Ao traditional village governments

The Ao tribe have three different types of traditional political institutions such as the *Putu Menden* (generation rule) among the Chungli group, the *Samen Menchen* (meat share rule) among the Mongsen group and the *Yanga Samen* (age-set system rule) which is also called the *Samen Menchen*. The village polity and distribution of power is determined by the type of traditional institution that is followed. The Mongsen group has the *Samen Menchen* system of government whereby the founding clans of the village occupy the top most positions and are in power for ten to fifteen years after which the younger people take over. Among the Chungli group the *Putu Menden* system of governance is prevalent and in this system a number of age-set grades are clubbed together into one 'generation'. A father and son cannot be of the same 'generation'. There are five such 'generations' and each 'generation' rules for twenty to twenty-five years (the span of years differs from village to village). In this system too the founding clans occupy the top positions. There is another system of governance based purely on the age-set system found in Changki and Khar villages in the Changkikong range. In this system the age-set grades move up progressively every three to five years and when they reach the traditionally prescribed grade to be in the village government, the members are automatically inducted into the village government regardless of whether they belong to the founding clan or not.

In the *Putu Menden* (Chungli) and the *Samen Menchen* (Mongsen) there is a clear distinction between the founding clans and the clans that settled later who are also known as 'latecomers'. The founding clans hold all the powers while the later settlers are relegated to the lower ranks. However in the *Yanga* (age-set) system there are no such distinctions for each person gets to be in the village government regardless of whether he belongs to the founding clan or not. This type of village government is based on the age-set system and as the grades move up progressively every three years or so, the councillors are drawn from the age-set system directly, when they reach the traditionally prescribed age-set grade that automatically ensures entry into the village government.

Yanga Samen (Age-set rule)

Yanga Samen is a Village Government formed by members

of an age-set grade. This form of traditional village government is found in only two villages among the Ao tribe. Each age-set moves up progressively and in due course of time when a certain age-set grade is reached, the members of that age-set grade automatically become village councillors, first as assistant councillors then as the senior councillors who will be responsible for the village administration in every sphere. The village councillors are assisted by the *Gaon Buras* who are elderly village statesmen drawn from the clans in the village.

This form of village government is found in Changki and Khar villages in the Changkikong range. In Changki the Council is of a single tier for when a particular age-set grade reaches the *Samenthi* (senior councillors) stage they assume power while the age-set group below them known as *Samen Nuzaba* (junior councillors) becomes assistants to them. For three years the *Samenthi* stay in office after which they have to retire from office and the *Samen Nuzaba* takes over.

The *Yanga* system that is practiced in *Khar* village is however different in that three age-set groups form a larger group known as '*Jubang*'. There are altogether about ten '*Jubang*' having different names. A '*Jubang*' remains in power for ten years and the Councillors are appointed on clan-wise basis and the Council is composed of four tiers such as *Samenza, Jenyim, Chametcha* and *Amajangr* (Ao,1980:117-144).

Changki *Süngdakba* and *Ayim Anet* Political organisation

Before we discuss the age-set system of Changki, it may be pertinent to give an explanation of the political organisation of the village so that a better understanding may be arrived at as to the role that the age-set system plays in the Changki polity.

At the village level the people are organised at the khel levels, that is ***Süngdakba*** (upper) and ***Ayim Anet*** (lower), *khels*. The division of the village into *khels* came about through the formation of the village. The term *khel* is derived from Assamese, which roughly translated, means geographical division.

In the beginning, the village was established at ***Süngdakba*** which is now the upper khel. The lower *khel* was established at a later stage as has been explained in the preceding chapter. The lower *khel* is known as ***Ayim Anet*** (two villages) due to the fact that the last group (comprising of five clans) which migrated and settled in the lower *khel*, came with a recognised '*Emli*' or system of village governance. This group belonged to the Chungli linguistic group and had their own system of customary laws and governance, as well as their own dialect and in effect the lower *khel* came to be regarded as being composed of two separate villages, hence the name ***Ayim Anet*** (two villages). At present although the lower *khel* is still referred to as ***Ayim Anet*** (two villages), over the years the Chungli group were assimilated into the Changki fold and adopted Changki customs although in certain aspects such as in inheritance rules they differ from the other clans which has been explained in the preceding chapter on kinship.

Each *khel* is a distinct social and political organisation with its own *Samen Menchen* (village government), rules and regulations. Similarly each khel has its own age-set system and the functioning of the *khel* administration is separate and independent.

Changki Age-Set System

In Changki the age-set system or the *Yanga* is an important component of the political set-up for the Village Councillors are drawn directly from the age-set grades. In the earlier chapter on kinship we have stated that clan membership forms the basis of a man's identity and social standing. In addition to this, for a man to be recognised as a bonafide citizen of the village with civil rights and duties, he must enter the age-set system. Only then will he be considered a part of the *Senso*, which interchangeably means citizen or citizenship. Once a male is registered as a member of the *Senso* of the village he will have all rights to the village lands and rivers and will be able to participate in the village polity. Women are not organised into formal age-set grades and they have no rights as far as village governance and polity is concerned.

In the age-set system all the boys who have reached the age of sixteen or so, enter the *Yanga* or age-set system. For three years they will remain in the same age-set grade and the first age-set grade is regarded as the recruitment period. After three years the age-set grade will move up progressively to the next grade and this will continue till the last grade is reached. The members of each grade will remain the same throughout.

In Changki the *Yanga Samen* (age set rule) is commonly called *Samen Menchen* (general term in Mongsen dialect for village government). We have explained that the age-set grades move up progressively every three years. As each grade move up, their responsibilities and duties towards the village administration increase as well as their hierarchical power.

The lower grades are answerable and accountable to the higher grades while the higher grades wield authority over the lower grade by commanding obedience and respect. As each grade has well defined duties, responsibilities and roles, the powers are also well defined so we find that when the age-set grade of *Samen Nuzaba* is reached this automatically means the entry into the village government with all the duties and responsibilities as well as powers.

Once the stage of ***Samen Nuzaba*** (roughly in the chronological ages of 44-47) is reached this grade becomes the junior councillors of the *Samen Menchen* (Village Council). For three years they will remain as the assistants and this period is considered to be the training period before they assume power as the ***Samenthi*** (48-51 years). The *Samenthi* grade becomes the senior councillors and technically this grade becomes the overall power and authority in the village political affairs.

In the political sphere we find that the two age-set grades of the ***Samen Nuzaba*** and ***Samenthi*** remain in power for just six years. Three years are regarded as the training period while the next three years are considered to be the period of ruling. The two grades combined together are called the ***emchachari***, which in Changki dialect means 'rulers'. The *Samen Menchen* comprises of the permanent male residents of the village.

The village age-set system as recorded by the researcher in the village in 2002 is given in the following. Certain age – set grades of both Süngdakba (*Luko* or upper *khel)* and Ayim Anet (*Lulang* or lower *khel*) are called by different names in the respective khels.

The age-set grading of Changki as shown in Table 15 gives the list of the fourteen age-set grades found in Changki as well as the chronological ages. We find that serial numbers 1, 3, 4 and 10 have different names for the grades while the rest are uniform.

Table 15
Changki Ayim Asem Changri Yanga (Changki Age-set grades)

Sl. No	Süngdakba (Upper *Khel*)	Ayim Anet (Lower *Khel*)	Chronological Age
1	Nuzabari Jungpori	Süngpori	16 – 19
2	Tekhüpba ori	Tekhüpba Ori	20 -23
3	Achangcharoba	Pangkhang	24 -27
4	Aphakcharoba	Kitsüng Nuzaba	28 -31
5	Azüakhang Nuzaba	Azü-Akhang Nuzaba	32 -35
6	Azü-Akang Tezenba	Azü-Akang Tezenba	36 – 39
7	Alikhun	Alikhun	40 -43
8	Samen Nuzaba	Samen Nuzaba	44 -47
9	Samenthi	Samenthi	48 -51
10	Risüden	Risütemba	52 -55
11	Empiba Ho	Empiba Ho	56 -59
12	Maozenba Nuzaba	Maozenba Nuzaba	60 -63
13	Maozenba Tezenba	Maozenba Tezenba	64 -67
14	Nokimungba	Nokimungba	68 and above

In the following, the functions and duties of the different age-set grades are given:

1. **Nuzabari Jongpongri/Süngpori**: - From the age of 16 –19 years all boys enter this age grade. The duty of this age grades is to do manual jobs such as fetching water, cutting firewood and run errands for the elders. Whenever there are meetings or communal works to be done in the village, this age grade is responsible for passing on information or messages in the village. For

example, on the eve of an important village meeting, this grade will be responsible to find out who is in residence in their respective khels and to give the list to the older grades. They will also collect three pieces of firewood from all the households to be used for the cooking and so on in such meetings.

2. **Tekhüpa Ori**: - This age grade from the age of 20-23 is responsible for night duty. Whenever there are emergencies and messages are required to be taken to other places outside the village, this age-set grade is called on to do this job. This grade is also responsible to call people residing in Changki *lusa* (territory) such as Longnak and Longtho for the meetings. In the event of deaths, should the death occur in other places, this age-set grade would accompany the dead to the final resting place. This is their *aküli*, which translated mean that this is the exclusive duty of this grade.

3. **Achangcharoba /Pangkhang**: - This group of 24-27 years of age has the specific task of collecting rice from each household when guests are to be entertained by the village. They are responsible for the hospitality to be accorded to village guests and on such occasions supervise the younger grades to carry such tasks.

4. **Aphakcharoba /Kitsüng**: - 28-31 years of age. This grade is considered the marriageable age grade and when one marries a new household is set up but he continues to be a member of the group. The job of this grade is to collect bamboo mats from the household whenever the village needs to erect temporary shelters as when medical teams visit and need separate cubicles for male and female patients. They also do other jobs assigned to them and at certain times they are responsible for distribution of work to the lower ranks. The age-set grades of Achangcharoba/Pangkhang and Aphakcharoba/Kitsung

are the back-up support for the lower grades under them, which often work under their supervision.

5. **Azü-Akang Nuzaba**: - 32-35 years of age. The Azü-Akang Nuzaba and Azü-Akang Tezenba are the junior and senior grades whose duties are the same. The Azü-Akang Nuzaba or junior grade is like the apprentice who learns on the job. The importance of these two grades lies in the fact that they are the grades whose duty it is to know the village boundaries, demarcate the jhum sites every year, collect the taxes for the Village Council and maintain the accounts and audit registers of the village. In effect through these age-set grades every male member of the village learns about the village boundaries and territory of Changki, for the male members move up progressively every three years. These two grades are responsible for the *Kisü-Lusü* duties. *Kisü-Lusü* means the jobs related to the household (*kisü*) and territory (*lusü*). For example, they will set a time for house, granary, *kilangmi* (open bamboo platform) repairs as well as for clearing of community paths, demarcation and allocation of jhum lands. The younger Azü-Akang Nuzabari age-set grade will do the errands at the bidding of the older Azü-Akang Tezenba and are in effect undergoing a training period. But both the grades will work in tandem related to the same specific jobs. Once the date and time for repair work, to collect materials from the jungle and so on, has been selected the younger grade will give the information to the villagers through the village crier (*Yimpiuri*).

6. **Azü-Akang Tezenba**: - 36-39 years of age. This age-set grade is considered to be experienced and mature enough to speak and act on behalf of the village. This group carries all the important messages. They survey and select each year's '**pok**' (the year's demarcated area

for jhum cultivation), they collect fines imposed by the Council, they allocate collective labour and it is this group that maintains the accounts of the village. The village registers such as audit reports, *Senso* register and so on are also in their safe keeping, although technically the *Samenthi* (senior councillors) age grade is in charge of such registers.

7. **Alikhun**: - 40-43 years of age. This age grade is the official load carrier of the village who accompanies the Council members on tours. The upper two age grades immediately above this age grade are the "**Emchachari**" or the village leaders. So in their capacity as village leaders they have to go from place to place on official duties. Therefore when they travel, the duty of **Alikhun** age-set grade is to carry the luggage of the older age grade, (this was more applicable in the olden days when traveling was on foot and therefore the necessity for porters to carry loads was needed). This is an important training period for the Alikhun who follow their seniors on official duties and thus learn the dealings of various official works. This age-set grade is the envoy to other villages in cases related to inter-village affairs. This age-set grade also takes care of all emergency work in the village. Under the supervision of this age-set grade, the rest of lower grades do all the community works.

8. **Samen Nuzaba**: - 44-47 years of age. The "**Samen Nuzaba**" are the junior executive body members and are required to do the bidding of the "**Samenthi**", which is the grade immediately preceding the **Samen Nuzaba** grade. The **Samen Nuzaba** or the junior councillors whose tenure is for three years in effect undergo training in the intricacies of village/khel governance. The **Samenthi** age-set grade will always be accompanied by this grade so that all menial works such as errands and

so on will be done by them. This age-set grade is also called '**Jenliba**' which translated mean those who run errands, for basically that is their duty and they have to undertake all tasks assigned to them by the **Samenthi** (senior councilors) grade. However government employees are exempted from the duty of the **Samen Nuzaba**.

9. **Samenthi**: - 48-51 years of age. The **Samenthi** age-set grade is the traditional leaders of the village under whom the village administrative, executive and judicial work is carried out. The revenue/tax collections as well as policies relating to village development work are decided by this grade. All judgments and decisions are pronounced by this grade. In effect this grade is the decision making body in the village.

The **Samen Nuzaba** and **Samenthi** age grades are called the **"Emchachari"** (rulers/administrators) and traditionally they are the village leaders who form the executive body of the village. However government employees are also exempted from the duty of the **Samenthi**. The reason why the government employees are exempted from the duties of these two age-grades is that as Councillors their job is full time and they have to be in the village at all times.

10. **Risüden/Risütemba**: - 52-55 years of age. This age grade is responsible for mobilizing search parties or rescue teams in case of accidents such as drowning and so on.

11. **Maozenba Telakba**: - 56-59 years of age. To oversee the guarding of the village, that is, they will mobilize, organise and supervise the lower grades for guard duties. This is more so during the wet rice cultivation season when most of the villagers leave the village to work in the fields 16-18 km away from the village. At this time of year only the old, infirm and very young are left in the village. Therefore guards called ***Nokhimongri*** are

organised to guard the village. This age-set grade is responsible for organising the ***Nokhimongri*** guards.

12. **Maozenba Temenba**: - 60-63 years of age. This age grade is responsible for organizing and directing the different lower age grades for community works such as clearing of the village path, repair of village gates and so on.

13. **Empiba Ho**: - 64-67 years of age. This age-grade set is responsible for organising the ***Mezetri*** (guard) of the village during *Ingkho Mapang* when the males are exempted from village duties as per the traditional age-set system. *Ingkho Mapang* literally means 'time to earn' which is explained in detail in the next chapter on economy. During this time the males can go away from the village for their own individual works and as the village is deserted, this age-set grade is given the task of organising the guard duty of the various age-set grades in the village and to look after minor official duties of the Village Council which also remain suspended during this period.

14. **Nokimongba**: - 68 and above. They are considered the retired citizens and are relegated the status of village elders and are treated with deference.

The systematic grading of the age-sets with specific roles and duties ensures that each male in the village learn leadership skills and responsibilities by experiencing the manual jobs from a young age and gradually progressing through various stages where every aspect of village life is learned - be it the village boundary, relationship with other villages, the maintenance of village law and order, administration and being at the helm of power and so on. This is a highly institutionalized form of division of labour where from boyhood to maturity the males learn to work for and protect the village community.

Once a boy enters the age-set system in the village he is also known as *'Emjangkhet'*, *'em'* meaning village, *'jang'* meaning legs and *'khet'* meaning hands, thus it means that once the males enter the age-set system they become the legs and hands of the village, meaning the work force. In each age-set grade, the oldest member is chosen as the leader. Sometimes when the services of all the members of an age-set grade are not required, the leader of that particular grade will select a few of his age mates and will then direct them to carry out the necessary duties.

As we have explained earlier the progressive change of grades in the age-set system occur regularly. Every three years there is an event called "***Ho Tsüngtepba***". This is the time when new entrants to the age-set system or the *Yanga* are inducted. With the new inductions each grade moves up progressively to the senior grade. This is a solemn and important occasion for in this event, the "*Emchachari*" or the village leaders give way to the next generation of leaders while the new entrants to the ***Ho*** or ***Orirachet*** (another term for the age-set system) is inducted. The occasion is marked by a simple ceremony where meat is distributed to every household in the village.

The outgoing ***Samenthi*** (senior Village Council members) age-set grade collects the funds from among themselves to purchase three pigs. The pigs are killed in the house of the eldest member of this age-set grade and the pig's head is given to him. The meat called "***Jongpongsa***" is then distributed to each household in the village. In a piece of bamboo three token pieces of meat consisting of fat, lean meat and bone are skewered and this is hung on the front door of each household where the male members are to be inducted into the next age-set grade or will enter the age-set grade. If due to some unforeseen circumstances a household, where a male member is to be promoted or to be inducted into the age-set grade is not given this meat, then as a fine three more pigs will have to be killed and the distribution of meat carried out again. The ***Samen Nuzaba*** (junior Village Council members) carry out the distribution of the meat. It is only after this ceremony that the ***Samen Nuzaba*** take the office of the ***Samenthi*** (senior Village Council members).

When the ***Samen Nuzaba*** takes over, the outgoing ***Samenthi*** shows them the village boundaries and all the village lands. The audit books and registers are handed over to them too. At the time of "***Ho Tsungtepba***" the other age-set grades are also allowed to kill pigs and have a feast among their age-set grade. This is not mandatory but if they so wish, they are allowed to have this feast. When the ***Samenthi*** step down and are promoted to the next age-set grade, the older age-set grades give them titles or "***Naroküm***" according to their performance when in office.

It is at this time that the different age-set grades get an opportunity to come together and renew their bond of friendship among themselves and for those who stay outside the village, this is the time when they get to meet their age mates and thus establish lifelong bonds. This is a celebration where a boy entering the age-set system is formally recognised as a man with attendant duties and responsibilities. The age-set system determines a man's position in the village and sets the patterns of social behaviour, civic duties and political responsibilities.

The oldest member in each age-set grade is responsible for assigning various tasks as per their grade to the age-mates and he is the one who will be sought by the older age-set grades to delegate certain jobs to his grade. He will be held responsible for negligence of duties.

In Changki there is another system of grading based on ***Naroküm***, which means title. Every title has a meaning and it is interesting to note comparisons are made to birds, animals or flowers. The titles are conferred on the junior age-sets by the senior age-sets after assessing the activities of the group while running the village government and the qualities looked for are honesty, loyalty, courage, clarity in village government laws and bringing of trophies to the village (this was more pertinent during headhunting days) and so on.

The manner of the grades receiving the ***Narokiim*** or title differs vastly between the ***Süngdakba*** (upper khel) and ***Ayim Anet*** (lower khel). The names of the titles in the upper and lower khels are different and although the titles are still in usage most of the meanings of the titles are not known by the younger generations.

In ***Süngdakba*** **(upper khel)** there are different ***Naroküm*** or title that each age-set grade can 'buy' from the older grades. These ***Naroküm*** are assumed by a grade till such time that they remain active participants in the village administration. When they reach old age and are exempted from village duties and taxes, the ***Naroküm*** that they have assumed can be handed over to any of the lower grades, if they are approached. The elders holding such a title may be very few in number, as most of their peers may have died out. The lower grade can treat these elders by giving meat or even cash and thorugh this process of *lilaba* ('buy') they get the titles. The title remains with a particular age-set grade until given away and these are not individual titles.

The ***Süngdakba*** (upper *khel*) ***Naroküm*** or titles are as follows:

1. **Saküb Ori:** Saküb means skin of buffalo and mithun. In the head hunting days shields were made of the treated skins of these animals besides those made of bamboo and cane. Shields made of animal skins were considered special for it was quite a rarity, due to the fact that the skins are considered a delicacy and most often it was eaten. This title was conferred on the group that

was considered tough, hard to defeat and feared by the enemies.

2. **Milen Changri Ori**: Milen is a kind of rare small bird known for its beauty, especially its colourful crown. It is known for being selective in its feeding and nesting, therefore rarely seen. In conferring this title, the group is acknowledged as being distinctive and distinguished.

3. **Nametaki Ori**: Nametaki is a fish which stings when carelessly touched. The fish is ferocious and cunning. Therefore this group is conferred the title attributing these qualities.

4. **Jongmi Changri Ori**: Jungmi is a rare and beautiful orchid usually found in the deep forest growing on high trees. The group scaling great heights is usually conferred this title.

5. **Mepung Changri Ori**: Mepung means wind. Mepung is always light and swift. This title is given to compare the group as light and fast as the wind in their duties and activities.

6. **Otsüngchangri Ori**: Otsüng is also a local bird, black in colour but with a red beak and with white-tipped feathers. It roams in couples usually inseparable. It is known for its intelligence. If trained properly it is said that it can produce human sounds – but it may be noted that this bird is not a parrot or a myna. The group conferred this title is considered to be loyal and intelligent.

7. **Sangpang Changri Ori**: Sangpang is a rare kind of berries which grow on shrubs and from a distance can be seen as red blossoms. These berries are a delicacy for birds and are used as bait to trap the birds. The group conferred this title is considered to be clever and tactful in executing their duties.

8. **Onet Changri Ori**: This is also a rare and beautifully coloured bird. This bird is characterized by being a follower of Miri bird, considered to be the king among birds. Thus the group given this title is considered to be loyal and the dutiful keepers of law and so on.

9. **Miri Changri Ori**: Miri is a local bird, black in colour and with a tail that has two decorative elongated feathers bird. It is a grand looking bird and it is supposed to be king among local birds. It is said that the other birds follow the Miri and is definitely the leader. Thus the group that showed great leadership qualities was given this title.

10. **Sati Changri Ori**: Sati means elephant and in comparison to it, the strongest and mightiest group was given this title.

11. **Medem Changri Ori**: 'Medem' means of same accord and also means of a good number. Therefore this title signifies a group comprising of a good number of members and working in cooperation and complete understanding among themselves.

12. **Tsüngi Changri Ori**: 'Tsüngi' is a carnivorous animal like wolf or hyena. It lives in packs of five or six in number and hunts as a group. Once they choose their prey they persist in following it even for days and weeks till they hunt it down. Thus this title means those who are persevering and hard working.

In ***Ayim Anet*** (lower *khel*) the names of the ***Naroküm*** or titles are bestowed upon the outgoing ***Samenthi*** (senior councillor) age-set grade by the older grades preceding them based on their performance as '***emchachari***' or village rulers/ administrators.

The ***Ayim Anet*** (lower *khel*) ***Naroküm*** or titles are as follows:

1. **Nanga Changri Ori**: 'Nanga' is a kind of bee, which makes its nest in large groups, and this bee is known for its ferociousness. Thus the group that is fierce in protecting the village and in carrying out its duties strictly is given this title.
2. **Medem Changri Ori**: 'Medem' means of same accord and also means of a good number. Therefore this title signifies a group comprising of a good number of members and working in cooperation and complete understanding among themselves.
3. **Mepung Changri Ori**: Mepung means wind. Mepung is always light and swift. This title is given to compare the group as light and fast as the wind in their duties and activities.
4. **Longsa Changri Ori**: In the ancient days of headhunting a warrior from Longsa village had taken the head of a Longkumer woman from Changki village who was noted for her beauty and especially her long hair which reached down to her ankles. In retaliation the Changki warriors captured alive the Longsa head hunter in the vicinity of Ungma village and killed him. This successful act of taking revenge was considered great and thus the title was given to those bringing such repute to the village by the group running the village government.
5. **Tsüenongdang Changri Ori**: During the headhungting days Changki village fought a long protracted war with the Lotha tribe and Changki village although fighting alone never allowed the Lotha warriors to set foot on Changki soil and thus successfully defended the village. Thus this title is given to those who defend and protect the village.
6. **Kucha Changri Ori**: 'Ku' means belongings or luggages;

'Cha' means to check. During *Ala Chela* or *Tsürang Tsüok* (community fishing). During such fishing expedition, while returning there is a strict rule that one cannot carry more than one item of newly made articles such as bamboo baskets and plates and so on. This rule was made so as to ensure that everyone attended to the community fishing duties and did not neglect assigned responsibilities during such time by taking time out to collect raw materials from the jungle to make such articles. The checking was done by *Azü Akhang* age-set grade at a particular point and if anyone had more than one article it was destroyed on the spot. Thus this title means those who check meticulously and ensure that everyone carried out the village rulings.

7. **Moya Changri Ori**: Changki people call the Sema tribe 'Moya'. Moya people are notable in their warfare as ferocious, persistent and having great tactical prowess. Therefore the title is given to those showing such qualities.

8. **Miri Changri Ori**: Miri is a local bird, black in colour and with a tail that has two decorative elongated feathers bird. It is a grand looking bird and it is supposed to be king among local birds. It is said that the other birds follow the Miri and is definitely the leader. Thus the group that showed leadership qualities was given this title.

9. **Sangpi Changri Ori**: 'Sangpi' is the name of a small jet-black bird known for its lively and intelligent in the air. It is also known for its fighting prowess wherein it can defeat even bigger birds. This bird is also seen to be leading groups of other birds. Thus the group which shows intelligence and who are fierce fighters with good leadership qualities are given this title.

We find that there are two categories of age-set system in Changki. One is based on the compulsory traditional ***Yanga*** system, which moves up progressively every three years. The other is based on ***Narokūm*** or titles, which can be 'bought' as in the upper khel or be given by older grades as in the lower khel. However the age-set mates remain the same throughout. It is also interesting to note that in ***Sūngdakba*** (upper *khel*) there are twelve ***Narokūm*** (titles) while in ***Ayim Anet*** (lower *khel*) there are only nine ***Narokūm*** (titles). We also find that although most of the titles are different in the upper and lower khels, three of the titles (*Mepung Changri Ori, Miri Changri Ori and Medem Changri Ori*) are commonly used in both khels. ***Changri*** in Changki dialect means members and ***Ori*** means of the same age group.

Apart from the traditional age-set grading system and the giving of titles the other traditional aspect of the village is the role of the *Yimpuiri* who is the village crier. Till date the *Yimpuiri* is the one who makes official announcement. The traditional village government is also based on the customary laws and the mode of enforcing it is through fines. In this way social control is exercised and the smooth functioning of the village government ensured. The following passages give in detail these traditional aspects of village governance that is followed till date.

Yimpiuri – Village Crier

The *Yimpiuri* or the village crier is a very important functionary in Changki. He is the official mouth piece that gives necessary information to all the villagers. He is chosen from among the *Samen Nuzaba* or the junior councillors. The Village Council Chairman announces the time and date for meetings and will instruct the *Samen Nuzaba* (the junior village councillors) to make it known to the villagers. The *Samen Nuzaba* will select a *Yimpiuri* who has a good, loud and strong voice. He will then go from *kiong* (locality) to *kiong* and make the announcement verbally in a loud, clear voice. Such announcements are made from time to time, sometimes late in the night too. The *Yimten ozüng* (village government order) is also announced by the *Yimpiuri* or village crier. The job of the *Yimpiuri* is very important and is taken very seriously, for this is the only way through which the whole village will get information and necessary instructions. If any mistake is made by the *Yimpiuri* in the course of the announcement, he is liable to be fined heavily and chastised roundly by the Village Council. The office does not carry any monetary remuneration.

Customary Laws in Changki

The customary laws are unwritten which has been handed through the generations by way of the oral tradition. Earlier the customary laws were indisputable and an inalienable part in the lives of the people. However nowadays there is the choice of taking recourse in the law of the land from the lower courts such as the *Dobashi* courts, the ADC or DC courts in the district headquarters to the high courts and even the Supreme Court.

All citizens have the freedom to appeal to such courts if they so wish. But in the village we find that the customary laws are enforced and in general the people abide by the rulings based on customary laws. Some of the customary laws as we find is enumerated below:

1. Tenure of the Village Council is 6 years.
2. Non-Changkians are not eligible to be in the Village Council.
3. Fines imposed by the Village Council shall be 3 pigs and not less.
4. Fines for those caught stealing within the village will be Rs. 500/- while those caught stealing outside will be Rs. 1000/-

5. Rules of divorce: If a man wants to divorce his wife, he will walk out of the house with one dao, one spear and gun, if any. The rest of the household things will remain with the wife. If it is the woman who wants to divorce her husband, she will walk out with only what she is wearing. The sons will stay with the husband and the daughters with the wife.
6. 3 pigs will be fined on the spouse who commits adultery.
7. If a child is born out of wedlock and the boy refuses to marry the girl, he has to build a house for the child and the mother and pay all the village collections for 3 years.
8. If a boy and girl from the same clan have a child, they will be fined Rs.100/- If they decide to marry each other, they will be fined Rs.500/- and expelled from the village.
9. If a woman has a child from a non-Naga, 6 days after the birth of the child, she and the baby will be sent away from the village.
10. Hunting, fishing by using poison, taking stones, wood and so on by non-Changkians from Changki territory without permission will be fined Rs.500/-
11. If a person dies intestate, his nearest paternal relative will inherit his wealth or pay off his debts, if any.
12. Any non-Changkian who had settled in Changki but is desirous to leave the village for good forfeits all rights on the immovable properties he might have.

Customary Fines

The maintenance of law and order and the means through which social control is exercised is by imposing 'fines' on the wrong doers and defaulters. Fines were in the form of pigs, cows and paddy in earlier times. But nowadays in certain cases they are supplanted by money.

The fines imposed are for certain crimes are given below:-

1) **Meraksa** (telling lies)

2) **Süokzükba** (cheating)

3) **Merokzükba** (setting wild fires)

4) **Kilamet** (adultery)

5) **Aki rongba** (house fire)

6) **Yimten raksaba** (violation of village rules)

7) **Yimten kakba** (violation of the general assembly or village *mungdang* decisions or collective decisions)

The fines for serial **No. 1 to 7** are not fixed; they are realized according to the seriousness of the case and may vary from case to case. The Village Council will fix the amount of fine after the matter has been thoroughly investigated. However the fines for the following crimes are fixed by the Village Council:

8) **Ayim chencha** (village fine for minor cases) is Rs 30

9) **Aomet** (stealing) Rs 500 if the theft is within the village and if outside Rs 1000.

10) **Kilamet** (adultery) 3 pigs, which are over 50 kgs.

11) **Mibenlangba** (murder) Rs 5000

12) **Mungdang kakba** Rs 5000 for violation of the general body decisions or collective decisions

The fines imposed for other violations vary according to the seriousness of the case. In the case of murder after the fine is meted out, the accused is then forwarded to the district courts for further trial and judgment.

Fines or '***tekang***' (absent fee) of Rs. 30 are also imposed if any one does not carry out community works such as ***emphi waba*** (clearing of village paths) or ***tsülu endi phiro waba*** (clearing of paths to the rice fields) without valid reasons.

The imposition of fines served as a deterrent as well as punishment for in the olden times there was no recourse to incarceration or other ways of punishing the wrong doers. In the present too fines are still the method used as the means of social control for it has societal implications as the social standing of a person is tarnished. Even if the fine is just Re. 1/- the shame associated with it is great and the phrase "*chenja jano*" which roughly translated means 'the one who was fined' alludes to the questionable character of the person.

There is another way of exacting punishment when a person does not repay a loan or steals from another person. In such cases the *Samen Nuzaba* will carry out the act of seizing the spear, dao and *noklubo* (which roughly translated means dao holder) of the wrong doer. In the event that there are clansmen of the wrong doer among the *Samen Nuzaba*, it is the clansmen who will take away the things from the house of the wrong doer. These are associated with manliness as it were and taking them away means that he is symbolically stripped of his manhood. This is the ultimate insult that can be meted out to a man.

A wrong doer when caught will be summoned by the Village Council to appear in the village court which is in the community hall. Even if a person is rich or occupies high office if he is in the wrong he will be summoned by the Village Council. A person found guilty and is fined by the Village Council. Being fined he will have to go out of the community hall whereby a *Samen Nuzaba* (junior councilor) will follow him so as to instruct him on how to speak to the Village Council members when he pays the fine. If the *Samen Nuzaba* member cannot instruct him to say the proper words, the *Samen Nuzaba* member is publicly chastised.

If any of the *Samen Nuzaba* members does not perform the duties assigned to them properly, then the whole grade is punished by fining each one of them Rs. 10/- for dereliction of duty. If any *Gaon Bura* or Samen Menchen member is charged with and fined *Aomet* (stealing) he is discharged with immediate effect from office and is also excommunicated from the church.

When the fines are realized half of the money is divided between the Village Council members while the other half goes into the Village Council fund. If in case pigs are fined the head of the pig is distributed among the *Gaon Buras* turn wise according to seniority. The rest of the meat is equally shared among the other councillors.

Traditional Samen Menchen (Village Government)

Traditionally the Village Government was formed by the *Samenthi* and *Samen Nuzaba*, age-set grades called the *Samen Menchen* comprising of the permanent male residents of the village. Interestingly we find that although the non-Nagas, who were adopted and given clan and village membership, become part of the village age-set system and move up progressively along with he others, when they reach the grade of *Samen Nuzaba* and *Samenthi*, they are not allowed to take part in the *Samen Menchen*. They may perform some tasks allocated to them but they cannot take part as *Emchachari*, or rulers. The reasoning is that although non-Nagas have been given membership, they have not been given citizenship and thereby cannot take part in the village government. Another rule is that the children of these non-Nagas are not allowed to marry Changki people. However, the non-Nagas who settled in the village before 1961 and were adopted by various Changki clans are allowed to take part in the village government and their children are allowed to marry Changki people. With regard to other Naga tribes, who were adopted by various clans and had settled in the village, they are allowed to be part of the *Samen Menchen*.

The *Samen Menchen* oversees the functioning of the village and for dispensing justice when offences and crimes are committed. But the *Samen Menchen* cannot arbitrarily make decisions, for following the traditionally democratic system of governance, the people's participation in the decision making process is also taken into account. The people participate in the Village Government through the *Ayim Asem Mungdang*, which translated means the Village General Assembly. It is compulsory for all Changki village male residents to attend the *Ayim Asem Mungdang*. In such meetings the agenda is read out and debated upon. The decisions taken are based on consensus among the people and the ruling is regarded as *Yimten Ozung*, which roughly translated mean 'people's verdict' or village government rule made on the basis of consensus.

Interestingly we find that the in the political institution of the village we find that women are not included in the decision making processes. In the proceedings of the Village Council women cannot sit in the meetings, in fact they are not even allowed into the Community Halls when such meetings take place. Even during the *Senso Mungdang* (general assembly of all Changki people) the women cannot take part. In the policy and decision making processes we find that women have no voice.

We find that the position of women in the political set up of the village is very low and their participation in the decision making processes negligible. We find that the women folk themselves regard the village political and administrative activities as the job of the men folk and although they can discuss such matters with their husbands and other male relatives within the confines of their homes, they do not participate in public life.

If we examine the age-set system we find that the allocation of specific duties and tasks assigned to each age-set grade involves all work starting with manual tasks such as fetching water and firewood, cooking, cleaning and so on. The self-sufficiency that the age-set system gives to the men provides for an exclusive and independent all male bastion that restricts the presence of women and segregates them totally, at least in the realm of the village polity.

On the other hand the men in the village find that their duties and responsibilities are heavy and often take up all their time. This is especially true for the younger generation of men who make up the main work force. The tasks allocated to each age-set grade are specific and the age-set grades are tradition bound to perform such tasks. Some of the younger men have left the village and settled in other towns because they found the village works interfered with their private lives and found such village works too hard. The men are kept occupied with village works concerning community works, economic activities and political responsibilities as well as church activities throughout the year. The men are on call everyday, for should the Village Council Chairman or councillors summon them they will have to follow the orders and carry out the jobs assigned to them even if it interferes with their own private work. That is one reason why government job holders are exempt from where the two age-set grades of junior and senior councillors are drawn. From a very young age the men in the village are trained to carry out the responsibilities and duties for the traditional and customary functioning of the village government requires that each Changki man who is a permanent resident of the village contribute to the smooth functioning of the village administration.

The Gaon Bura Institution

Although the age-set system in Changki still forms an integral part of the polity, certain changes have been incorporated that has modified the traditional village government. The first change was the incorporation of the institution of *Gaon Bura* introduced by the British in 1882 so as to make their administrative work easier and conducive to maintaining law and order.

The main functions of the *Gaon Buras* were to collect the annual house tax from their respective villages for the British government, settle cases of civil and criminal nature according to their respective tribal customs and established usages, and were responsible for the maintenance of law and order in their respective village jurisdiction (Sema,1992:32). As the *Gaon Buras* were village chiefs or headmen they could carry out the orders of the British colonial rulers and make the administration of the villages easier for them. 'The *Gaon Buras* were appointed by the Government and they became the direct link between the British colonial administration and the villages. The powers and functions of the *Gaon Buras* as representatives of the colonial administration were determined by the Government. The *Gaon Buras* had no participation in the formulation of the policy regarding their own affairs. On the other hand, the *Gaon Buras* only received directions and supervision from the British district officers. The words *Gaon Bura* has been taken from the Assamese, *Gaon* meaning village and *Bura* meaning elder. It simply means village elders.

Another institution introduced by the British was the *Dobashi* institution. This institution served both as an instrument of pacification of the Nagas and as a native team of intermediaries between the rulers and the ruled. *Dobashi* literally means two languages. Thus the *Dobashi* was the interpreter. The British had instituted the *Dobashi* system as early as in the 1840's as part of an effort to create good relations with the Naga tribes, the object being to promote goodwill and understanding with the Nagas.

However this institution was discontinued in the 1850's only to be reintroduced and made permanent in 1881. The institution of *Dobashi* was an integral part of British administration. Its personnel were paid colonial employees who were primarily used as a link between the native population and the colonial administrative officers (Sema, *op.cit*,:34)

In Changki the *Gaon Bura* institution was established in the 1880's after the British introduced it in the Naga Hills. The exact date cannot be ascertained but the first Changki *Gaon Bura* chosen was **Rongseniken Changkiri** of the lower *khel*.

In the beginning only one *Gaon Bura* was chosen but in the intervening years the *Gaon Buras* began to be selected on the basis of clan and soon became the representatives of the clans. The *Gaon Buras* were the only links with the British administrators and it was through them that the official orders and information was passed on to the people.

As the traditional *Samen Menchen* is based on the age-set system whose tenure is for six years only, (three years as junior councillors and three years as senior councillors), the *Gaon Bura* whose tenure was more or less permanent and being the representative to the British administrators they were found to be necessary for the village administration and was therefore included in the *Samen Menchen*, although they were not part of the grade that automatically ensured entry into the *Samen Menchen*. In this way the *Gaon Bura* institution became an important component of the traditional village government.

The *Gaon Buras* are representatives of the clans to the *Samen Menchen* and are therefore selected by the clans on individual merit. Men with leadership qualities and oratory skills were selected as *Gaon Buras* to represent the clan. The *Gaon Buras* are also usually retired army personnel, teachers and government employees. These men are experienced public speakers and leaders and as the traditional *Samen Menchen* drawn from the age-set system stayed in power for a duration of only six years, the *Gaon Bura* institution gained prominence for the *Gaon Buras* are permanent members of the *Samen Menchen*. Under the circumstances the *Gaon Bura* institution became a powerful and influential component of the Changki village government. When a *Gaon Bura* becomes too old or ill to function, he may be replaced by another representative who is selected by the respective clan members.

In the upper *khel* there are six *Gaon Buras*; two are from the Longchari clan; two from the Amri clan; both of these are the founding clans while two are selected from the Alingri clan. In the lower *khel* there are also six *Gaon Buras*; two are selected from the Tsungliri group comprising five clans, two from the Metsulosang group comprising two clans (Metsüri and Losangri), one from the founding clan Changkiri and one from the Emrem Changki clan.

The Dobashi selected is from the Longchari clan and is attached to the Dobashi Court in the Deputy Commissioner' office in Mokokchung.

GAONBURAS (2007)

***Süngdakba* (Upper *khel*)**

1. Amri Clan :- a) Jendiraba
   b) Limameri
2. Longchari Clan :- a) Sademtsüngba
   b) Imchameren
3. Alingri Clan :- a) Imrongsüngba
   b) Lanuteka

***Ayim Anet* (Lower *khel*)**

1. Changkiri Clan :- a) Rongsensashi
2. Metsülosang Clans :- a) Metangkaba Aonok
   b) Tekatiba Medemtsüngba

3. Tsüngli Clans :- a) Imnameren Ningdangri

b) Longriniken Molieri

The **Chairman** of the **Changki Village Council** is **Limameri** from the **Amri** clan of the lower *khel*. As Longnak area is under the jurisdiction of the Changki village government, there is one *Gaon Bura* representing **Merakiong** (which is the common name used for the Longnak area), namely Menangnoktsüng Amri.

It is interesting to note that in the age-set system, the clan system does not have any part in the segmentation of the village into age-set grades. But in the *Gaon Bura* institution the clans play a major role for the *Gaon Buras* are representatives of the clans.

The traditional *Samen Menchen* is drawn from the age-set system and technically they are the ones who hold the reins of power in the village as per the tradition but in reality the powers and influence lie with the *Gaon Buras*.

The *Gaon Buras* in Changki village are the respected village elders, the representatives of all the clans. Each *Gaon Bura* is identified by the black and red waistcoat and red blanket that they wear. They act at the behest of the Government as quasi-officials and they are not paid any salary but the prestige and power that they enjoy at the village level is immense.

The traditional *Samen Menchen* is given its due respect and they take part in all the decision making processes but they are handicapped by the fact that they are in office for only six years, three of which are spent as assistants.

The institution of *Gaon Bura* and its powers and functions were further enhanced by the introduction of the **Village Council** and its incorporation into the traditional system of village governance. To understand how the *Gaon Buras* have superceded the traditional Samen Menchen as far as its powers and functions are concerned it might be useful to look into the details of the Village Council and Area Councils Act and the salient features of the Act.

Changki Village Council

Under the Constitution of India, provisions for safeguarding social and religious practices, customary justice and landed property of the Nagas are included in Article 371 A (1). This article deals with the special provisions with respect to the state of Nagaland.

"371A. (1) Notwithstanding anything in this constitution,

(a) No Act of Parliament in respect of –

(i) Religious or social parties of the Nagas,

(ii) Naga customary law and procedure,

(iii) Administration of civil and criminal justice involving decisions according to Naga customary law.

(iv) Ownership and transfer of land and its resources, shall apply to the state of Nagaland unless the Legislative Assembly of Nagaland by a resolution so decides." (Government of Nagaland, 1971:60).

This Act states that the processes of dispensing justice, administration of the villages and land ownership and transfer will be according to the Naga customary laws. In effect the customary laws are recognised as legal and binding. Only the State Legislative Assembly can amend the Act. As such no amendment of this Act has been promulgated so it may be taken to mean that this Act has been accepted by all sections of Naga society.

After Nagaland attained statehood in 1963, the Village Council was recognised by the State Government and promulgated through the Nagaland Village, Area and regional Councils Act 1970.

Nagaland Village, Area and Regional Councils Act 1970 was extended to the districts of Kohima and Mokokchung for at that time there were only these two districts and the then Naga Hills Tuensang Area (NHTA). It was only in 1973 that the three districts were divided into 7 districts. The Act was to consolidate the constitution of Village, Area and Regional Councils to regulate the functions and duties and for matters connected therewith. Some of the salient points of the Village Council as enumerated in *The Nagaland Code*, Volumn II, (First Edition) 1971 are as follows:

Village Council:

1. **Constitution**: Every recognised village shall have a Village council

   Explanation: Village means and includes an area recognised as a village as such by the Government of Nagaland. An area in order to be a Village under the Act shall fulfill the following conditions namely:

   a) The land in the area belong to the population of that area or given to them by the Government of Nagaland, if the land in question is a Government land or is given to them by the lawful owner of the land; and

   b) The Village is established according to the usage and customary practice of the population of the area.

2. **A Village Council shall consists of members chosen by villagers in accordance with the prevailing customary practices and usages**, the same being approved by the State Government, provided that hereditary Village Chiefs, Gaon Buras and Angs shall be ex-officio members of such Council and shall have voting rights. (Government of Nagaland,1986:61).

The Constitution of the Nagaland Village and Area Councils Act states that it is mandatory for every recognised Naga village to have a Village Council. The specifications for constituting it are simple - that the land belongs to the village and that the village is established according to the usage and customary practice of the population of the area. The Village Councils as promulgated by the Government of Nagaland is a part of the decentralization process whereby the village administration are based on the traditional system of village government but will be additionally accountable to the civil administration.

The qualification for members is that they have to be bonafide citizens of India and above 25 years of age and the tenure of the Village Council is five years which is extendable to one year by the State Government by a notification in the Gazette. The members hold office for the stipulated tenure but should there be a vacancy another member may be appointed provided he remains in office for the remainder of the period till the Village Council is dissolved on completion of its tenure.

In the Act it is clearly stated that the established traditional institutions continue to function as Village Council according to respective custom and usages and the selection of the Chairman and Secretary are left to the discretion of the Village Council.

Wide ranging functions and powers are conferred upon the Village Council for developmental works as well as administration of justice which are backed with provisions for adequate resources with which to conduct their work:

The Village Council shall have the following powers and functions:

1) To formulate Village Development Schemes, to supervise proper maintenance of water supply,

roads, forest, sanitation, education and other welfare activities;

2) To help various Government agencies in carrying out developmental works in the village;

3) To take development works on its own initiative or on request by the Government;

4) To borrow money from the Government, Banks or financial institutions for application in the development and welfare work of the village and to repay the same with or without interest as the case may be;

5) To apply for and receive grant-in-aid, donations, subsidies from the Government or any agencies;

6) To provide security for due repayment of loan received by any permanent resident of the village from the Government, Bank or financial institution;

7) To lend money from its funds to deserving permanent residents of the village and to obtain repayment thereof with or without interest;

8) To forfeit the security of any individual borrower on his default in repayment of loan advanced to him or on his commission of a breach of any terms of loan agreement entered into by him with the Council and to dispose of such security by public auction or by private sale;

9) To enter into any loan agreement with the Government, Bank and financial institutions or a permanent resident of the village;

10) To realise registration fees for each litigation within its jurisdiction;

11) To raise funds for utility service within the village

by passing a resolution subject to the approval of the State Government:

Provided that all monetary transactions shall be conducted through a scheduled Bank or the Nagaland State Co-Operative Bank;

12) To constitute Village Development board;

13) Power to do certain Acts in the event of an epidemic.

On the outbreak of an epidemic or infectious disease Village Council shall initiate all preventive measures.

Administration of Justice

(1) The Village Council constituted under the Law in force from time to time shall administer justice within the village limits in accordance with the customary law and usages as accepted by the canons of justice established in Nagaland, and the law in this respect as enforced from time to time.

(2) In case of disputes between villages falling in different areas or districts two or more Village Councils may settle a dispute in a joint session or refer it to the appropriate authority. (ibid:62-63).

From the above points enumerated we see that the functioning of the modern state machinery is incorporated into the administration of the village using the age-old traditional power structure and based on customary laws concerning civil and criminal justice as long as they are applicable and are deemed appropriate. The modern system has been adapted and interwoven into the traditional village political framework without disturbing or doing away with the customary and traditional ways of village governance. The developmental programmes and allocation of funds, resources and implementation of such activities are through the Village Council and the Village Development board.

The Village Council also facilitates the smooth functioning of the district and state administration in the rural areas and serves as a link between the state and the villagers through the block/sub-divisional and district headquarters. This is enumerated in the paragraph concerning village administration.

(1) The Village Council shall be auxiliary to the administration and shall have full powers to deal with internal administration of the village:

(a) Maintenance of law and order

(b) In serious case offender may be arrested but such person shall be handed over to the nearest Administrative Officer or Police Station without undue delay;

(c) To report to the nearest Administrative officer occurrence of any unnatural death or serious accident;

(d) To inform the presence of strangers, vagabonds or suspects to the nearest Administrative Officer or police Station;

(e) To enforce orders passed by the competent authority on the village as a whole;

(f) To report the of break of epidemics to the nearest Administrative Officer or medical Officer;

(g) No transfer of immovable property shall be affected without the consent of the Village Council. Written record of this shall be maintained by the Village Council.

The Village Council is under the supervision and control of the Deputy Commissioner/ the Additional Deputy Commissioner or Sub-Divisional Officer (Civil) in-charge of the Sub-Division, Extra Commissioner or Circle Officer within his jurisdiction.(ibid:64).

The above directives ensures that the Village Councils assist the district administration in maintaining law and order, facilitating health measures to contain diseases and to oversee the overall smooth functioning of the village.

In Changki following the directives as given in the Village and Area Council Act the people have constituted the Changki Village Council comprising of the traditional *Samen Menchen* drawn from the age-set system as well as the *Gaon Buras*. The Village Council is known as '*emchachari*' which means rulers. Thus the *Samen Menchen* is synonymous with the Village Council.

The Village Council Chairman is selected from among the '*emchachari*' but in Changki we find that the Council Chairman from the very inception of the Village Council continues to be selected from among the *Gaon Buras*.

We find that in Changki the *Gaon Buras* being educated leaders who had had exposure to the outside world and its workings, most *Gaon Buras* being retired army personnel, retired teachers or government employees were increasingly called upon to carry out the work of the Village Council in dealing with the district HQ offices in Mokokchung and thus they became an essential feature of the Village Council. The *Samen Nuzaba* and *Samenthi* who had progressively moved up the age-set system in the village were mostly agriculturists who may have had some degree of education but were not too well versed in the ways of the bureaucracy and state machinery. Furthermore, the *Samen Nuzaba* and *Samenthi* were in office for only six years, three of which were spent as junior councillors undergoing training. The *Gaon Buras* on the other hand had no such fixed tenure. Thus with the introduction of the Village Council Act, the institution of *Gaon*

Bura became a permanent fixture in the traditional village government and in many ways became more powerful.

In the Village and Area Councils Act the tenure of the Village Council Chairman has been stipulated as five years but in practical terms the tenure varies from village to village. In Changki we find that the tenure is not fixed and since 1972 when the Act came into being, there have been eight Village Council Chairmen in the village with the present Chairman holding office for a second term.

The exact dates of the terms held by the various Chairmen could not be given as no records as such were maintained in the village but the names are given below in the order of tenure held by them:

1. Imkongwati Longchari (upper *khel*)
2. Metongmeri Changkiri (lower *khel*)
3. Imchatsüng Longchari (upper *khel*)
4. Tinumeri Amri (upper *khel*)
5. Imotiba Longchari (lower *khel*)
6. Tajenyuba Changkiri (lower *khel*)
7. Pongenliba Alingri (upper *khel*)
8. Lanuteka Alingri (upper *khel*)
9. Tajenyuba Changkiri (lower *khel*) (second term)

It is observed that the majority of the people who have held the office of Chairman belong to the three founding clans: Longchari Amri and Changkiri and apart from two persons the rest are from the upper *khel*. The others belonging to the Alingri clan are said to have arrived in the village just a few days after the three founding clans established the village and as such are accorded due respect and honour.

The tenure of the Changki Village Council Chairman is not fixed (though as per the Government Act, it is supposed to be for five years) but it is not permanent either. The tenure of the Chairman depends on how effective he is as a leader and as long as he enjoys the confidence of the other Council members. The Village Council chairman can be removed from office if he is ineffective or mismanages the office. The chairman may also resign on personal grounds.

The Changki Village Council comprises of the **Süngdakba** (upper *khel)* and **Ayim Anet** (lower *khel*) ***Samen Menchen*** (village government). The Village Council chairman Tajenyuba Changkiri, selected from among the Gaon Buras is assisted by two secretaries, one from each *khel.* They are Imnasangba from Süngdakba (upper *khel*) and Tekasünep from Ayim Anet (lower *khel).* There are twelve *Gaon Buras*; six from each khels. In the composition of the Village Council we find that there are representatives from each *khel* in the traditional political structure. The number of senior and junior councillors is unequal as only those who are not government employees and who have reached the respective age-set grade are inducted and given the responsible of holding the highest office in the village polity.

Case Study

During the research work the Changki Village Council Chairman was Tajenyuba Changkiri, aged 70 years then and he was the first person in the village to hold the office of Council Chairman for the second term. His first term was from 1994 – 2001. He resigned from the chairmanship in 2001 as there were some people who worked against him and therefore to put an end to the 'bad blood' as he put it, he resigned. However in 2003 he was again nominated by the village council members and his nomination was sent to the Additional District Commissioner (ADC) which was forwarded to the District Commissioner (DC) in Mokokchung, the district headquarters, and he was appointed by the DC. The office of Village Council Chairman does not entail any pay from the state government.

Tajenyuba Changkiri did his schooling in Jorhat Christian High School, Rajabari as his father worked as a Supervisor (1940's) in the Jorhat Mission Compound run by the American Missionaries. Tajenyuba came to Changki village and taught in Mission School Changki from 1954, then moved on to Sangpangmen Government Primary School Changki where he taught from 1957 to 1991 when he retired as the Head Master. In 1990 he was awarded the National Teacher's award for which he had to go to Delhi to collect the award from the President of India. As it was his first visit to Delhi he was accompanied by his *Temnakja* (sister's son). In 1992 he was selected by his clan as a *Gaon Bura* and in 1994 he became the Village Council Chairman. He is proficient in English, Hindi, Assamese, Nepali and Bengali languages and was also an all round sportsman. He was married to Sentimenla Longkumer and they had five children. When his wife died he married her youngest unmarried sister Imdangtila and they have two children.

The official duties that Tajenyuba has to attend to are often related to various office matters. All necessary documents from character certificates to recommendations and verifications that the people require to send to the district headquarters will have to be signed by him. Without the signature of the Chairman nothing official can be undertaken. Every village assembly is chaired by the Village Council Chairman and he conducts the meetings where decisions are made collectively after which the final decision is pronounced by the Chairman. Some minor matters can be disposed off by the Village Council Chairman but for all major matters the consensus of the *ayim mungdang* (village general body) is required. As most of the official work pertains to constant interaction with government officials the Chairman has to make frequent visits to the district headquarters as well as to the state capital, Kohima. In all these visits the Chairman is always accompanied by a few select council members such as *Gaon Bura*, *Samen Nuzaba* (junior councillor) and *Samenthi* (senior councillor). The expenditure for all these trips is realized from the Village Council fund.

The Village Council Chairman looks after the welfare of the villagers and whenever people visit, the hospitality extended in the form of refreshments are borne by the Chairman as no funds are given for it. Any visitor to the village will have to approach the Chairman first and as the Chairman does not have a separate office, he entertains all visitors in his house. The chairmanship is more along voluntary service and Tajenyuba says that very often he has to depend on his wife to look after the rice field and farm that they depend on for their livelihood. All his children are married and have their own families and fields to look after. However Tajenyuba said that he likes his job especially travelling and meeting new people. He said that the most interesting part of his job was in discharging the right judgment when cases come up to him.

With regard to inter-village conflicts he said that as the boundaries of each village is well demarcated and the people have genuine respect for land there have been no serious conflicts with other villages. However should such conflicts arise, neighbouring villages will stand as witness and take oath. Such cases may be referred to the *Dobashi* court under the district administrative control. The inter-village relationship is based on friendship and respect for each other's boundaries of land and rivers. The work of the Village Council is never ending and the council members meet every Sunday at Alingtemen which is a small hall in the middle of the village demarcating the upper from the lower *khel*. Here the weekly reports are given and discussed and matters relating to cases within the village are taken up and the dates are fixed for holding the village court to try the cases.

From the case study of the incumbent Village Council Chairman we understand that the village government is run along the traditional system of village government but most of the work is now taking on the mechanisms of the bureaucratic system with much file work and officialdom. In this way changes are taking place in the working of the traditional village government. The development works for the village and access to resources depends on the Village Council Chairman and his ability to network with the various levels of government officials. In many ways the Village Council Chairman has to take on the roles of civil servant, judge, politician and humble cultivator.

Powers and Functions of Changki Village Council

The Changki Village Council comprising of *Samenthi* and *Samen Nuzaba* as well as the *Gaon Buras* headed by the Village Council Chairman have overall powers to conduct the affairs of the village according to the customary laws within the village.

It is the *Samenthi* (senior councillors) who only can issue summons, pass judgment and give directives based on the customary law. However the summons or the verdict is given in the name of the *Samen Menchen* or Village Council and announced by the Chairman.

The role of the *Samen Nuzaba* is that of junior councillors and as such they are confined to do whatever works as directed by the *Gaon Buras* and *Samenthi*. They are not authorized to speak in public although in special cases they may be allowed to do so but only after they seek the permission of the assembly. If they speak out of turn or unnecessarily they are fined immediately by a small amount of money.

The *Gaon Buras* enjoy full powers with regard to development works on the intervention of the State Government, as they are the direct link to it. However the

Gaon Buras cannot sanction any financial matters as the financial authority rests solely with the *Samenthi*. The village funds are collected through the village household collection, the *Senso* membership fees, land tax, Changki valley Mill tax, Tzurang valley tax and so on.

There are 2 types of household collection among the villagers. The senior citizens who are above 70 years of age, widows and spinsters pay only half the amount, while the rest pay the full amount as decided by the A*yim Asem Mungdang* (general village assembly). The amount for the *ayim charu* may vary from Rs.300 to Rs.350 annually. A certain date and time is fixed by the Village Council and it is called '*ayim charu* which is announced through '*yimpiuri*' or public announcement made by the village crier. The *Samen Nuzaba* with detailed lists of each household makes the collection. On the collection date old and invalid people who cannot afford to maintain themselves will come with 50 paisa and giving that 50 paisa will ask for exemption from "*ayim charu*".

All those exempted from "*ayim charu*" will not have any voice in public meetings unless the *Samen Menchen* specifically requests him. They will also not cultivate or fetch firewood as not paying tax means complete exemption from all normal activities. On that day of the collection, the eldest *Gaon Bura* will host the day's hospitality sanctioned by the *Ayim Asem Mungdang*, the killing of a pig being the normal fare. The household collections are deposited at his house too.

The yearly audit held in March end is audited by people selected from the public such as schoolteachers, government jobholders and retired army personnel. When the audit report is ready a general assembly meeting is called in the village and after verifying the proper usage of the funds, an amount for the current year's collection is fixed. An annual house tax of Rs.20 is paid to the government. This amount is also collected by the *Samen Menchen* and deposited at the sub-divisional headquarter, Mangolemba.

In the Changki Village Council represented by the age-set grades of *Samen Nuzaba* and *Samenthi* as well as the twelve *Gaon* Buras, the Village Council Chairman presides over public meetings, when such meetings are held. The agenda is read out and discussion in the house takes place where everyone is given a chance to voice his opinion. The way the speaker addresses the house is formal and respectful. Any breach of decorum here is viewed seriously and a fine imposed. When there is a Changki *Senso Mungdang* or general assembly, all the villagers regardless of where they reside, (except the women and children), attend the meeting and each person regardless of clan, age or status is allowed to speak provided he follows the strict norms of public speaking.

When cases are tried, the guilty party as well as the injured party is summoned by the Village Council and each party given a fair hearing. Witnesses are called in and the evidence given for or against. After deliberation if the guilty party is found to be at fault a fine is imposed depending on the gravity of the case. If the injured party cannot give enough evidence or reasonable explanations then they are also liable to be fined.

In cases when the aggrieved party does not accept the verdict of the Village Council and decides to file a case with the district administration or any other higher courts, it is mandatory that the aggrieved party should give proper information to the Village Council. If not the case will be blocked and the offenders fined. If the aggrieved party after giving proper information goes ahead with filing the case in other courts, the Village Council gives the ruling that should they lose the case, the Village Council will take action and compensation has to be paid by the aggrieved party to the Village Council. In case the aggrieved party goes to court of law willfully without informing the Village Council, they are fined heavily. If any cases go to the DC court and other courts of the land a file will be created by the people concerned.

We also find that when disputes arise it is the norm of the aggrieved parties to call well-wishers, except Village Council and church members, who will try to negotiate so that a compromise is reached between the parties. In such cases there are no fines imposed. If any party should decide to go the Village Council with the case, the Village Council will first ask the verdict of the well wishers. They study the case thoroughly but usually the ruling follows the verdict of the well wishers. If a fine imposed on the guilty party by the Village Council is not paid and the party decides to go to other courts and loses the case, then the party has to pay the fine as well as the costs of the case for the Village Council too.

When disputes such as not paying of loans with interest, the parties are given a chance by the Village Council to settle the matter between the parties by fixing a date for repayment of the loan with interest. If the defaulter does not pay the amount by the time fixed, the case is tried by the Village Council and should the defaulter pay back the loan when the case is being taken by the Village Council, the case will not be withdrawn and the defaulter is fined, even if he has paid up the full amount. This is to deter the unnecessary wastage of the time of the Village Council as well as to uphold the sanctity of the Village Council.

The *Samen Menchen* (Village Council) is also subject to punishment by way of fines if they are found guilty of wrong doing. The *Gaon Buras* may be respected village elders but this does not mean that they are above the law. In the year 2003, a *Gaon Bura* was summarily dismissed from office for he was caught stealing log from the reserved forest. This meant that the church also took action by excommunicating him and his clan fined him heavily for bringing shame upon them.

Usually among the Ao the clans try adultery cases but in Changki, the Village Council tries the cases. In such cases, as soon as it comes to the notice of the Village Council, the parties are summoned and the case tried. Family and friends are allowed to stand as witnesses.

In the meetings called by the *Samen Menchen*, only the *Samenthi* members are allowed to speak. No one can speak in such meetings for such meetings take place when a final decision has been taken after calling the executive as well as the *Senso Mungdang* meetings.

The relationship between that of the *Gaon Buras* and the traditional *Samen Menchen* (traditional village councillors) is cordial and formal. The *Gaon Buras* being the elders have more authority by virtue of their age as well experience and as the Samen Menchen are in office for only six years, three of which are spent as assistants, they are guided and supervised by the *Gaon Buras* . The Village Council Chairman is also inevitably selected from among the *Gaon Buras*, so the *Samen Menchen* has little authority on its own. But as they work in cooperation and in tandem with each other, the combined forces of the *Samen Menchen* and *Gaon Buras* comprising the Village Council regulates the affairs of the village.

The Village Council dispenses its duties as per the customary laws, which have been the norm from time immemorial. The form of punishment is through fines, which usually involves pigs and payment of cash. We find that Changki village as in the rest of Nagaland has shown a high degree of adaptability and a readiness to incorporate new political and administrative reforms into the existing traditional village political structure to attain new goals without doing away with the old system. In this way by establishing relatively viable administrative units at the grassroots level like the Village Councils within the traditional local political framework, the possibilities for obtaining resources for development and for gaining access to wider patterns of participation in the decision making processes has been opened while the continuity of cultural identity is retained.

People's Participation in the Village polity

The traditional system of village administration is based on the active participation of the people where decisions are taken after open debates and discussions and a consensus is reached. Although the Village Council comprised of the traditional *Samen Menchen* and the *Gaon Buras,* the acknowledged leaders, it cannot pass any ruling without the consent of the people pertaining to the welfare of the people in general. With regard to maintenance of law and order, disputes over property, divorce and so on the Village Council acts according to customary laws which is indisputable. The people's participation in the village polity is not confined to the permanent residents of the village alone. The Changki people living outside of the village are also expected to participate although the participation may be limited. To show how this takes place, it will be relevant to explain how the people have organised themselves at the village level and outside of the village.

At the village level the people are organised in the following manner:

a) at the clan level

b) at the *khel* level: **Süngdakba** (upper) and **Ayim Anet** (lower)

c) at the *Ayim Asem Mungdang* (Changki Village General Assembly) level.

At the clan level each clan has its own committee which oversees the clan property and settles disputes within its jurisdiction. The clan committees in the village have office bearers such as Convener, Secretary and Treasurer and executive members the number of which can be from five to more than twenty members depending on the numerical strength of the clan. The clan committee at the village level also maintains a register where names of the male members living within as well as outside the village are entered.

At the khel level we find that both *Süngdakba* and *Ayim Anet* have their own traditional *Samen Menchen* (village government), *Gaon Buras* and age-set systems. Each khel has its own independent and separate set of rules and regulations pertaining to its jurisdiction. However when it comes to the village as a unit, both the khels will discuss the matter at hand and will formulate rules and regulations through consensus.

At the *Ayim Asem Mungdang* level all male residents of Changki village take part in the village polity; their participation is through the *Ayim Mungdang* or the village general meeting. It is compulsory for every male to attend the meeting. In these general meetings the people are free to speak and even air their grievances or complaints. The people can also question the *Samen Menchen (Village Council)* and if there are anomalies in the conduct of the *Samen Menchen*, the people can impose fines on them too.

The Changki people residing outside the village are organised in the following manner:

a) Changki Union level
b) Clan level
c) Changki *Senso* level

There is a Changki Union in every town wherever there are Changki people. The Changki Union caters to the welfare of the people and in times of need and trouble as well as for celebrations and other events it is the Changki Union that provides support through physical and material support. Each Changki male is registered with the Union and pays annual membership fees. Once a man is entered in the Union register, his family is also automatically registered. Each Changki Union has a President, General Secretary as well as a Treasurer. The meetings are held whenever the need arises. The Changki Union also holds Changki Fellowship services every Sunday.

In this way the sense of community living and participation is kept alive even in the towns. Apart from this each clan has its own Union too and it is through the clan unions in the towns that the members are included in the age-set system. The clan committee in the towns maintain a register where each the names of the male members are entered. This is turn is sent to the village clan committee who will in turn make sure the names are registered in the village clan register thus ensuring that the members entry into the village age-set system is automatic. This is so for once the names are entered in the clan register; the village clan committee makes sure that the names are also entered in the village register. The members living outside of the village may be part of the age-set system but they are not assigned any duties or roles for practical reasons. It is only those living in the village who are actively involved in the village age-set system and the *Samen Menchen*.

We have stated that all males have to enter the age-set system to become *Senso* (citizen) and that to be counted as a member of the village all males require clan membership.

Clan membership is through birth while entry into the age-set system depends on the chronological age of the person. When the males enter the age-set system, they are considered to have become responsible citizen. As citizens their names are entered in the clan registers and a token membership fee is taken from them. It is the duty of the clan members responsible for maintaining the register to see that every member's name has been entered in the village Senso register too, which is maintained clan-wise. Each Changki male regardless of where they live pay a membership fee of Rs.10 annually now. In this way all the Changki males become a part of the village *Senso*.

The participation of the Changki males who are non resident villagers in the affairs of the general village polity, no matter where they reside, is through the *Changki Senso Mungdang* (*Senso* – citizens; *Mungdang* – general assembly). The meetings are always held in Changki village and all Changki males are expected to come to the village for the meetings.

The *Changki Senso Mungdang* is the general public meeting. All males who have entered the age-set system are eligible to attend this meeting. Whenever a *Senso Mungdang* is called all the Changki Unions are notified and each Union is responsible for intimating the same to each member.

It is mandatory that every Changki male, wherever he may be residing, attend the meeting. In the event that a person has settled too far away in other states and finds it inconvenient to come for the meeting at short notice, he is exempted. The ties with the village are kept intact in such ways and every Changki male have a responsibility and duty towards the village through participation in the *Senso Mungdang*.

The *Changki Senso Mungdang* (Changki general body assembly) also has a **Senso Menchenphuri** which roughly translated mean, General Body Office Bearers, comprising of all the Changki males, regardless of where they reside. The *Senso Menchenphuri* comprises of a President, Vice President, Secretary, Assistant Secretary, one Treasurer and one Finance Secretary selected from within the village itself. The *Senso Menchenphuri* officials hold office for a period two years.

Apart from these officials the *Senso Menchenphuri* is also comprised of the "*Sanen Luden*" or Executive Committee. The Executive Committee is made up of two representatives each from the Mokokchung, Dimapur and Kohima Changki Unions and one each from the other Changki Unions within Nagaland. As Changki village is also taken as a unit, representatives are sent to the *Sanen Luden* from the village itself. The representatives comprise of two *Gaon Bura*, two *Samenthi* (senior councillors), two *Samen Nuzaba* (junior councillors) and four members from the general public, that is, two each from the two khels. The *Sanen Luden* holds office for two years.

The *Senso Menchenphuri* has overall power to take decisions on matters pertaining to matters discussed by the *Changki Senso Mungdang*, which is final and binding. Among the *Sanen Luden*, the representatives from the *Samen Menchen* (Village Council) have the power to impose fines as per the customary law and to mete out punishments.

The President selected from among the office bearers of the *Senso Menchenphuri* who are permanent residents of the village has the power to call the *Senso* meeting whenever the need arises. When such meetings are called, it is the duty of the *Samen Nuzaba* (junior councillors) to personally go to each Changki Union and give the letter of intimation for the meeting.

In these meetings every member has a right to speak but certain protocols are observed so that decorum and decency are maintained. Proper permission is ought when anyone wants to speak from the President and the manner of speaking is formal and respectful. The person speaking in such meetings must keep to the point he has raised and cannot make long speeches and no one can interrupt someone who has been granted permission to speak.

The traditional political set up and the manner in which the people have organised themselves include every Changki male. Through the *Senso Mungdang* the Changki people residing outside the village maintain links with the village. Although people who do not attend the meetings are viewed in a poor light, not everyone takes active part in the *Senso Mungdang* and a few Changki people living outside the village do not maintain links with the village. However, anyone who does not attend the *Senso* meetings are fined Rs.100/- and it is mandatory for them to pay the membership fee of Rs.10 annually. It is through the *Senso Mungdang* that the people stay connected to the village and especially for the males, this is an important factor as their participation will give them recognition, status and respect within the village.

Case Study

In the earlier chapter on kinship we have discussed the problems arising due to the claims made by one clan that they were *the* original founding clan in the lower *khel*. The political fall out of this claim is best illustrated by the events that took place from 2001 onward. In the ensuing discord the claimants tried to break up the *Senso Telongjem* (solidarity of the people) as well as the *Senso Menchenphuri* (General Body Office Bearers) as the following details will show.

In 2001 when the *Senso Charu* (citizen membership fee) was collected, the Emrem Changki clan sent their membership fees using the name of the Changkiri clan. In effect they were openly declaring themselves as the Changkiri clan. This issue was brought to the *Senso Mungdang (*general body assembly*)*, on October 25th 2001. In this meeting, the question of how two clans having the same name could submit membership fees separately was raised. After much discussions and debates, the President, following the consensus/verdict of the general body, made the final decision and declared that the clan led by Tajenyuba G.B. (*Gaon Bura*) as Changkiri, and Lanutemsu as Emrem Changki.

After the *Senso Mungdang* verdict, the Emrem Changki on their own will took the matter to the court of law, that is, the district judiciary Mokokchung under DC in the form of appeal against the *Senso Mungdang* judgment. It was only when the DC court summoned Tajenyuba as the respondent of the said appeal that the matter came to be known. As it was the verdict of the *Senso Mungdang* (general body) as a whole, and not the verdict of the respondent cited, Tajenyuba referred the matter to the *Senso Menchenphuri* (General Body Office Bearers), as it was in contravention to the *Senso* verdict and decision. Therefore the *Senso Mechenpuri* had to call a *Sanen Luden* (executive committee) meeting whereupon it was decided to hold again a *Senso Mungdang* (Changki general body assembly), on 18th January, 2002.

The *Senso Mungdang* in the meeting concluded that the Emrem Changki clan members had not honoured the customary law by going to the court of law without publicly declaring their intention of going to a court of law. This was a complete breach of Changki customary law, the act of which is a serious offence inviting the penalty of a fine Rs.5000/- the customary fine for *Mungdang Kakba*, which is a fine for violating the general assembly's decision. But when the members of Emrem Changki clan did not comply, the *Senso Mungdang* requested the Village Council action as is customary to seize from the possession of the Emrem Changki *Gaon Bura*, Imtajenba, a dao and spear as a token of imposing the given fine and kept in the custody of the Changki Village Council.

In the meantime, as the case was already in the District Magistrate's court the *Senso* (general assembly) decided to fight the case and as the case was initiated by the Emrem Changki clan, it became *Senso* Vs Emrem Changki. Further, to fight the case, the *Senso* also decided to collect funds from all the Changki *Senso* members, in all the centres, including the Emrem Changki clan, as they were part of the *Senso*. The *Senso Mungdang* also selected a committee and authorized it to handle the case on behalf of the *Senso Mungdang*.

Accordingly the *Sanen Luden*, as is the practice, in a subsequent meeting passed a resolution to collect a sum of Rs.300, inclusive of all *Senso Mungdang* related expenses, the court case expenses being one of them, per household and fixed May 31st 2002 as the deadline. Despite the deadline fixed, many centres having Changki Unions, corresponded with the *Senso* office, asking for more time to collect the funds. When the Mokokchung Changki Union as one of the centres sought clarification on the matter only after the deadline expired, the *Senso Menchenphuri* (General Body Office Bearers) did not entertain their quest, reasoning that it would be out of the way to do so when the official deadline had already expired. However the *Sanen Luden* (Executive Committee) was called by the *Senso Menchenphuri* on 21st June 2002 and the matter was discussed wherein a resolution was made to extend the deadline to the 15th August 2002 and authorized the *Senso* office to hand over the list of names of those failing to pay to the Village Council. This was in keeping with the customary procedures wherein the Village Council is the only authorized body to impose any such penalty against offenders. In other words, the decision was taken by the *Senso Mungdang*, and the execution carried out by the *Samen Menchen*. Now the duty of the *Samen Menchen* was to ensure that all the members paid the *senso charu* (general body fund collection) but with a penalty for not conforming to the deadline.

Samen Menchen (Village Council) therefore had to summon the people who still did not pay the *senso charu*, centre-wise, and as Mangkolemba and Mokokchung were closest, the people from these centres were the first on the list. While members from Mangkolemba came on the date fixed, the people from Mokokchung did not come. Instead the Mokokchung Changki Union sent in a letter seeking clarification to the *Senso Menchenphuri* (General Body Office Bearers) with only a copy for information to the *Samen Menchen* (Village Council). This was an act of blatant defiance of the Village Council's authority by the Mokokchung centre.

Therefore the *Samen Menchen* called for a *Ayim Asem Mungdang* (village general assembly) in the month of October 2002, as is generally done in such an event. The village general body unanimously decided that the Mokokchung Changki Union had defied the authority of the Changki Village Council and therefore the *Changki Yimten* (people's court) took the matter into their hands that is the matter was now in the hands of the people's court. The *Changki Yimten* fixed a date and time and summoned the Mokokchung Changki Union to present themselves at Changki.

However on the appointed day, the Mokokchung Changki Union did not come and the *Samen Nuzaba* (junior councillors) was sent from the village to Mokokchung to fetch them. The Mokokchung Changki Union did not comply and due to the insolence and the disrespect shown to the village government and the blatant and willful contravention of accepted customary laws, the *Changki Yimten* (people's court) de-recognised the Mokokchung Changki Union.

In reply, the Mokokchung Changki Union took recourse to legal action and took recourse to the court of law. When the summons came to the *Changki Yimten* (people's court) from the court, another *Ayim Asem Mungdang* (village general meeting) was called and it was then decided as the

Mokokchung Changki Union was directly challenging the village government, the Mokokchung Changki people would be barred from entering Changki territory (*enki tsüba*) and from October 2002, the Mokokchung people were barred from entering Changki territory. The *Changki Yimten* passed a resolution that offenders would be fined the highest penalty of Rs.5000/- and that they would be ousted from the Changki *lusa* (territory) by the *Samen Menchen*. The *Changki Yimten* resolutely stood by their decision but knowing full well that penalty imposed on the offenders would lead to contempt of court as the matter was in court, the *Changki Yimten* recorded the names of those who violated its ruling so as to take action only when the court matter was settled.

In the meantime, the church elders played the role as peace makers and in early 2004, the Mokokchung Changki Union, on their own volition, withdrew the case from Mokokchung ADC court as well as from the Kohima Bench. However in the withdrawal of the case from Kohima Bench, the reason cited by the Mokokchung Changki Union was that the union had amicably settled the matter with the *Changki Yimten,* which was untrue, for the union had withdrawn the case on the intervention of the church workers.

When the withdrawal papers pertaining to the case reached the village, a *Ayim Asem Mungdang* (village general meeting) was called wherein it was resolved to remove the *enki tsüba* (barring entry into Changki territory) strictures on the Mokokchung Changki Union.

However as there were still other matters to be settled with the Mokokchung Changki Union, it was summoned by the *Changki Yimten* at a later date in May 2004. The issue in hand was to ascertain whether Mokokchung Changki Union did the right thing in defying the *Changki Yimten lenla* (Changki customary code of law). At the hearing in the customary court the Mokokchung Changki Union admitted their offence on the following grounds:

1. Not complying to the summons of the *Samen Menchen* by the union
2. Violations of *enki tsüba* (barring of entry into Changki territory) by individuals from Mokokchung
3. Citing false reasons when withdrawing the court case.

In case of offence number one, Mokokchung Changki Union was fined Rs.60 as customary penalty. The normal Changki customary penalty is Rs.30, if the matter is resolved at the *Samen Menchen* level, but as the case pertaining to the Mokokchung Changki Union had reached the *Changki Yimten* the fine was doubled.

In case of offence number two, the 44 individuals from Mokokchung who had violated the *enki tsüba* (barring entry into Changki territory) strictures were fined Rs.500 each (total Rs.22,000). It may be mentioned that the fine for *Yimten Kakba* (violations of village rule) fixed at Rs.5000, but showing *emli langba* (mercy/humane considerations) the *Changki Yimten* imposed only Rs.500.

In case of offence number three, the Mokokchung Changki Union was fined Rs.5000 for violating village rule (*Yimten kakba*). But this fine imposed was *Tepang Chenja* (oral fine), meaning that although the fine was imposed, on their plea for mercy, the cash amount was returned to the union but the action was recorded as oral fine. This means that although no fine was taken in cash, it is still considered as having been fined.

Apart from the customary fines, when anyone goes to court of law against another but eventually withdraws the case or loses it, it is the customary practice that compensation be paid by the one who withdraws or loses the case to the other party. In the case of the Mokokchung Changki Union Vs *Changki Yimten*, as the Mokokchung Changki Union withdrew the case, they were automatically bound to pay compensation to the *Changki Yimten* for the expenditures incurred. But on the pleas and entreaties of the union, the *Changki Yimten* on their part decided to bear the burden of the case expenses by showing mercy (*taochi*). After settlement of the issues cited above, the *Changki Yimten* on appeal from Mokokchung Changki Union revoked the earlier resolution wherein the union was de-recognised.

From the Mokokchung Changki Union case, we understand that the traditional customary law based on *Yimten Emli*, (people's verdict), *Yimten Ozung* (village rule), *Samen Menchen (Village Council)* and *Senso* (citizenship) still play a very important role in the lives of the people. The *Samen Menchen* (Village Council) is the apex body under which all units function and its influence crosses over the boundaries of the parent village to all the other places where Changki villagers may be settled.

The *Samen Menchen* (village government) does not govern arbitrarily; following the traditional democratic norms it takes into account, the people's will and verdict. The traditional decision making authority is the *Ayim Mungdang* (village general assembly), where direct participation of the people takes place in the decision making process. The *Samen Menchen* (Village Council) administers judicial discretion on consensus (*obang utepba*) and precedence as the case maybe. Here again the concept of '*emli*' (system of governance) is deeply ingrained in the executive function of the *Samen Menchen*. In the traditional village administration the concept of *emli langba* (humane considerations) also plays a major role. From the very beginning the *nikla* (objective) of the village government was for the welfare of the people as well as to keep the authority of the village government strong. Therefore in awarding penalty and punishments the underlying objective is to serve as a deterrent to others from committing such offences again.

The latest development of the inter-clan dispute is that the Emrem Changki clan refused to pay the *Ayim Charu* (village tax) and as per customary laws since they willfully did not pay the tax they were removed from the *Changki Senso* signifying that they were no longer considered to have citizenship in Changki. The clan also went to court but the *Changki Senso* refused to attend the court on the premise that as the customary laws and usage is enshrined and recognized by the Constitution, the final word will be the verdict given by the Changki Senso and thereby no other ruling will be recognised or entertained, thus reinforcing the sanctity and supremacy of the customary laws.

Village Development Board

Another major change that was incorporated into the traditional village organisation was the introduction of the Village Development Board (VDB). The Village Development board was the brainchild of the former Chief Secretary of Nagaland A.M. Gokhale, based on a theory that had been conceptualised by his father, Late Madhav Gokhale, in Phek district. The VDB rules were formulated and passed by the State Assembly in 1980 and amended in 1994. The salient features of the VDB are as follows:

It is formed under the aegis of the Village Council in every recognised village of Nagaland with tenure of five years, unless dissolved by the Village Council earlier. A VDB Secretary and other members are appointed, at least two of them women members. It is entrusted with assisting the village council in formulating and implementation of development schemes on an annual basis. Grant in aid is provided by the government yearly, the quantum of which is assessed by multiplying the number of the total households in the village into the allocation per household. There is a minimum and maximum ceiling to this grant in order to avoid discrimination, 25% of the total grant to the village is reserved for Women's Programmes.

The yearly allocation, when received by the Village Council Chairman, is announced in a general public meeting of all denizens of the village. The infrastructure needs of the village are short listed. At least one scheme must compulsorily be income generating. It is mandatory for all VDBs to hold monthly public meetings for review and monitoring of ongoing projects. The minutes of such meetings are submitted to the District Commissioner (DC) regularly. Unless absolutely unavoidable, all work under the VDB is executed by the community. The profits are either shared equally or kept in the village account. The DC is the Chairman of all VDBs in the district.

Every VDB has a bank account in which the DC and the VDB Secretary are joint signatories. Any drawal is to be authorised by the Village Council in the form of resolution signed by all the VCMs and VDB members. Besides this, each VDB is required to have Fixed Deposit (FD) account under the Matching Cash Grant (MCG) Scheme. The government matches all deposits in the FD with a like amount credited into the same account, up to a limit of Rupees two lakhs. This account functions as an effective contingency fund in times of emergency or shortfall.

More importantly, this entire procedure provides an ideal platform for unusual interfacing between the financial institutions, the government and the villagers. Although initially set up to execute work under the Department of Rural Development, today the VDBs have become the indirect instruments for most field level departments, covering the entire gamut from public health services to roads and bridges to essential public services like power, water supply and so on within the village.

Since its inception, the VDB has established itself within the firmament of the Naga village setup. One can discern the reason why. Its strength lies in its simplicity and logic, easily acceptable to the Naga ethos and psyche. This aided the transition to practical application of the theories of micro level planning and de-centralization. Moreover, the traditional Village Council hierarchy shifted responsibility from simple 'legal administration' to the wider and modern trend of 'development administration' (Government of Nagaland,1989).

In Changki the VDB is composed of the Village Council Chairman who is also the Chairman of the VDB and a secretary and members selected from among the villagers, the selection of whom is made by the Village Council. With consultation of the Village Council, the VDB will formulate projects for village development. After proper discussion and approval from the '*Ayim Asem Mungdang*' or village general assembly meeting, the project will be submitted to the Block Development Officer (BDO) who will then take it up to higher authorities. When the sanctions come, the VDB or the Mass Management Committee as it is also called will look after the schemes in its execution and implementation. All committees in relation to village development works are controlled by the Samen Menchen or Village Council, both in terms of materials and finances.

The VDB in Changki has 3 sub-committees namely the Finance Committee, the Youth Development Committee and the Women Programme Committee, which are all separate cells with allocation of a certain amount of funds. The Village Council Chairman is the Chairman in all the sub- committees.

The first developmental work carried out in Changki through the VDB in 1980 – 1981 was the construction of the community hall followed by the construction of the village gate in 1981 – 1982. The other construction works through the years were the building of two more community halls cum dispensary, community granary, public toilets, repair of LP school etc. Other activities were purchase of paddy under food programme, development of pineapple plantation and banana farm and construction of community fisheries.

The programmes for the women included income generating schemes such as piggery where the women were given loan to buy a pigling each. The loan was repaid after a year when the pig was sold off at a profit. The piggery scheme has become very popular with the women in Changki. The weaving unit scheme was also introduced and funds were allocated for purchase of sewing and knitting machines for starting sewing and knitting units. However this has not proved to be very profitable and this scheme has been stopped.

The pottery scheme which has been going on from the beginning of the VDB programmes (1980's) in the upper *khel* generates some income but more importantly through this scheme the art and skills involved in making the traditional Changki pots is being preserved. In the lower *khel* the pottery scheme was introduced from 2004 only.

Another income generating scheme run by the women is the money put up for loan with interest. The women had bought paddy from the money allocated to them in the earlier scheme. At first the paddy was loaned out on interest but as this involved too much labour, time and required a granary for storing the paddy, the paddy was sold off and the money is now being utilised for giving out on loan with interest.

For the youth the scheme included school agro-forestry VDB educational tours, construction of volley ball and basket ball courts and holding of village sports meet and so on. The funds that come under the VDB programme are for Changki village as a unit. But internally, the money is shared in equal amounts between the upper and lower khels. From the funds allocated to each khel, 25% is allocated to the women of both the khels respectively.

The introduction of the *Gaon Bura* institution, the Village Council and the Village Development board has brought about changes in the traditional political organisation of Changki. The *Gaon Bura* institution was incorporated into the traditional *Samen Menchen* and gradually gained prominence especially with the introduction of the Village Council. The Village Development board being an auxiliary part of the Village Council brought about developmental progress in the infrastructural aspects of the village. All these have contributed towards bringing the village in closer contact with the outside world through interactions with the administrative bodies and in a sense widened the political sphere of the village.

Communitization Process

The strength of rural Naga society lies in the richness of its social capital which consists of strong community and village bonds and this is best exemplified by the Village Councils which is the apex body of village governance. The smooth running of village affairs is ensured by the highly organized division of labour, where contribution and service are the hallmarks of participatory community works. Capitalizing on this the Village Development Board (VDB) was set up in 1980 for effective grass root level planning and development. As the VDB took root and thrived another concept was introduced known as "communitization" introduced in 2001 and enacted in 2002 as the ***Nagaland Communization of Public Services and Institutions Act 2002***. With this certain powers of management were delegated directly to the user community, that is, the assets of the government were transferred to the community through an MoU.

Since the community owns the institutions and is responsible for its management, albeit with supervision, there is a vast improvement in the functioning of the institutions. Communitization in short is the partnership between the government and the user community where decentralization, delegation, empowerment and capacity building is the core idea. This concept is based on the triple "T" approach. **Trust** the user community. **Train** them to discharge their newfound responsibilities. **Transfer** government powers and resources in respect of management.

In Changki the communitization process began in 2003 with the Village Education Committee followed by the Village Electricity Management Board and the Village Health Committee.

The Village Education Committee has a chairman appointed by Village Council, secretary and 5-6 members from the village community. As Changki people recognizes the importance of education, earlier all the Government Primary Schools & High School had their own managing boards from the locality (e.g. Sangpangmen GPS had its own management board with people from the locality as members etc) and as such the responsibilities of seeing to the functioning of the schools were undertaken by such management boards. However with the coming of the communitization of the schools, only one committee was constituted to look after all the 6 schools in the village. The workload for the committee is reportedly too much and its functioning has not been as smooth particularly regarding the transfer of teachers. As of now the management boards from the localities are still looking after the functioning of the schools but as these boards are not recognized by the government, certain issues cannot be resolved. The villagers are of the opinion that these boards should also be included in the Village Education Committee so that the schools can be monitored properly and so that certain loopholes can be taken care of.

With regard to the Village Electricity Management Board there is good progress, the collection of revenue is regular and those failing to pay the bills as well as misuse of funds by the committee are penalized by the Village Council. The repair and maintenance jobs are undertaken earnestly and as such the electricity supply is more or less regular.

The Village Health Committee in Changki has not been constituted till date and it is the Village Council that looks after the overall functioning of the Primary Health Centre. The health care sector is also making good progress. Earlier the government used to send consignments of medicines but it never reached the village. However now the government sanctions a sum of Rs.10,000 monthly and the dispensary in-charge lists the required medicines after which the medicine is bought, after proper verification and checking by the Village Council. So far the medicine supply is good and the PHC is well stocked for immediate relief. The duty of the primary health centre functionaries is also checked by the Village Council which is then reported to the concerned department and if the persons are found to be irregular, their pay is cut accordingly. The salary of the PHC functionaries is also paid only after the Village Council gives its go ahead.

Modern Electoral Process and Party Politics

The modern electoral process that was introduced with the formation of the state of Nagaland in 1963 has also brought about a new dimension to the polity of the village.

Traditionally leaders like the *Gaon Buras* are selected on the basis of clans as well as through consensus. The *Samen Menchen* is directly recruited through the age-set system as per the customary practice. But with the introduction of adult franchise and party politics the system of election by ballot came into practice into the village, for the village is part of the 29 Jangpetkong Constituency of Mokokchung district. This constituency comprises the villages of Changki, Chungliyimsen, Khar, Mongchen, Dibuai, Waromong and includes Alongkima, which is the area's administrative sub centre, Mangkolemba, the district sub-divisional centre and Longnak and Merakiong polling stations.

The role of the women in the state election process and party politics is also quite different from that of the role and position of women in the traditional village polity. Each village has its own women's wing where the women actively work for the party. However when it comes to actual decision-making and governance the women are still to get their due. Most times the women are relegated to cook and serve, although they can participate in public meetings and so on.

It is interesting to note how the people have adapted the modern electoral process and moulded it into the traditional way of selecting and now electing their leaders. For example, anyone who wants to stand for election from the Jangpetkong range will first apply at the constituency level that is at Mangolemba and with the recommendation from the constituency, his application will go to the district and then to the central headquarters. A special committee for every political party will be constituted which will select candidates for the constituencies and will distribute the party tickets. The Indian Congress party and the regional Nagaland People's Front (NPF) are the two main parties holding sway in the village.

Once the party tickets are distributed the candidate will declare his intention in his own village. That is if he is from Changki he will first inform the Changki Village Council of his plan, either on his own or through the party machinery of the constituency. The intending candidate(s) will then actively garner the support of his clansmen and villagers within the village and in the surrounding villages. The clan elders can also campaign for their candidate by trying to convince the other clans to support the candidate. The support base for the candidate in the villages is more often than not along clan lines. However it does not mean that all the clansmen will give support nor is it mandatory.

In the earlier chapter on kinship we have discussed the schism created due to the dispute between the Changkiri and Emrem Changki clans. We find that this schism is most evident in the electoral process of party politics in the village. The Congress MLA from this constituency is a member of the Emrem Changki clan who has been returned to power for the 4th consecutive term on the Congress party ticket and through political leverage the cleavage within the village has been further deepened.

In fact due to the deepening crisis within the village, the three founding clans of Changki, that is, the Longchari, Amri and Changkiri got together in 2001 and resolved not to help the Emrem Changki in politics anymore and *en masse* supported the regional Nagaland People's Front (NPF) party. This decision of course had its ramifications with some members of the founding clans resenting the decision, as they were supporters of the Congress party.

The intra and inter-clan animosity arising out of political differences has brought about further breakdown in the relationships among the villagers and Changki has been reduced to two opposing parties along political party lines. Along with the antagonism created due to the clans' dispute, the party politics has also heightened tensions arousing suspicion and distrust among the people. We find that here is a deep-rooted politicization of the village more or less based along clan lines. Political affiliations to parties have played a divisive role in the village polity causing inter and intra clan rivalries. It was observed that such political affiliations went along the emotionally charged loyalties to family and clan and so on.

5

ECONOMY OF CHANGKI VILLAGE

Mills (1926:107) stated that 'the Ao is before everything an agriculturist. Be he a mission teacher, a carpenter or a government servant he farms his fields. Rice is his staple food. In it wealth is reckoned and from it he obtains his food and his drink.' Smith (1980,reprint:196) also wrote that 'agriculture has been the chief occupation, and it has been an honourable one, from which he does not turn easily. The missionaries have found it difficult to get men to give up the time needed to secure the training which would make them good teachers and preachers.' Writing about the pre-colonial pattern of village economy, Sema (1992:1320) said 'the autonomous village that the British encountered were in the main primitive economic units with a system of subsistence agriculture which provided them with barely enough for their needs.' The people were largely engaged in agriculture where the household economy was self-contained. Control of means of production and labour was held by the producers themselves and exchange was in the form of labour and products (ibid:132). Although agriculture was the principle occupation, the people were also part time craftsmen. All made their own ornaments and handicrafts such as baskets, mats, wooden plates, furniture and other household requirements. With the establishment of British rule in the Naga Hills, the improvement in law and order between villages and especially the ban on headhunting, had a direct bearing on agriculture. Earlier it was the custom that able bodied men guarded the villages but as headhunting was stopped and there was peace, they could now concentrate on agricultural production, and they could go farther afield to cultivate rice. The trade and commerce also improved with the plains people and with improved and extensive means of communication and transport facilities, markets began to be developed especially in the border areas with Assam.

With the advent of Christianity and education, employment avenues were also opened and many Nagas were employed as pastors, school teachers and as low level clerks in the colonial administration. However the majority of the Nagas were largely engaged in agriculture. This trend has continued and the 2001 census shows that in Nagaland out of a total population of 1,988,636, the rural population is 1,635,815 which is 82.26 percent of the total population. Out of the total number of workers of 849,982, the total number of cultivators is 544,432, which is 64.05 percent of the total number of workers (Census 2001). Thus we find that Nagaland is traditionally an agrarian society. In Mokokchung district we find that out of the total population of 227,230, the rural population accounts for 196,026 and out of the total number of workers projected at 108,779 the number of cultivators is 65,366 (Census 2001). Changki village which falls under Mokokchung district is also an agrarian society where the mainstay and primary occupation of the people is agriculture.

The primary economic activity of Changki society is the agriculture practice of wet rice cultivation. In Mokokchung district there are only two valleys where wet rice cultivation is practised, namely, Changki in the Changkikong range and Tuli, in the Langbangkong range. The Changki valley is situated 11 – 16 km from the village settlement area covering an area of 12,895 sq km where wet rice cultivation is practised which is the mainstay of the people. Earlier jhumming was the traditional agricultural practice and as the Changki territory is vast covering an area of 148.615 sq km, the jhumming area extends to 71.1075 sq km (jhum fallow land: 63.425 sq km plus current jhum land: 7.675 sq km) and so the jhum cycle could take up to twenty years and the land could be left fallow for that period. This meant that there was enough fertile land for cultivation and through the practice of jhumming the people could cultivate enough rice which is the staple food of the people. The primary agricultural practices of both the jhum cultivation and wet rice cultivation provided the people not only with enough food but also surplus leading to a favourable economic condition for the people.

In addition to the traditional economic activity of agriculture, many new ones have emerged. There are teachers working in the Government Primary schools, the Government High School as well as in the private Mission school, some are working as 4th grade government employees in the Department of Horticulture Fruit Canning factory, the PHE (Public Health Engineering), Electrical department, Wasteland department, and PWD (Public Works Department) and as the offices are located at Longnak 16 km away from the village these people commute daily from the village. There are also petty shopkeepers running small businesses and in the village there are twenty petty shops, twelve in the lower Khel and nine in the upper Khel, which sell essential commodities like salt, oil, pulses, tea, sugar, milk as well as paan, cigarettes, sweets and village produce like vegetables and fruits. Many people are also taking up horticultural activities such as pineapple, arecanut and orange cultivation. As Changki has coal deposits, the coal business has also been taken up by the land owners on whose land the deposits have been found.

Although there are now many new occupations the agricultural practice of wet rice cultivation is still the backbone of the economy in Changki and it is rather surprising that this agricultural practice of wet rice cultivation began only in the late 1920's. This was due to the direct intervention of the British administrators. The annexation of the Ao territory by the British and the incorporation of the Ao area within the British jurisdiction in 1889 had direct consequences on Changki village in many ways. Changki village was established atop a peak, as was the norm in the ancient time for defense purposes, and the people practiced jhum cultivation. The valley below the village was not utilized at all for agricultural purposes due to the reason that wild animals caused immense problems by attacking the villagers and there was also the ever-present danger of being beheaded by neighbouring foes. Even when the practice of headhunting was stopped, the Changki valley was not utilised due to the simple reason that the people did not know about wet rice cultivation and its economic viability.

When the British surveyed the land in the late 1920's they found the Changki valley to be fertile and conducive for wet rice cultivation. An official order was passed and under duress the villagers began to practice wet rice cultivation. The British brought over labourers from neighbouring Assam who worked alongside the Changki villagers so that the villagers could learn the skills of wet rice cultivation. In the beginning the new agricultural practice was not very profitable as wild elephants inevitably destroyed the crops. But in due time this menace was contained and soon high returns brought economic prosperity to the villagers changing their lives.

As agriculture is the primary economic activity of Changki the land holding system of Changki is examined.

Land holding system

The traditional land holding pattern has its origin in the village formation for the clans who first founded the village first selected the sacred and ceremonial site where they could worship and conduct religious rites. Common sites were also selected for the *Ariju* or male dormitory. After this they had the first choice of claiming sites for their homes as well as for cultivation. The land was thus distributed following this system. Other clans who settled in the village were also given land by the founding clans which then became *their* clan land.

The traditional land holding system in Changki falls under the categories, enumerated in the following:

1. **Village sites:**

At the time of establishment of the village certain areas were demarcated for common use such as the place for worship, recreational purposes, meeting place for the *Samen Menchen* or village government, the male dormitory and forests for jhumming, and the surrounding hills and jungles falling under the village territory. In the olden days the village square was also a common site where the spoils of war were put on display. Such lands cannot be sold or transferred unless with the consent of the Village Council. The people can use the common forests for jhumming, collection of raw materials for construction of houses and so on. For commercial purposes such as logging or collecting fire wood for sale the permission of the Village Council is required. The wanton destruction of the village land is a serious offence and heavy fines are imposed for such crimes.

2. **Clan lands:**

The first comers or the founding clans had the pick of the sites in the village for home sites and land for cultivation in the surrounding forests. Such claims became the inalienable right of the clans for perpetuity. The clan lands cannot be sold or transferred to another clan. The senior members of the clan get first priority for cultivation and for collection of fire wood from the nearest woodland of the clan. The clan members can use the clan lands freely and if there is surplus land they can lease out the land to others, not necessarily members of the clan, for cultivation on payment of land tax. Among the founding clans, for example if in one clan there were three brothers, the eldest would get the biggest plot and the rest distributed among the younger brothers. The eldest brother's share would then be passed on to his descendents.

The clan land holdings are also gifted to *Temnakja* (sister's sons). If the *Tiou Tukori* (maternal uncles) belongs to the founding clans, they may give portions of the clan lands to their *Temnakja* (sister's sons). These lands then become individual lands belonging to the *Temnakja* and his descendents.

3. **Khel lands:**

The village is divided into two sectors the upper khel and the lower khel. Each khel has a common site for recreation such as games and sports, house sites, sentry house, graveyard and the community hall of the *Samen Menchen* or village government. In the olden days each khel had places of worship too. Such sites are public lands and cannot be utilized for any other purposes except for common public activities.

4. **Individual lands:**

Through the ages as clan members worked on the land allocated to them continuously the land became individual land passed on from father to son and so on. Individual sites can be either homesteads in the village or *tsülu* (wet rice fields). Private lands are thus obtained through inheritance, purchase from clan members, and division of common land belonging to the clan, occupation of new land and so on. Such lands can be sold to anyone who is a Changki and the transaction is between the buyer and the seller, without any interference from clan members or the village authorities. The sale of such land is conducted with witnesses from both parties in order to ensure that should any dispute arise, they would vouch for the transaction. Nowadays people also take the precaution of writing deeds of sale for such transactions.

The distribution of land use in Changki is demarcated as village community forest, jhum fallow land, current jhum field, reserve forest, wet rice cultivation fields, private plantation, orchard and residential sites.

Table 16
Distribution of land use in Changki *lusa* or territory

Land use	Area (Sq. Km.)	Total area (percent)
Village Community forest	41.745	28.09
Jhum fallow land	63.425	42.68
Current jhum field	7.675	5.16
Reserve forest	13.875	9.34
Wet rice cultivation fields	12.895	8.68
Private plantation	1.150	0.77
Orchard	1.850	1.24
Residential	6.00	4.04
Total	**148.615 Sq km.**	**100.00**

Source: Dr. Sapu Changkija, 2001: Centenary Souvenir of Mission School 1901 - 2001

From Table 16 we find that the jhum land is 63.425 sq.km or 42.68 percent of the total area and stretching up to about 10 miles away from the village. Interestingly the wet rice cultivation area is only 12.895 sq.km or 8.68 percent of the total area.

Lumelen – Land Taxes

Just as land holding is based on the founding of the village, the land tax is also based on the traditional pattern that has been in practice for ages.

The taxation of land is merely on a token basis and as a sign of ownership so that there can be no disputes later on. As the areas are demarcated clearly between the village, clan and individual lands, the land tax imposed is a token amount so that anyone who works the land will know that it is not theirs to do as they wish. Taxes as understood here include the land tax paid to the Village Council as well as the money paid to individuals for the use of their land. The following land tax system is given in detail below:

1. **Ajen** (East): The land to the east of the village upto *Tzüeit* river bordering Aliba and Mangmetong villages has no taxes levied upon it. It is the **emlu** or village lands. Anyone who cuts the **mezen** or virgin forests first can claim it as theirs but if they do not continue to cultivate the land then any others who cultivate it at a later stage can claim it as theirs.

2. **Achep** (West): The land to the west of the village which slopes down upto the *Tzüong* river and the wet rice cultivation fields, has direct ownership rights; for anyone who cuts the **mezen** or virgin forests first can claim it as theirs. If they do not continue to cultivate the land, others who may want to use the land for cultivation can do so with due permission from the owner and with a payment of land tax which is Rs 2/-

3. **Tsülu** (Rice fields): Both sides of the bank of *Tzüong* River are used for wet rice cultivation. However to the

east of *Tzüong* river, land ownership is permanent while to the west of *Tzüong* river, there is no permanent ownership, that is anyone who cultivates the land do not have to seek permission from the previous cultivator nor do they have to pay taxes. However the Village Council has enforced a new ruling that anyone who does not cultivate the land for three years on either side of the *Tzüong* River forfeits their right to land ownership and anyone can claim the rice field as theirs and cultivate it. This is so because the rice fields are close to each other and if a plot land is left untended the overgrowth can cause a great deal of difficulties for the neighbouring cultivators as the network of paths and irrigation canals that connect the plots of rice fields gets blocked. This ruling came about as some villagers migrated to other places and hence there was no one to cultivate the rice fields.

4. **Tzürang Valley:** The Tzürang valley in the Longtho area of Changki *lusa* (territory) comes under the category of village land. The area which was the last portion of virgin forest in Changki was opened for development to the Changki citizens. Interested parties were allocated fifty to more than a hundred acres of land for cultivation of tea, orange and other cash crops. The area was opened in the year 2000, with the stipulation that if the person who had taken land in his name does not develop the land by the year 2006, the said land would revert back to the Village Council and it would be again allocated to other people. The land tax for the area is Rs. 25/- per acre per annum, which is collected by the Village Council.

We find that the demarcation, usage and distribution of land under the category of the *emlu* or village land is managed by the Village Council and individuals can acquire the land if they have the resources to cut the forest and develop the land. In this way individual ownership of land comes about, whereby the owner can do as he pleases with the land, including selling it to any interested party if he so wishes. However the sale of the land is restricted to Changki people only. No outsiders, that is, non-Changki people are allowed to buy any land in the Changki territory.

The owner of a plot land can also allow fellow villagers to use the land on the payment of '*lumelen*' or tax, which is paid annually, the rate of which is fixed by the Village Council. Certain bamboo groves, forests and kitchen garden plots are allowed to be used in this manner. The produce of the land belongs to the one looking after it but the land belongs to the owner who is paid a fixed amount of money yearly. This is very clear to the people for land is considered sacred and any litigation concerning land is avoided. It is believed that should any man or woman make false claims on land or encroach on land belonging to others or desecrate other people's land, great misfortune befall on these people and for generations they are cursed. The respect for the land and sense of ownership is so great that in the adjoining rice fields, which are separated by a narrow path or streamlet, and where the ripened rice stalks fall into neighbouring plots; should the neighbour's stalks of rice be cut by mistake when reaping, the stalks belonging to the neighbour is left on his plot to show that it was an accident.

Land is highly valued by the Changki people for the land is the source of livelihood, production and wealth. Landlessness exists for there are a few people, mainly young married couples, who do not own private land such as house sites and wet rice fields; but even if a person does not have private land, he/she can always make use of the clan land or the village community land. Land is transferred from father to son and in the event that a man does not have a son, the land goes to the next brother which is then transferred to *his* son. The land and its use is restricted to Changki people only, that is, outsiders cannot purchase or use the land which ensures that the land within Changki territory is protected from being exploited by outsiders, including Aos from other villages.

Case Study

Traditionally the land is owned by the males and is passed on from father to son. However as one case study will exemplify, females too have a right to work the land and live off its produce. Imnalemla Longkumer (60) cultivates a two acres plot of rice field on sharecropping basis. She is a school teacher and has two children. She was divorced about 19 years ago. She lives in her father's house which she helped to build and when her father was very ill and on his death bed in 1996, he requested his only son (Imnalemla's only brother) to allow her to cultivate the rice field that he owned as long as she was alive. Her brother Lanusüja Longkumer (73) has since then allowed her to cultivate the rice field which his father had worked and she also continues to live in their father's house in Tsüngli *kiong* (locality).

Imnalemla keeps an Adivasi worker and his family in the rice field, with whom she shares the produce on a 50-50 basis. However when she dies the rice field and house would automatically go back to her brother or to his sons. Her children would have no right to the rice field or to continue to live in the house as they belong to a different clan.

From the case study we also find that the agricultural production is based on independent households where norms regarding the land holding are followed but the actual production from the land depends only on the household/ family i.e. the land may be given for sharecropping or be worked by the family itself. In the agricultural processes it is the nuclear family that is central to the production factors and although other family members may help in times of severe crisis most of the work is done independently.

Agricultural Seasonal Calendar

As we have stated earlier, in Changki the people are dependent on agriculture and in many ways the agricultural season sets the pace of village life which is shown in the Changki seasonal calendar in Table 17.

Table 17
Seasonal Calendar of agricultural activity in Changki village

Month	Local name	Activity
February	Phenphüo	a)Slash & Burn (jhumming) b)Ingkho Mapang (Period set aside for earning)
March	- do-	-do-
April	-do-	do-
May	Tsükla	a)Preparation for wet rice cultivation b)Sowing of jhum areas
June	-do-	-do-
July	-do-	- do-
August	Mezheü	a)Wet rice cultivation b)Harvesting of jhum areas
September	-do-	-do-
October	-do-	-do-
November	Mungphüo	a) Harvesting b)Collection of brooms, repairs of house/animal sheds etc
December	-do-	-do-
January	-do-	-do-

We find that in the Changki seasonal calendar there are four seasons and the year has been divided into three months each. The detailed explanation is as follows:

Phenphüo – This is the dry season when nothing can be cultivated during the dry months of February, March and April. In this period the jungles are cut for jhumming in the month of February and left to dry, which is burned in the month of April. This is the season for *Ingkho Mapang* which means that everyone is free from village work and can go out of the village to do business and attend to personal works. A detailed explanation on *Ingkho Mapang* is given later in the chapter.

Tsükla – This is the season when preparations are made for wet rice cultivation such as ploughing, making nurseries for rice seedlings etc. as well as *lüthen* that is, sowing of rice in the *tukonglu* or jhum area. May, June and July are the months when such activities are carried out.

Mezheü – The months of August, September and October is the time when *tsülu* or wet rice cultivation work is carried out in earnest. This is also the time when the rice is harvested in the *tukonglu* or jhum area.

Mungphüo – This is the cold season starting in the month of November and continuing through December till January. People harvest the paddy and begin to transport the paddy from the rice fields to the village. In this season the people go to the jungles to collect broomsticks called *ungkolulu* in the Changki dialect and palm like fronds which are converted into brooms called *sera kipharu* used for sweeping the compounds. People also go to work as daily wage earners for collecting firewood, building houses, pig sties, making *kilangmi*, which is an open platform made of bamboo attached to the house. All major repair works around the house, *athi* (granary) and in the *tsülu* such as repair of irrigation canals and bunds are done during this time.

Everyone in the village collect firewood for the whole year during this time as firewood is still used for cooking rice, meat and so on. Nowadays almost every household has LPG cooking gas connections.

As agriculture sets the pace of the village life it might then be useful to explain the agricultural processes of the jhum and wet rice cultivation in detail and the kind of relationships that emerge in the process of production. In the Changki agricultural activity the *Yangtep* was an important aspect. *Yangtep* was the formation of small working groups comprising of friends and good neighbours of the same age. This provided for a work force from the olden days within the community. In each family the father would be part of his age-set grade *Yangtep,* the mother part of her age mates (informal groups) and so too the children according to their age. These groups would work in each others plots on a rotational basis so that the plots would be prepared in the shortest possible time. Thus the division of labour based on age groupings was formulated through the *Yangtep* system.

As jhumming depended on hard physical work over a vast area which was mostly virgin forests especially in the olden days, the *Yangtep* system formed the basis of the agricultural work force in the village and provided the means through which community participation and camaraderie was maintained as each person was dependent on the other for survival. The *Yangtep* system was utilized during the period of burning the forests, sowing of paddy grains and weeding. However when it came to the period of reaping or harvesting the ripened paddy, it was the responsibility of each family for reaping their own plots. The reasoning was simple; if a person neglected his own plot of ripened paddy to work on another's plot, his crop would be eaten by birds, insects etc or destroyed by wild animals etc. Thus at the time of reaping the *Yangtep* system was not made use of.

The *Yangtep* system provided the people with companionship, help and support for jhumming, especially during the olden days when headhunting was still prevalent, for it meant that the people had to leave their homes in the village to go far away into the jungle where there was the ever present danger of being attacked by other villagers in search of heads, as well as being attacked by wild animals and also the possibilities of unforeseen accidents. Thus moving about the jungle in a group gave the people a sense of security. The physical and psychological hardships and privations that the people underwent were compensated by the mutual help and cooperation that the *Yangtep* system provided.

The *Yangtep* system was carried over and continued even when wet rice cultivation was introduced. As wet rice cultivation also requires a good number of labourers the *Yangtep* system proved to be advantageous. As explained earlier those who make up the *Yangtep* work force are usually good friends belonging to the same age group. The group will work on each others fields especially during ploughing, *ama rakba mapang,* that is, at the time when the seedlings are taken out from the nursery plots and tied in bunches in readiness for planting in the rice fields, transplanting of seedlings and during weeding.

Today we find although the *Yangtep* is practised by the Changki people, it is on the wane. The person on whose field the *Yangtep* is carried out will provide tea and snacks for refreshments and for the midday meal will provide meat and other items. The others who are working on his field will bring their own cooked rice, either wrapped in leaves or packed in tiffin boxes. Bringing one's own cooked rice is a custom that is part and parcel of the *Yangtep* system.

In fact it is a tradition among the Changki people that when they go out of the village they will carry enough rice for themselves so that the host does not feel the pinch. This is part of the *liba liru yimya* (norms of social behaviour). The person on whose field the group is working will not do much work on the field for he/she will be busy making tea or cooking for the group and seeing to other small works. As pointed out earlier, the *Yangtep* system is not practised at the time of reaping the paddy. This is the time when birds can cause havoc so as soon as the paddy is ripened each family will undertake the reaping on their own.

Tukonglu (Jhumming)

Tukonglu literally means 'dry rice field'. The cultivation of rice and other crops by the jhumming method does not depend on irrigation as in the wet rice cultivation. Hence the name *tukonglu*, for jhumming takes place in the hills and rugged mountainous areas.

The Village Council decides upon the selection of the year's *Tukonglu* area (jhum area) for cultivation, known as *Pok*. The *Azüakhang Tezenba* age-set grade (the sixth grade) assisted by the *Azüakhang Nuzaba* (fifth grade and the junior interns to the sixth grade) carry out the survey for the demarcation of the jhum area, and supervises the distribution and management of the *Pok* like allotting plots to the families and maintaining buffer zones against wild animals and creating such zones for burning of the cleared jungles before sowing. The burning of jungles is especially handled very carefully as wild fires can occur causing extensive damage to the area and even to the village for sometimes the demarcated area for jhumming is very close to the village.

The agricultural season for jhumming begins in the *mungphüo* season in January when the jungle is cleared. After felling the trees, the area is left to dry in the *phenphüo season*, throughout the month of February. In late March/ early April the burning of the jungle begins and it is only after burning of the cut jungle that the land is cleared and prepared for cultivation. Immediately after the area is burned and cleared, maize, yam, tapioca, ginger and other vegetables such as tomatoes, variety of beans, bringjals and chillies are planted, which is done by the women. The men build temporary huts and sheds, called *athi*.

Towards the end of April sowing takes place. The grains are broadcast and the soil lightly hoed using a *'tuktsü'* (small hoe) to cover the grain with the soil. Towards the end of May when the shoots begin to sprout, transplantation may be undertaken as the randomly broadcast paddy may be growing too close to each other. In August weeding takes place and all this work is done mostly by the women utilizing the *Yangtep* system. Harvesting begins in the last week of September and this is the time that the men do most of the hard manual work. The harvested paddy is tied in bundles and the men beat the bundles on the ground so as to separate the paddy grains from the stalks. The women collect the grains, winnow it and both men and women carry the paddy loads on their backs in *akhang* which are conical baskets carried on the back with the support of a head strap.

The agricultural implements used are simple and procured from Mariani which is the nearest market town in Assam. The villagers order the necessary implements by giving the design that they require or want to the blacksmiths. For jhumming the main implement used is the *dao*, which is akin to a machete used as a tool as well as weapon. It is used for cutting trees, slashing overgrowths, cutting bamboos, as well as for domestic purposes. Another implement used in the jhum fields is "*ayah*", or a scraper where a thin piece of flat iron is looped over a Y shaped wooden handle and which is used to scrape the weeds. A small hoe called "*tuktsü*" is used for clearing bushes and tilling, and the "*tukorang*" or a bigger is used for digging and leveling the land. The *Tsükera* or the sickle is used for cutting the paddy during harvesting.

In the process of jhum cultivation the men are responsible for cutting the forest and for burning the dried forest area. While clearing the forest in readiness for jhum cultivation the big trees are cut for firewood and the big rocks are quarried for building retaining walls or to use in the building of houses and taken to the village. The men also help the women in weeding and lastly to stand guard over the paddy as it ripened, against birds and wild animals. Sometimes the men would guard the paddy the whole night as in the earlier days elephants were a menace. The women are responsible for clearing the burned forest of small bushes and to ready the plot for cultivation. The sowing of paddy grains and weeding is the job of the women. The children are relegated to helping the parents in the sowing of paddy grains, planting of other vegetables and to carry loads of firewood back to the village.

From the information gathered we find that for jhum cultivation the varieties of rice cultivated in the jhum fields are of the indigenous variety. The indigenous paddy is called '*Aonglu ajak*' and the varieties found are *Aboara, Narila* (white and black variety), *Mesürong Malang, Aonglu Malang, Malang Tenakla, Longrah, Manen* and *Tangmajak*. In the *Tukonglu* (jhum field) the various crops and vegetables grown are maize, tapioca, yam plants, sweet potatoes, chilies, tomatoes, pumpkins, spring onions, beans and so on.

Over the years the wet rice agricultural practice became the mainstay of the villagers and jhumming slowly became an activity that only a few families practiced for wet rice cultivation proved to be more useful and profitable from the economic point of view. Earlier the people would practice both jhum and wet rice cultivation. They would consume the *tekonglu* rice and sell the *tsülu* rice and in this way managed to run the household and send their children out to other places for further education.

However this practice has also stopped as the people themselves prefer to eat the *tsülu* rice and so people concentrate more on the wet rice cultivation. Wet rice cultivation also involves less hard labour, and unlike in the jhum areas which are sometimes deep in the jungles, the wet rice fields or the *tsülu* areas are located close to the state highway and most *tsülu* have motorable roads. This means that the people do not have to carry the paddy themselves as they can hire a mini truck or if they have vehicles of their own they can transport the paddy from the fields to the village on their own. We find that the practice of jhum cultivation is almost negligible in Changki as the following table shows.

Table 18
Distribution of households practising jhum cultivation

Year	No. of households Upper Khel	No. of households Lower Khel	Total	Percentase
1999-2000	12	5	17	3.20
2000-2001	12	6	18	3.40
20012002	0	0	0	0
2002-2003	16	6	22	4.14

In Table 18 we find that the number of households practicing jhum cultivation is less than five percent of the total population while in the year 2001-2002 none of the families took up jhum cultivation. The reason cited was that the *pok* (jhum) area demarcated for that year was too far from the village and the people preferred to concentrate on the wet rice cultivation and horticultural activities.

Tsülu - Wet rice Cultivation

The *tsülu* (*tsü* meaning water and *lu* meaning field) or

wet rice fields are located in the *Tzüong Tsüpak* valley, 15 - 17 km from the village. The footpaths leading from the village to the fields are called *Kümbalani Endi* and *Changpang Aling* in the lower khel and *Namen Endi* and *Aliban Endi* in the upper *khel*. These footpaths are maintained by clearing the overgrowths and repairing the steps periodically by an order of the Village Council who will declare the date of cleaning the footpath by the community. The *tsülu* area is along the state highway so the people can also reach the *tsülu* by vehicle.

As wet rice cultivation is dependent on river irrigation in the *Tsülu* the neighbouring cultivators form groups to dig and maintain irrigation canals, using the natural sources that flow through the fields and to release or drain the water in accordance to the cultivation cycle. Bamboos conduits are used as irrigation pipes while to dam the water, mud, stones and hay are used. Canals are dug and to divert the water to various plots of rice fields a pipeline of bamboo conduits is utilized to bring the water from the nearest river and as the rice fields are divided into "*thepdang*" which are low bunds that has been raised using earth, cow dung and hay to make small plots so that the water can be retained, the pipeline serves as the boundaries between adjoining rice fields. Each cultivator is dependent upon the cooperation of the other for the irrigation of the rice fields as the fields are close to each other and the network of canals and bamboo conduits pass through each other's fields.

For the wet rice cultivation ploughing of the land begins towards the end of May. The fields are ploughed using the traditional plough pulled by bullocks. It is interesting to note that the ploughing is done by hired labourers from Assam at Rs.100 per day. After the fields are ploughed, the fields are left to dry out for a week, after which it is ploughed again. After the second ploughing, the land is leveled by tying strips of split bamboo measuring 6' – 7' harnessed and pulled by the bullocks. Then the land is irrigated by the traditional system of irrigation canals.

The process of growing the rice seedlings is by keeping a sack of paddy for one to two days in a well, or a small pond or stream. The sack is kept well covered till the paddy begins to sprout. Meanwhile a small plot called the *puthia mukojen* is ploughed and leveled and left to dry and the sprouting paddy are planted there by scattering the sprouting paddy on this plot towards the end of June. This is the nursery plot where the seedlings grow which takes about two weeks. When the rice is ready for planting towards the end of July to first week of August, the field is drained, ploughed again and leveled for transplantation.

For one week newly planted fields are not irrigated so that the seedlings do not get dispersed or get drowned. After this stage the fields are irrigated, followed by weeding after two to three weeks, after which the fields are drained. Two or three days later the fields are irrigated again and the rice is left to grow. The second weeding takes place just before cultivation. The rice takes three months to mature that is from August to October. Harvesting takes place from November to beginning of December. It may be mentioned here that no fertilizers are used, as the soil is fertile due to the silt deposited by the various rivers and its tributaries.

For the wet rice cultivation the plough pulled by bullocks is commonly used to prepare the land for cultivation. The traditional method of cultivation is still the norm. Everything is done manually from the transplantation to the harvesting of the paddy. The sickle is the main implement used during harvesting. The sickle is used for cutting the paddy and the cut paddy stalks are collected in the *moütsüjen* which is a circular area that has been leveled and hardened by spreading cow dung paste thus cementing the earth into a hard surface. The *moütsüjen* is in front of the *alu athi* and it is here that the paddy stalks are spread out. The bullocks are made to trample over the paddy stalks by a man who uses a stick to direct the bullocks in circles around the *moütsüjen* till the grains separate from the stalk from the trampling of the bullocks. After two or three days of making the bullocks trample over the paddy stalks in this manner the grains are ready to be collected. The grains are put in *mülok* or baskets and winnowed (*zenba*) till the grains are cleaned of all extraneous material. Once the paddy is cleaned, it is put in sacks and kept in the *alu athi*. The paddy is transported later by hiring the mini-trucks at a convenient time. In the olden days the paddy was transported by the people in *akhang* or conical baskets carried on their backs supported by a head strap.

The harvested paddy is kept in the *alu athi* or field granary-cum-living quarters till such time as it can be transported to the village. The *alu athi* is an integral part of the paddy fields, as it serves as a temporary granary till such time that the paddy is transferred to the village, as well as sleeping quarters for the cultivators and their helpers.

In the wet rice cultivation the varieties of rice cultivated in the *tsülu* are *Kuki, Amosjak, Lahijak, Nagaland Special, Khatajang, Endoor Hali, Shial-hali, Bordhan* and so on.

In the *tsülu* near the *alu athi* or the granary cum rest house, the people maintain a small orchard cum kitchen garden called *somni* where oranges, arecanut trees, papaya trees, guava trees, palm trees, etc as well as some vegetables are grown. It is here in the *somni* that the well and/or pond is dug. It is also turned into a small fish pond by some of the people. This is a place where the people relax when they take breaks in between the work in the rice fields and also where the people can grow vegetables and fruits for domestic consumption as well as for selling.

The wet rice fields are fed and irrigated by the river Tzüong along with its tributaries. The rivers are small and the tributaries are mainly streams. The tributaries of Tzüong are *Mejangjuet, Zaong, Longpen, Chechet, Longnak, Kotakkülemba, Tzümeremba, Ofinak, Aotzü, Jungjen, Engtsü, Ako Terokongba, Chembi, Tzüsasa, Mesütsüng and Tzüsemsa.*

The wet rice fields are also fed by the tributaries of the Tzürang River such as *Lithi, Tongtong, Arepjemba, Tzürangmen, Satiait, Longtho and Tsenririokzükba.*

Another source of water is the Tzüeit River with its tributaries such as *Kuromen, Chempongtzü, Tzümet, Chalem, Chanaing, Heni, Longlangba, and Aitzü.* The wet rice cultivation is carried out in the *mezhüo* season.

We find that the rice fields are also clearly demarcated between the upper and lower khels. The rice fields belonging to the upper khel are *Tsümerem, Lutiba, Tsürongrong, Longnak, Longnakchuie, Chechet, Mangkosüng* and *Tsüsasa* while the names of the rice fields belonging to the lower khel are *Chembi, Mangkosünglulangba, Ingtzü, Nakaola, Alongkaba, Langpaliokba, Chiengba, Chaniti, Otsüngpong, Aotzü, Imtsüngchang, Jungjen and Nokzaba.*

In the wet rice cultivation we find that the gender division of labour as found in the jhum rice cultivation does not exist. Men and women undertake all the tasks equally, even the transplantation of the rice seedlings and weeding. The fact that wet rice cultivation is economically viable could be the reason that both men and women work hard together.

Sharecropping

In Changki the majority of the people are cultivators who also own the fields. However we find that sharecropping is also practiced. There are two types of sharecropping practices; one is called "*Athi*" which means that the owner of the rice field will share equally with the person working the field that is fifty percent of the harvest is given to the sharecropper. The owner will provide the plough cattle and all the necessary requirements but from the fifty percent the monetary expenses borne by the owner is deducted from the paddy cultivated, thus the owner of the paddy field sometimes gets more than his share and more importantly his fields are cultivated and there is enough paddy for the annual consumption. In this way the owner of the paddy fields gets his harvest without expending much.

The other sharecropping practice is called "*Tikka*" which is like a contract. That is the share is usually in the ratio of 30 percent for the owner of the rice field while the person working gets a share of 70 percent of the total produce. In this practice the owner of the field will also provide all the necessary requirements. If the owner gives the field on "*Tikka*" he will stipulate the number of tins he will take from the field worked at the time of handing over the rice field on contract basis which would be approximately 30percent of the estimated total yield. Even if the produce is very little that year due to unforeseen circumstances, the owner will still take the amount he had stipulated at the time of giving the rice field on contract.

The practice of sharecropping is particularly prevalent among the old people whose children have left the village and settled in other places. There are also people who have settled outside the village but have ancestral homesteads in the village and rice fields who practise sharecropping by entrusting the work to relatives in the village. Sharecropping also came into practice when the Village Council enforced a new ruling that anyone who does not cultivate the *tsülu* for three years on either side of the *Tzüong* River forfeits their right to land ownership and anyone can claim the rice field as theirs and cultivate it. Thus in order to retain their paddy fields the people took to sharecropping.

We observed that the sharecroppers who worked the fields for the old people as well as those working in the public sector in the village and for others settled outside the village were mostly Adivasi's from neighbouring Assam. They live in the rice fields in the *Athi* with their families and some have been working in the same fields for many years. The villagers who do not have their own paddy fields, mainly the newly wedded couple who are yet to get their share of the rice field plots from their family also took to sharecropping. The number of Changki people who work other people's fields on sharecropping basis is very few.

In Table 19 where the household wise distribution of agricultural land is given we find that although the majority of the villagers own their own agricultural land some of the villagers practise sharecropping. We find that 11.59 percent people of the total population in the lower khel give their fields for sharecropping on Athi basis while in the upper khel it is 8.22 percent of the total population. In the Tikka sharecropping pattern we find that there are less people practising this with only 2.17 percent of the total population giving their fields in the lower khel and 3.42 percent in the upper khel. The uncertainty of a good crop and the fact that the sharecropper will have to give the stipulated amount of paddy to the owner of the field even if the harvest is not good makes this pattern less attractive economically.

Table 19

Household wise distribution of agricultural land

	Frequency		Percentage	
Sl. No. Upper Khel	**Land Use pattern**	**Lower Khel**	**Upper Khel**	**Lower Khel**
1. Own Land	238	129	86.23	88.36
2. Athi (sharecropper)	32	12	11.59	8.22
3. Tikka (sharecropper)	6	5	2.17	3.42
4 Land taken on lease	0	0	0	0
Total	**276**	**146**	**100**	**100**

The paddy produced from two acres of land is on an average about 300 to 400 tins (one tin of paddy is approximately 10 kg) but this is dependent on the fertility of the particular rice field. There are about two families in the upper khel and two from the lower khel who cultivate about nine to ten acres of land and whose annual produce is on an average 1000 tins. Apart from these families the rest of the villagers on an average produce 300 to 600 tins per annum.

Between 1999-2000 and 2002–2003 the amount of paddy harvested was approximately 67,700 tins of paddy to 69,450 tins as indicated in Table 20.

Table 20
Distribution of annual production of Paddy and contribution to the Church

Year	Total production	Increase	Percentage increase	Tithe: 10% contribution to the Church
1999-2000	67,700 tins			6770 tins
2000-20001	67,890 tins	190 tins	0.27 (+)	6789 tins
2001-2002	69,000 tins	1110 tins	1,60 (+)	6900 tins
2002-2003	69,450 tins	450 tins	0.64 (-)	6945 tins

Note: 1tin is equal to approximately 10 kg of paddy

In Table 20 we see that the annual production of paddy is within 67,700 tins to 69,450 tins. In the years 2001-2003 we see that the yield was higher than in the other years taken into account. In all the fluctuations in production does not vary much.

The average of the total yield was calculated on the basis of the Tithe or thanksgiving which is 10 percent of the total produce that the people offer to the churches in Changki.

After giving the *Tithe* the rest of the paddy is stored in the granaries. According to the needs of the family, the paddy is taken out from the granaries, dried and then taken to the rice mills for husking. If there is a surplus it is sold mostly to the people living outside the village.

The sale of surplus paddy and the income generated from it is shown in Table 21. The paddy is sold at Rs.50 per tin. This is also an average taken from the Tithe given to the churches in Changki.

Table 21
Distribution of household annual income from paddy production

Production per tin	Income in (Rs)	No. of household: lower khel	No. household: upper khel
0-150 tins	0-7500	76 (27.53)	28 (19.17)
150-450 tins	7,500 – 22,500	174 (63.04)	96 (65.75)
450 – 750 tins	22,500 – 37,000	24 (8.70)	20 (13.70)
750 and above tins	37,500 and above	2 (0.72)	2 (1.37)
Total		**276 (100)**	**146 (100)**

In Table 21 where the distribution of household annual income from paddy production is given we find that the number of households whose annual income was between Rs.7,500- Rs.22,500 was highest in both the upper and lower khels with 65.75 percent and 63.04 percent of the total population respectively . Those earning between Rs. 22,500 to Rs. 37,500 are 8.70 percent in the lower khel and 13.70 percent in the upper khel. Those earning Rs.37,500 and above are just 0.72 percent and 1.37 percent in the lower and upper khel respectively. It is also indicated that on an average the people in the upper khel earn more from the sale of paddy.

We find that on an average the upper khel people work their own land and hardly go in for sharecropping. The following case studies cultivators from the upper khel and lower khels shows that agriculture is the mainstay but other forms of income generating activities supplement the family income.

Case Study

Assamwati Longchari is 39 years old. He is from the upper *khel* and lives in Nasenongti kiong (locality). He is married to Chubatola Amri (34) and they have three children, two sons (14 & 12 yrs) and one daughter (9 yrs) who are all studying in the village school. He studied up to class X and as he grew up in the village, working on the family *tsülu* or rice fields was nothing new. After his marriage he was given a *tsülu* plot of 6 acres by his father and since 1990 he and his wife has been working the rice field. From this rice field Assamwati Longchari procures 450 tins of paddy. Although he does most of the *tsülu* (wet rice cultivation) work himself, as the rice field is big, during the ploughing and cultivation period he hires labourers.

Assamwati works the land just as his parents and grandparents worked the land but there are certain changes that have made his work lighter and easier. For instance, he does not walk the 11-16 km trek from the village down to the *Tzüong Tsüpak* valley where the rice fields are located. He takes the village bus when it makes trips to Mariani or to Dimapur as the rice fields are located on the highway going towards Mariani. Otherwise he walks the short distance to the X junction (Wachen) and hitches a ride on any vehicle that is going down to Mariani. When the paddy is harvested, Assamwati does not carry the paddy up from the rice fields to the village on his back with the help of a head strap as his parents and grandparents did. He hires a mini-truck at Rs.450 per trip or if he happens to meet an empty truck coming up towards the village, he transports the paddy at Re.1 per tin. The entire paddy has to be transported to the village as it is in the village only that he can sell the surplus and store the rest for family consumption.

Apart from rice cultivation, Assamwati also works as a carpenter. He is a gifted ironsmith/craftsman and has started his own tiny factory where he makes simple iron implements and furniture. During the slack agricultural season Assamwati hires himself out for carpentry work at Rs.150 per day. His wife, who stays at home to look after the children and home, rears pigs which are sold whenever they need the extra cash. She also keeps chickens. Assamwati has also planted 1400 areca nut trees and other fruit trees like mango, orange and jackfruit in the *Somni*, which is a small orchard cum kitchen garden, located in the rice fields.

Assamwati is kept busy not only with working the land but as he belongs to the Azü-Akang Tezenba age-set grade, he has the responsibility of carrying out the duties traditionally specified for his age-set grade. He is the oldest in his age-set grade so his duties and responsibilities are heavy. He is also actively involved in the church. Besides looking after his immediate family, he has to take care of his parents and also his parents-in-law in numerous small ways.

Assamwati says that he does not really nurture any ambitions for his children. He leads a comfortable and secure life working the land and using his talents. As he has also developed the land by starting an orchard on a rather big scale, he is of the opinion that his children would not have much difficulty in getting adequate returns from it as well as from the rice fields. However he said that if his children desired they would be free to explore other avenues of employment.

On an average Assamwati's expenditure for the rice fields comes to about Rs.5000 annually while the income from surplus paddy is approximately Rs.14, 500 (250 tins at Rs.50 per tin). The income from sale of pigs, chickens, vegetables and so on as well as from working as hired help is approximately Rs.8000. As they live a simple and do not have to spend so much on food, Assamwati and his family lead a relatively comfortable life.

In contrast, another case study of a cultivator in the lower *khel* reveals that size of family and rice field have a direct bearing on the income and relative comfort of a family. Tekaongdang Tzüdiri (55) and his wife Imkongtemsüla Longkumer (43) have five sons and two daughters between the ages of 22 and 3. They own 3 acres of rice field, which is not very fertile, from where they get approximately 280 tins of paddy. This amount is just about enough for the family for one year and they are wholly dependent on it. They do not have other sources of income except from working as hired help whenever such work is available.

Adding to their burdens is their eldest son who is 22 years old is infirm. When he was 18, he fell ill for a long time and at one time was more or less paralysed. But although he regained the use of his limbs, he is mentally challenged and requires constant medical care which his parents cannot afford. He had been treated now and then with the help given by his grandparents but as they cannot give cash regularly his ailment has been largely unattended. His siblings are all in school and his parents hopes rest on the second son whose education in Dimapur is being sponsored by a relative. Tekaongdang hopes that after class XII his second son would get employment in the army and that he would help his other siblings. Tekaongdang and his wife are of the opinion that only education would free the children from the cycle of poverty and the two children who show promise are being sent to the Mission School in the village. Their monthly fees comes to Rs.175 each, and the fees are paid for from the money Tekaongdang and his wife earn from working as daily wage labourers and from selling wild vegetable which they collect from the jungles, as well as bananas and arecanut from the few trees in their *somni*. The other children are sent to the government primary and high schools which is free of cost except for the uniforms and some books.

During the *tsükla* (May, June and July) *mezhüo* (August, September and October) agricultural season the daily routine of Tekaongdang and his wife for *tsülu* or wet rice cultivation work follows this pattern: Imkongtemsula wakes up at 3.30 a.m., light the fire, wash up and cook food. By 4.30 a.m. she has packed the necessary implements in the *Aiengkho* which is a short cylindrical basket with a head strap carried on the back, mostly by women. Tekaongdang too helps around the house by preparing the pig's swill and feeding the pigs. The children are then woken up and sent to do errands or to fetch water, as they still cannot afford to put pipes they have to depend on the public water tap, after which they get ready for school.

Tekaongdang wears a belt made out of a woven strap to which is attached the *noklubo*, a dao holder which is a rectangular wooden piece which has been carved and split in the middle so that the *anok* or dao (machete) can be slipped into it. The dao is the common implement used for all types of work from cutting the arecanuts to clearing jungles etc. Tekaongdang also uses a *charong*, a long walking stick which is used to clear the path of undergrowth etc and a bag containing tobacco, arecanuts, torch light and so on.

After eating and also packing the day's provision they leave instructions to the older children to do the household chores and take their youngest son across to Imkongtemsula's parents whose house is opposite to theirs. They then leave the village by about 5:30 a.m. to trek down to the valley below to the rice fields located roughly 13 km away from the village. When Imkongtemsula was still breast feeding she used to carry her child on her back tied by a *nubusü* (literally baby carrying cloth).

It takes about an hour and half to reach the *tsülu* following the path that has been used for ages. The paths leading to the rice fields from the upper khel are called *Namen Endi* and *Aliban Endi,* while the paths from the lower *khel* are called *Kümbalani Endi* and *Changpang Aling*. Tekaongdang and his wife use the *Changpang Aling* path. In the *tsülu* husband and wife work side by side, taking a break at midday for a meal, after which they work the field again. As they cannot afford to pay the daily wages for hired help, they do all the work except for ploughing for which they pay Rs.100 per day. Ploughing takes a month or so and their expenses come to about Rs.3000 as they also have to feed the workers.

By 5 p.m. to 5:30 p.m. they stop work, have tea and refreshments and start their trek back to the village, which is uphill all the way. They do not sleep in the *tsülu* for in the summer the heat and the mosquitoes cause too much discomfort, besides their children need them. As they trek to and fro to the rice fields, they also collect wild vegetables and fruits growing in the wild and these provide a side dish during mealtimes and most times they sell these to supplement their meager income.

In this way Tekaongdang and his wife eke out a living. At times of extreme need their relatives come to their aid and sometimes old clothes are sent to them by relatives living outside of the village. Both husband and wife work extremely hard and somehow they have been able to educate their children which are their top priority.

The two case studies show that belonging to the founding clan has its advantages. Assamwati and his wife belong to the two founding clans in the upper khel, Assamwati to the Longchari clan and his wife to the Amri clan. For Assamwati, land and its usage will never be a problem for he can utilise his clan's vast land holdings with due permission from the clan elders. He can also take the produce from his father-in-law's land after getting permission. His additional skills also mean that he can earn a good living and as such he does not have to worry too much about the future of his children for they belong to the founding clan and the children's *Tiuo Tukori* (maternal uncles) belong to the other founding clan.

In contrast Tekaongdang and his wife belong to the clans who settled in the village later on. Therefore their access to land is limited and being not too well educated and with no additional skills their future is not too secure.

Nokhimongri – Village Guards

As stated earlier the agricultural season for wet rice cultivation starts from the *tsükla* season (May, June and July) when the land is prepared for cultivation. The peak is during *mezheü* season (August, September and October) when the seedlings are prepared, transplanted and so on. At this time of the year especially the *mezheü* period the villagers are all kept busy in the rice fields.

During this period the village guards called the *Nokhimongri* stay back in the village to do village guard duty. The *Nokhimongri* are not drawn from the age-set system but the *Mozenba Telakba* grade (11th age-set grade) is responsible for organising the guard duty of the *Nokhimongri*. The village guards are selected house wise that is in one locality, about ten houses are selected serially and the males told of the *Nokhimongri* duty. All the males who have *Nokhimongri* duty cannot go to the rice fields or go out of the village for personal works, unless it is very important for which they will have to seek the permission of the Village Council. The *Nokhimongri* sit in the village council hall, in the upper and lower *khel* respectively, as this is a venue that is known to everyone, including children. The reason is that should accidents occur or someone dies, the news will be first reported to the *Nokhimongri* who will then depute the younger males to take the news to the relatives working in the rice fields. The duties also include fire prevention.

The duration of *Nokhimongri* duty is for one day, as the *mezhüo* (monsoon) season is the main agricultural season for the villagers. As every house with male residents are counted for *Nokhimongri* duty, the rotation of such duty move serially from one locality to the other and when the last house in the last locality has been counted for this duty then it starts all over again from the first house. Thus the villagers can leave their homes to go far away to the rice fields secure in the knowledge that some responsible people will be there in the village to take care of emergencies should they occur.

Agro-based activities

So far we have discussed about the economic activity based on agricultural production, processes and the way the people have organised themselves for this activity. But in recent years other economically viable activities have been undertaken with the intervention of the State government and banking agencies such as the Horticulture Department, Government of Nagaland, National Horticulture board and NEDFI (Northeastern Development Financial Institute).

The Horticulture Department, Government of Nagaland, established the Changki Valley Fruit Preservation & Canning factory at Longnak, in Changki territory as the area is located in close proximity to fruit growing areas in and around Changki valley. The idea was for the industrial utilization of the surplus fruit and for marketing the processed fruits. However due to mismanagement and neglect this factory as of now is defunct and is causing major problems for growers of horticultural produce.

Horticultural activities in the form of pineapple and areca nut (arecanut) cultivation in Changki area have also been taken up by the Changki villagers. Pineapple cultivation was first introduced by the Rural Development Department in 1992. An interest free loan of Rs.5000/-, to be paid in installments spread over a period of five years, was also offered to encourage cultivation of pineapple.

The pineapple farms are located at *Athabang* in the *Longnak* area. There are approximately twenty pineapple farms comprising of plots that range from one to five hectares run by the villagers. The expenditure of a farmer having about five hectares of land for pineapple plantation amounts to approximately Rs. 9000/- while the profit margin from one hectare in a season is about Rs.12,000 to 14,000/-. The pineapples are sold within the price range of Rs.3 – Rs.6 depending on the size. The pineapples are sold to the Fruit Canning Factory at Longnak run by the Horticulture Department, Government of Nagaland; the contractors for Assam Rifles from Jorhat, in neighbouring Assam also buy the pineapples wholesale, and a private fruit preservation factory in Mokokchung also buys the pineapples.

The Rural Development Department, Government of Nagaland, has constructed a Market Shed solely for the sale of pineapples at *Athabang* on the main road as it is the State Highway connecting Mokokchung, Tuensang, Mon and Zunheboto districts. Within the village too, the pineapples are sold as well as in the main intersection on the state highway linking Nagaland to Assam and serving as the junction from where the road leads to other villages in the Changkikong range and Mokokchung etc. This area is called X junction and is located in the Changki area.

Although arecanut has been grown by the villagers in the *Tsülu* (rice field) areas for ages as it is consumed on a large scale by the villagers; plantation of arecanut on a large scale and for commercial purposes is a recent development. The Horticulture Department, Government of Nagaland, is actively encouraging this enterprise by giving out free arecanut seedlings from the year 2002, as well as soft loans for developing arecanut plantations. NEDFI (Northeast Development Financial Institute) is also encouraging the development of this enterprise by giving soft loans for plantation in Longtho, in Changki area. The areas under intense arecanut cultivation are in *Athabang, Alongkaba, Engtsü, Chungjen, Chiengbalukong* and *Longtho*, in the Changki area.

The Horticulture Department, Government of Nagaland also introduced the model projects in *Tasangli* simply called the *Tasangli* Project on land belonging to the upper khel people in the Longnak area. Altogether nine people have started arecanut cultivation with a subsidy of Rs.3000 per acre. The same department has also given subsidies to the lower khel people at *Aotzu* known as the *Aotzu* Watershed Project, near the *tsulu* (wet rice fields) area where the beneficiaries totalling seventeen people have taken up mixed crop cultivation such as orange, arecanut cultivation, jhum paddy cultivation as well as tree plantation.

Both the projects were started in 2002 on an experimental basis and the subsidy for the first year was given to the beneficiaries of both the *Tasangli* and *Aotzu* projects. The project was for three years but so far only the subsidy for one year has been given. However the beneficiaries who have undertaken the projects are looking after their fields on their own as the land belongs to them.

The Horticulture Department, Government of Nagaland, has also taken up mixed crop cultivation on a project in the *Tzurang Kulemba* Kong area on land belonging to the village community. There are about forty beneficiaries from the upper and lower khel and this project known as the Center of Excellence was started in 2003 for a period of three years. The community land has been distributed to individuals who have the resources to develop the land.

Bananas are also grown but it is on a small scale and it is mostly for home consumption. From the year 2003 some individuals have taken up orange plantations with the help of the Horticulture department, which supplies seedlings and technical know-how. These orchards are located in the *Tzürang* valley and are privately owned.

It may be noted that although the village community land belongs to the village where the residents have the right to use the land with the Village Council acting as the caretaker/guardian of the land, once the decision is taken to distribute the land by the Village Council, the land is allotted to individuals. The individuals who apply for the allotments are those who have the resources to develop the land. The Village Council has a rule that the land allotted has to be developed by a certain period of time after which the land is reverted to the Village Council if nothing is done on the land.

The distribution of community land is allocated on the basis of the individual's ability to develop the land. From this we understand that the distribution of land is on the basis of individual wealth and resources. Once the land has been allocated the ownership of land becomes the individual's and it becomes private property.

The intervention of the state government and the banking sectors have had a positive impact in that the villagers have taken up other allied agricultural practices but there have been certain drawbacks too. The main drawback appears to be lack of organised endeavor in marketing and lack of technical expertise especially in the horticultural activities and the high expectations of the villagers for immediate economic returns.

Ayu – (Kitchen Gardens)

In Changki most of the kitchen gardens are not situated near the houses due to lack of space as the houses are huddled close to each other and as the lay of the land is such, the steep and rocky spaces are not viable for any productive activities. The villagers look for open spaces surrounding the village and in the lower *khel*, the kitchen gardens are located at *Longtsüen, Tsünglaong, Narisobo, Amotsüba* and *Sangban.* The kitchen gardens in the upper *khel* are located at *Longkiküm, Aok Enmong, Lichaba Korang* and *Endisang.* Whoever wants to start a kitchen garden takes permission from the owner of the land or the clan elders and after proper permission is taken, the kitchen garden is started. They cultivate pumpkins, maize, yam, tapioca, bananas, ginger, squash, beans and cucumbers.

The kitchen garden produce are meant not only for home consumption but also for selling, although the sale of such produce is on a very small scale. As mentioned earlier, there is no market within the village so people rely on the produce of the *ayu* for their own consumption. However certain items may be sold when the people need the money. The kitchen gardens also produce fodder for the pigs such as tapioca; the leaves are cut into small pieces and cooked along with wheat bran and some rice, while the tubers are chopped finely or grated and dried so that it can be fed to pigs during the winter season

Besides the cultivation of rice there are many other crops being grown. The crops and cropping pattern shown in Table 22 gives the details.

Table 22
Crops and cropping pattern

Sl. No	Types of crop	Months for sowing	Growth period	Month of harvesting	Purpose
1	**Rice (jhum)**	April/May	4 months	September/October	Non commercial
2.	**Rice (wet rice)**	July/August	4 months	November/December	Commercial and non commercial
3	**Maize**	March	3 months	June/July	Non commercial
4	**Yam**	March	8 months	November/December	Non commercial
5	**Tapioca**	March	8 months	November/December	Non commercial
6	**Bananas**	May/June	6 - 7 months	Every 6 months	Non commercial
7	**Tomatoes**	March and in September	6 months	Every 6 months	Non commercial
8	**Beans**	March and in September	6 months	Every 6 months	Non commercial

(Contd...)

Sl. No	Types of crop	Months for sowing	Growth period	Month of harvesting	Purpose
9	**Chillies**	March and in September	6 months	Every 6 months	Non commercial
10	**Oranges**	March	3-4 years	December	Non commercial
11	**Arecanut**	May/June	7 -10 years	Throughout the year	Non commercial
12	**Papaya**	June/July	1-2 years	Throughout the year	Non commercial
13	**Pineapple**	Any season	6 months	Every 6 months	Commercial
14	**Palm trees (*sera tong*)**	June/July	1-2 years	November-January	Commercial
15	**Broomsticks (*ungkholulu*)**	May	7 months	January-February	Commercial

In Table 22 we find that that out of the fifteen items of crops grown only four were for commercial purposes. These four items are pineapple, *ungkholulu* broom, palm trees from where *sera kipharu* (broom) is made out of the palm fronds and rice grown in the *tsülu* (wet rice fields). As rice is the staple food, only the surplus produce is sold.

Piggery

Apart from the crops grown for consumption which are sometimes sold in a very small scale, the people also rear pigs. The rearing of pigs is like a hobby for some of the people while for the majority it is a practical way of investment. In practical terms the rearing of pigs takes care of the kitchen waste like peels of vegetables as well as the chaff of husked paddy. In terms of investment the people spend a lot of energy and time foraging in the forests nearby for wild edible plants to be mixed in the pig swill and taking care of the kitchen garden to grow tapioca; as well as the money spent on buying wheat bran which has to be procured from Mariani in Assam.

We find that piggery is another source of income for the villagers. Almost every household rears pigs for sale. The live pigs sold are @ Rs. 55/- per kg. Usually the pigs are reared upto a weight of over 100 – 200 kg. Pork meat is rarely sold for it involves too much work and furthermore it is more profitable to sell live pigs. However when pigs are killed and sold, the rate is Rs. 60/- per kg. A pigling cost Rs.1000/- and as it is more profitable, the people rear sows. Those who rear pigs for breeding purposes take one pigling in lieu of money after the pigs have been successfully crossed.

The pigs are fed wheat bran, which is procured from Mariani and a bag of 30 kg costs Rs. 230/-. The villagers forage in the nearby forests for fodder as the pigs are fed green vegetations as well as rice and wheat bran. The kitchen wastes such as vegetable and fruit peels etc are collected for the pig's feed. The pigs feed consists of a mixture of green vegetation, boiled rice and wheat bran and are fed twice daily, once in the morning and once in the evening. Most of the villagers tend small *ayu* or kitchen gardens, wherever space permit, to grow tapioca as the leaves can be fed to the pigs during summer and in the dry season, the tubers are cut finely and dried, cooked and fed to the pigs. The tapioca tree is also used for making pig sties.

The pigs are sold during weddings, village or community celebrations and other events, Christmas and New Year celebrations and so on. The Village Council fixes the rate of pigs sold and no one can raise or lower the rate. Even during the wedding season when the pigs are in high demand, the rates remain fixed.

People rear at least two pigs at a time and the piglings may be bought at different times, therefore the pig that has grown up to 100 kg or so will be sold off first and a pigling bought to replace it with the money procured from the sale of the pig. A trend started by the teachers of Sangpangmen Primary School in Changki, is fast becoming a viable economic activity with regard to piggery. As everyone, including the teachers' rear pigs for extra income, the teachers have devised a way through which they can earn extra income on a regular basis.

The school teachers began the pig *phak jaba* trend by contributing equal amount of money to buy a pig, which was bought from within the circle only and so the owner of the pig also contributed his/her share of the *phak jaba* money. Once the pig was killed and cut the meat was shared equally among the group. For example, a group of ten teachers will pool in equal amount of money to buy a 100 kg pig, costing Rs.5500. The meat will be cut in equal shares of 10 kg and distributed among the group. If a member finds 10 kg of meat too much for personal consumption, he/she is free to sell the meat to others.

Thus through this pig *phak jaba* system the people resolve the problem of selling the pig as well as buying the meat, for there is no market within the village itself where meat can be easily bought. Most of the villagers buy meat from Mokokchung for the village bus makes daily trips to the town. Other people in the village have also started to form small groups of ten people or so who will buy the pig from within the group and sell the meat on equal shares.

As of now pigs are reared by individuals on a small scale mainly for personal consumption. But a piggery on a large scale has been started in the *tsülu* (wet rice field) area by Sademenba, a young entrepreneur from the lower khel, from the year 2003.

Apart from the traditional occupation of agriculture the Changki villagers also do various works which has been traditionally a source of income for them. The following are the traditional non-agricultural activities that Changki people undertake:

Basket Weaving

Basket weaving is an income generating traditional occupation which is undertaken by males only. As agriculture is the main occupation for the villagers there is demand for such woven products. However as most people know how to make baskets the income from this occupation is not very high and as the baskets lasts for years, the demand may not be too great in the village. But there is a demand from people residing outside the village so there is a steady income from basket weaving. The people who weave baskets for sale could not give the exact number of bamboo and cane products each year but on an average they earn about Rs.2500 – Rs.3000 per annum. There are various types of woven products such as:

1. *Mülok* – This is a basin like basket made out of *aling* or fine strips of bamboo. The standard size of this basket is about 8" in height and with a diameter of about 1'.2". This is used for collecting vegetables and for storing small amounts of rice. This is also the standard used for measuring paddy when it is bartered or given on loan. Such baskets may vary in size from very small to large. The standard size *mülok* costs Rs.50 per piece.

2. *Apha* – This is a flat triangular shaped tray with the pointed part of the triangle raised to about 6" and made out of *aling* (bamboo strips) and used for cleaning rice. The *apha* costs Rs.100 per piece.

3. *Likhu* - This is a flat circular tray type that is used for drying vegetables, herbs, meat etc. It is also made out of aling and costs Rs.120 per piece. It is smaller than the apha but the work is finer and thus is more expensive.

4. *Changyangru* – This is a flat circular sieve 1'.6"in diameter made out of *aling* and which is used for cleaning rice. The fine grains called *changping* are collected to be fed to pigs. The sieve costs Rs.50 per piece.

5. *Aphak* – This is a mat made out of aling and used for drying the paddy. A standard *aphak* measures 5'by 3' and costs Rs.350- Rs.400 per piece.

6. *Akhi* – This is a finely woven conical shaped basket with a head strap used for carrying paddy. The *akhi* is made out of *arhu* or cane and if the workmanship is exceptional good, such baskets are water proof too. The *akhi* costs Rs.250-Rs.300 per piece.

7. *Aiengkho* – This is a smaller cylindrical shaped basket with a head strap used for carrying firewood, agricultural implements etc especially for jhum

cultivation. It is made out of *aling* and costs Rs.150 per piece.

8. *Aben* – This is a fish trap made out of bamboo cut into fine sticks and it costs Rs.120 per piece.

9. *Tsüenkho* – This is a small cylindrical basket with a strap that can be slung over the shoulder used by women to carry small things such as edibles, vegetables or meat for cooking in the *tsülu* etc. It is made out of cane and costs Rs.60 per piece.

10. *Akut* – These are woven baskets with covers made out of bamboo strips where dry chilli, dry fish, dry meat etc are stored. It costs approximately Rs.60.

11. *Jangkut* – This is an large oblong basket with a cover made out of cane which was used in the earlier days to keep clothes etc. This is not in usage anymore.

12. *Manukhi* – It is a very large conical shaped basket made out of bamboo strips which is used to collect paddy especially in the jhum fields. It costs about Rs.500-600.

13. *Ajem* – This is a large round storage container made out of bamboo, in which upto 100-150 tins of paddy can be stored in the *Athi*. It costs Rs.350-400.

14. *Anung* – it is also a storage container, smaller than the *ajem*, where paddy can be stored and even carried by people with the help of a head strap. It costs about Rs.250-300.

15. *Tsutakhopok* – This is a triangular shaped basket for carrying bamboo containers filled with water. This type of basket is rarely used nowadays.

16. *Sungkhokopok* – This is a basket which is square in shape with one side split with a strap attached for carrying firewood. As the basket is loaded with firewood,

the load can be secured with the strap. This type of basket is made of cane and costs Rs.70-80.

17. *Chakupa* – This is a flat rectangular tray type made out of bamboo used for winnowing paddy. It costs about Rs.70-80.

Pottery

Pot making is a traditional occupation undertaken by the Changki women. In the ancient days pot making was an important source of income; for the Changki women were the only one's who made earthen pots in the Ao area as the other Ao villagers considered it taboo. Thus from all the neighbouring Ao and even some nearby Lotha villages people used to walk for days on end to Changki village so as to barter their goods such as wild vegetables, paddy, yam, tapioca, ginger, fruits and so on for the pots.

The women who make pots use the same implements that their ancestress used. They also procure the clay from *Lithu* at the banks of *Tzümet* River, which has been the source for clay since time immemorial. The art of pot making has not evolved much for the same designs and implements are still in use. The pots are usually for cooking and some people still use earthen pots for cooking meat. In the olden days huge pots were made too for storing rice in the kitchen for daily consumption. Although there is still a demand for pots, the people prefer to use aluminum and other utensils. Pot making is also a tedious and long drawn process. **Sentiyangchetla Aonok**, who is 75 years old and is from Aliba *kiong* in the Upper *khel*, has been making pots since her childhood. She learnt the art from her mother who passed on the technique to her and her 5 sisters and they were once considered the best pot makers in Changki.

Sentiyangchetla Aonok explained that the pots are usually made during winter as in the dry season the pots are consistently dried and will not explode much when roasted in the fire. In the summer the humidity and the rains spoil the drying process. The process of pot making is long drawn and simple wooden and clay implements are used. In Changki the method of pot making is as follows.

Red and grey clay are mixed, with a slightly larger portion of the former, and well kneaded with water. A mass large enough to make a pot is then taken and worked on a board into the shape of a large round bun. This is picked up and rammed on to the left fist, the flat bottom being towards the fist. It is then shaped and worked with the right hand till it forms a sort of cap over the clenched left hand. Next it is put rim upwards on the ground, and further worked with the damped fingers of both hands, first with an upward scraping motion and then with a circular motion around the pot, the left hand being inside and the right outside all the time. When the rough shape of the finished article has been arrived at it is left in the sun to dry for an hour.

Hitherto, the clay being very soft, nothing but the fingers had been used to shape it. After it has hardened a little in the sun the final shaping is begun. For this a mushroom shaped stop (*putsüru*) of baked clay is held against the inner surface with the left hand and the outside tapped and smoothed with various shaping sticks till the requisite shape and thinness have been obtained. The first shaping stick (*puzükru*), which is used for the rough work, is a narrow flat piece of wood with a smooth surface. Next a stick (*puyakru*) with broad ends, like a double paddle, is used. The four flat surfaces of the paddle ends of this are deeply grooved in squares and lozenges. This gives a rough surface to the pot, and prepares it for the final smoothing stick (*ayaktsüngba*), which similarly has paddle-shaped ends, but with smooth ends.

After drying one full day in the sun the pot is ready for baking (firing). To bake the pots they are piled on a very low platform of bamboo, and dry reeds put under and all over them and lighted. The pots when finished are round bottomed with an overturned rim for lifting them off the fire. No ornamentation of any kind is applied. A ring made out of bamboo strips called *pusenru* is used to keep the pot so that it does not roll about.

Nowadays to get the pots to dry quickly instead of being dried for one full day in the sun, the pots are piled on the '*Kharo*' or the shelf-like contraption over the hearth and dried by the fire lit in the hearth till they are blackened. Before use the starch of the rice is boiled and allowed to overflow the pot. The starch is then spread all over the pot on the inside and outside for it hardens the pot and makes it more lasting. The pots usually used for cooking meat etc are sold for Rs.45 while the smaller decorative pots are sold from prices ranging from Rs.10 – Rs.25. The price of the pots varies according to the size. Pot making is mostly confined to the upper Khel women and they earn some income from it. Interestingly pot making is undertaken by the women in the upper khel only and there 6 full time potters in the Upper Khel. The average annual income from this occupation is Rs.5000 to Rs.7000.

The main reason that discourages pot making is that to collect the red and grey clay, the women will have to make a trek of 16 km to *Luthi* at the bank of *Tzümet* River which is steep and dangerous. The clay will then have to be dug and hauled back which is back breaking. It is also not economically viable as most people do not use the earthen pots for cooking, preferring the aluminium and other varieties of cooking utensils available in the market.

However the VDB (Village Development board) Women's Wing has undertaken a pottery scheme where the young girls are taught to make the pots. The reasoning is that the skills of this indigenous cottage industry should not be allowed to become extinct. Pottery was one of the distinctive features of Changki village and was also an income generating activity at one time. The pots made under this scheme in the upper khel are sold too and the annual income generated from each session of training is Rs.600-700. The lower khel started this scheme from 2004 only.

Weaving

Weaving of *Temoksü* (shawls) and *ani* (wrap around skirt) is another traditional occupation undertaken by the women. In the olden days cotton was harvested, spun and then woven to make *ani* (skirt) and *Temoksü* (shawl). However nowadays as the yarn is readily available in the market the women buy the yarn and weave the skirts making use of the same equipments and methods that their ancestresses used. Changki *awhani or* skirt and *taktepsü* (shawl) is distinctive from other Ao costumes. The *awhani* is indigo blue with red rectangular designs over regular spaces while the *taktepsü* is white with indigo blue stripes. An *awhani* costs Rs.650 per piece while the *taktepsü* costs Rs.300 per piece inclusive of the yarn and making charge. There are four professional weavers in the lower khel and three in the upper khel. To weave one skirt usually takes about a week. On an average in a month these women weave four skirts, the cost of yarn per skirt is Rs.200, and therefore the women earn Rs.1800.monthly. There is a steady demand for the traditional *awhani* (skirt) not only within the village but also from outside the village. Sometimes the women weave five to six *awhani* per month.

Commercial Development of Changki Valley

In recent years the extensive land holdings of Changki village in the *Tzürang Longtho* valley, which is owned by the village community has been opened for cultivation to all bonafide citizens of Changki village. Interested candidates had to register their names and had to pay only the registration fee of Rs. 2000. The land was allotted to the individual through a lottery system, so that there was no discrimination in the distribution of the land. It is interesting to note that those who were allotted land were all Changki people residing outside the village who had the means and resources to develop the land. In the year 2000, about six individuals were allocated about eighty to hundred acres each for starting tea gardens and vegetable farms while 4 individuals have been allotted about the same area in 2002. The fertile valley is already showing promises of yielding good crops of tea and vegetables but as yet all this is still at the experimental stage.

In the *Tzürang Longtho* valley there are now five tea gardens, one Aloe Vera farm and one orange orchard started by the Changki entrepreneurs. All the plantations are on a large scale meant for commercial purposes. The individual areas for the various plantations are approximately eighty to hundred acres. As of now the economic returns is yet to be assessed as the plantations were started only in 2002. The people who have started these plantations are Changki people living in Kohima, Dimapur etc. The workers on the plantations are non-local for the local people are not experienced nor have they shown much interest in these lines of employment. There is also a saw mill in *Longtho* run by a local business man based in Dimapur.

The area also got a boost through the initiative of NEDFI (North Eastern Development Financial Institute) and NHB (National Horticulture board), which adopted the area in the year 2002, as a viable economic sector for development and marketing of agricultural and horticultural produce. To make this feasible NEDFI in particular has taken the help of the Village Council and has issued micro loans to the farmers of Changki so as to help them get started in their endeavors, which is mostly horticulture. So far 119 farmers have received the loans. The Village Council screened the applicants and since they know them well, only those who were deemed to be fit and sincere were selected. The Village Council is also the guarantor for the beneficiaries of the loans. The NHB has also started a Centre of Excellence for Horticulture Model Project in this area in 2003. In this project the villagers who have been allotted land in this area by the Village Council are given orange seedlings, arecanut seedlings and so on and the department also imparts the technical know how from time to time.

We find that in Changki the people are also involved in a number of occupations far removed from agriculture and other land based economic activities. A few work outside Changki village as employees of the government, army and other private firms and the numbers of these are not given here.

Table 23
Distribution of non-traditional occupation of population in Changki village

Occupation	Frequency	Percentage to total population
Shopkeepers	20	3.77
4th grade govt. employees	60	11.30
Teachers	73	13.75
Primary Health workers	2	0.10
Nurses	1	0.50
Total	**155**	**28.81**

In Table 23 we see that non-agricultural occupations such as petty shop owners running small business ventures have been taken up. In the village there are twenty petty shops, twelve in the lower Khel and nine in the upper Khel, which sell essential commodities like salt, oil, pulses, tea, sugar, milk as well as paan, cigarettes, sweets and village produce like vegetables and fruits etc. Most of the things sold in the village are procured from Mariani, the border town in Assam, which is the nearest and most important market for the people of not only Changki and the Changkikong range but also of almost the entire Ao area.

We also find as shown in the table that apart from the shop keepers running small businesses, the majority of the people engaged in other occupations are salaried employees working in the public sector such as fourth grade employees, school teachers and primary health workers. Of the 73 teachers, 57 are employed in the Government Primary Schools as well as the Government High School. Out of these, 3 are non-Nagas while 4 are from other Ao villages that have been posted to Changki. Therefore 50 of the teachers employed are from the village itself. In the 1 privately run Mission School there are 16 teachers out of which 5 are non-tribals. Therefore there are 61 teachers who are Changki people.

There are two village buses, one from the upper khel and one from the lower khel, which are privately owned. These offer bus service to Mokokchung daily, twice-weekly service to Dimapur and tri-weekly service to Mariani on rotation basis. The introduction of the twice-weekly bus service to Dimapur from the village and back has been a boon for the people for they can now travel at their own convenience in the village buses. Through the availability of this transport system the village, in many ways, has been linked to the outside world. The influence of such links can be seen in the consumption patterns especially in ownership of assets and other household items.

From Table 24 we find that the possession of modern gadgets and facilities shows the consumption pattern of the villagers and we can gauge the absorption capacity of Changki villagers. Better transport and communication systems and interaction with the outside world have resulted in changes within the economic structure of the village and consequently on the lifestyle of the people. The four wheelers are not only for personal use but sometimes are also hired out especially when there are community works and in times of emergencies. The exact figures could not be given as there are no fixed rates as such. The two wheelers are owned by the school teachers and fourth grade employees who commute daily to their offices located at Longnak, 16 km from the village. The two mini trucks are privately owned and the hire charges are Rs.300 per trip. There are five generators out of which three are privately owned while two are owned by the two churches respectively. The community bus services which are privately owned, one from the lower khel and the other from the upper khel, have a roster whereby when one bus make trips to Mokokchung daily for a week, the other bus will make twice weekly trips to Dimapur. Thus we find that the villagers are mobile as well as being connected through the telephone which totals to 98 connections

Table 24
Distribution of ownership of assets and other household items

Sl. No.	Name of property	Frequency
1	Private vehicles: four wheelers and two wheelers four wheelers & 83 two wheelers	9
2	Community buses	2
3	Rice mills	8
4	Television	130
5	CD players & music systems	27
6	Refrigerators	25
7	Mini trucks	2
8	Generator	5
9	Telephones	98
10	Inverters	2

In addition to the income generated not only through sale of paddy and other land based production activities as well as the private and public sectors, we also observed that people earn as daily wage workers.

Table 25
Distribution of occupational wages among male and female workers

Sl. No.	Type of work	Wage rate (Rs/per day)	
		Male	Female
1	Carpentry	Rs.80 - 100	-
2	Tsülu	Rs.100	Rs. 65
3	Firewood collection	Rs.100	Rs.65
4	Coal	Rs.100	-
5	Logging	Rs.100	-
6	Stone quarrying	Rs.100	Rs.65

In Table 25 we find that the type of daily wage work is manual and requires hard physical labour. We also find that there is a disparity in the wages between the males and females. When asked about this the argument given was that the men do more hard labour. Most of the daily wage work is done in the *phenpüo* season (February, March and April), which is the slack agricultural season.

Changki is also endowed with coal deposits in its territory and the coal is dug out and sold to the tea factories in Mariani and Jorhat. Significant coal seams have been exposed northeast of Changki. The top coal seams of this area are 1.5 to 2.2 metre in thickness. The central portion of Longnak nala at about 1.5km from Athuphumi village in the Changki territory is rich in coal deposits. However, proper assessment and surveys have yet to be conducted. The extraction of the coal deposits is unorganised and unscientific leading to harmful after effects such as landslides and even pollution of the water streaming down to the fertile valley below where the paddy fields are located. Besides coal, the prospects for sand, clay and natural gas also have great potential for economic exploitation. The economic returns of the coal extracted are not as profitable, as might be expected for the businessmen from Assam who control the market and the digging of the pits pay only Rs.5000 per truckload to the Changki villagers who have no contacts with the outside traders, which is in turn sold to the tea factories etc for Rs.35,000 per metric tonne.

Ingkho Mapang (Traditional period for earning)

We have mentioned earlier that the Changki seasonal calendar sets the pace of village life. This can be best illustrated by the period of *Ingkho Mapang* during the *Phenpüo* season.

During the *Phenphüo* season which is the slack agricultural season, a month is allocated for *Ingkho Mapang* and is generally from the middle of February till the middle of March, after the jhum area is cut and left to dry. In this period the villagers especially the males, are exempted from all village works. It may be noted that the males are assigned various village duties according to their age-set grades which mean that every male participates in the overall administration of the village. Thus throughout the year the males are kept busy with their personal work as well as with village works. '*Ingkho Mapang*' literally means time set aside for working outside the village or '*Yayang*', which means to earn.

In the ancient days the people would go down to the plains to trade for a year's supply of salt and iron implements and these were exchanged with cotton, ginger, chillies and so on. As Changki is in the border area and in close proximity to Assam, such trade was carried out, especially with the Ahoms.

This period was also essentially a break from the monotony of village life and the hard agricultural cycle of jhum cultivation. During the British colonial rule the villagers would go down to the plains in Assam and work as hired labourers in the tea gardens or when roads were being constructed, they would work as labourers. Mackenzie (1979, reprint) quotes P.T. Carnegy, Assistant Commissioner of Jorhat (1873) who wrote to the Deputy Commissioner of Sibsagor describing the Nagas living in the hills adjoining to Jorhat as 'the people of all tribes known to us are great traders, and parties of them are continually to be met with in the cold season, when they bring down cotton, chillies, ginger and other produce and take away salt, iron, daos, fish and pariah pups. It is, I believe their appreciation of the value of this trade that makes the Nagas peaceable neighbours to us' (ibid:400) The Nagas mentioned are the Ao tribe and Changki was one of the villages situated in the border area that traded with the plains people.

During the *Ingkho Mapang* the *Samen Menchen* (Village Council) remained suspended and only the *Mezetri* or village guards stayed in the village to undertake certain duties such as to oversee that no untoward incidents or accidents occurred. The *Mezetri* were led by a senior among the *Empiba Ho* age-set grade (the thirteenth age-set grade) and volunteers from all the other age-set grades. If there were no volunteers' ten men from the first age-set grade to the tenth were selected to do the village duties during this period. The duty of the *Mezetri* was to act as sentry, messenger and to ensure that law and order was maintained in the village. They took turns to do this duty on a weekly basis where in the earlier days they would sit in the *Arju* (the male dormitory) from dawn till dusk. Nowadays the *Mezetri* sit on the terrace of the community halls.

In the discussion earlier on the processes of wet rice cultivation we had pointed that when the people are away in the rice fields the village is guarded by the *Nokhimongri* or the village guards. In the *Ingkho Mapang* period the village is guarded by the *Mezetri* who are also village guards.

The difference in the village guard duty during the *mezhüo* season (monsoon season) and *phenphüo* season (winter season) is that in the *mezhüo* season, the village guards are called *Nokhimongri* and their duty is for only one day and during this period the *Samen Menchenri* or Village Councilors are exempt from such duty. The *Nokhimongri* also work under the direct control of the Village Council, for the Village Council decides on the number of houses to be selected serially for such duty.

However during the *phenphüo* season the village guards are called *Mezetri* and the guards are drawn from the *Yanga* or age-set system and the duration of the *Mezetri* duty is for one week. The *Mezetri* can also include the *Samen Menchenri* or Villager Councillors except the *Gaonburas* and as such the *Mezetri* on duty are not under the control of the Village Council so they are free to decide how to carry out their duty, and to make their own roster for such duties.

On one of my visits to the village in 2002 I came across the *Mezetri* sitting on the terrace of the Panchayat Hall in both the *khels* who were making bamboo baskets, sharpening their dao and generally keeping themselves busy. They would sit in the terrace from dawn till dusk and this continued for a week till they were replaced by another group.

However on my visit to the village again in January 2004 I observed that the *Mezetri* village guards had worked out the roster in such a way that most of the older guards would carry on with their own works in the village without having to sit in the terrace of the Panchayat Hall having delegated the younger members to sit there.

We find that the even today the *Ingkho Mapang* system and the traditional customs associated with it is still prevalent in Changki. The *Mezetri* sit on the terrace of the village council halls in both the upper and lower *khel* from dawn to dusk. In addition the *Mezetri* undertake the charge of fire prevention duties for usually this is the dry and windy season and the danger of fire spreading through the closely packed houses is very real.

At dawn, afternoon, evening and nightfall the '*Yimpiuri*' or the village crier gives out the call to put out all fires after cooking or to be careful when lighting fire. The villagers are duty bound to tie three bamboo containers filled with water in the front of their houses so that should an emergency arise due to fire, each and every household would have water to douse out any fire, if it occurred in the village.

The last duty of the Village Council members before their office closes for the *Ingkho Mapang* period is to oversee that each and every household has these bamboo containers filled with water tied in the front of their houses. If any household does not follow this order, a fine is imposed. This is also a very dry period so having water filled in the bamboo containers ready for emergencies gives some sense of security to the people.

Apart from the traditional custom of doing village guard duties the people are also active in many works during the *Ingkho Mapang*. We observed that the people engage in various economic activities within the village and these activities are non agricultural work in nature. During this time as it is the period of earning, community works, apart from village guard duties, are not imposed, except for emergencies. We observed that people also do not give free '*jangkhet*' (worth of one's service) as is usually the norm.

The typical works carried out during this period are as follows:

Carpentry work: The males hire themselves out for carpentry work such as building or repairing houses, building pig sties, repairing or making new *kilangmi* (open bamboo platform), making furniture and so on. The males who go out to work taking with them their own *hatiar* or equipments charge Rs.150 per day for repairing or building houses, while those who do not take with them their *hatiar* charge Rs.80 per day. To build or repair pig sties the daily charge is Rs.100. For furniture most people usually supply the raw material such as wood so the carpenters take only the making charge which is Rs.2000 for a big bed and Rs.500 for a long bench which is the common furniture found in every Changki household. Other items made are *langpa* (ladder) and *langpang* a low rectangular stool made out of wood. *Süngden* is a wooden box, rectangular in shape in various sizes that is an important utility item in every Changki household. Rice as well as other food items is kept in this box so as to protect such items from rodents. The *süngden* is made in the village and the making charge varies according to size from Rs.500 to 1500.

***Süngkho* or collection of firewood**: Both males and females carry out this type of work. If a person does not have his/her own individual or clan land from where they can collect the firewood, they seek permission from those who have land and cut the wood for firewood with the understanding that one equal load will be cut for the owner of the land. One load of firewood is cut wood piled up 5 feet by 5 feet which is sold for Rs.600. In one mini truck three such loads can be transported to the village for Rs.300 to Rs.600 depending on the distance from the forest to the village. Those having land collect firewood for the whole year for their own use and if possible sell the firewood in the village for Rs.650 usually to old people and spinsters etc who cannot go to collect firewood themselves. In one season those having ample land can earn up to Rs.1800/- to Rs.7200/-. The usual practice is for the people to go to the forest and cut the wood and bring it up to the main road for easy loading into the mini truck. The wood is neatly piled into 5 feet by 5 feet piles ready for sale. People buy the firewood piled on the road and transport the wood to the village by hiring the mini truck on their own. Thus for one mini truck load of firewood the people pay Rs.2100/-. If the wood is cut in the forest above the main road, the cut pieces are thrown down to the road to be piled up into the standard load. However if the wood is cut in the forests below the main road, then daily wage earners usually females are hired for Rs.60 per day, if the firewood cut is a lot.

Construction work: If some major construction is being done such as the community hall, leveling of public grounds, laying of water pipes or repair of roads etc, the villagers work as daily wage labourers where males are paid Rs.100 and females are paid Rs.65.

Basket weaving: It is at this time that the raw materials such as bamboo and cane are collected and cut and seasoned etc suitable for basket weaving.

Broom making: This is also the time when the people go to the jungles to collect brooms and also palm like fronds for making brooms. Such brooms are made by the people and sold for Rs15-Rs25 and also supplied to the shops in Mariani, the nearest market town in neighbouring Assam.

Wood Carving: Wood carving is undertaken by the males who make decorative pieces, household items such as *thatsü* (a ladle made out of bamboo), *azü* (serving spoon for rice, made out of wood), *süngphu* (bowl like item with a stand made out of wood and used as a plate for eating as well as for making *chutney*), *achem* (a hollowed bowl type used for pounding rice, dried chillies, bamboo shoots), *mitüm* (wooden stick used for pounding), *maruk* (cups made out of bamboo used for drinking water as well as black tea), *aowphu* (a rectangular plate made out of the bamboo bark), *techempong* (a slim cylindrical container type made out of bamboo for pounding herbs etc for cooking), *charong* (walking sticks), *nokpang* (dao handles), *noklubo* (wooden piece tied to a belt for carrying the dao), *phabang* (axe handle), *saniru* (wooden block for chopping meat etc), *ami* (spear handle), *sachuk* (bamboo sticks meant for skewering meat for drying) etc. The *süngpho* costs Rs.160 – 200 depending on the size, the *achem* costs Rs.50-60, the *charong* Rs.30-40 and the *nokpang* costs Rs.25. Apart from these the rest of the items listed above are made by almost everyone and those who cannot make such things ask relatives and friends who make such things for free.

The other activities during the *Ingkho Mapang* are stone quarrying for retaining walls and so on as well as for *Longzak* which is a small slab of stone used for sharpening knives etc. The *Longzak* is made of a particular stone found mostly in Changki *lusa* (territory) and is therefore in great demand from other villages. These stones are chiseled into small slabs and sold for Rs.25 each.

As was observed this period is a very busy time for the villagers as they have to complete all personal works by the close of the *Ingkho Mapang* which is announced by the Village Council.

The importance of the *Ingkho Mapang* lies in the fact that for ages it was during this time that the villagers would go down to the plains in Assam and trade their produce such as rice, ginger, yam, tapioca and so on in exchange for a year's supply of salt and iron implements. After the British imposed the annual house tax it was from the wages earned during *Ingkho Mapang* that the villagers paid the annual house tax and also other village collections.

The tradition of *Ingkho Mapang* continues even today for the villagers, especially the male, being bound by the age-set system are hard pressed for time of their own as their duties for village works are very heavy and they cannot neglect their duties assigned to them as per the age-set system. Therefore the *Ingkho Mapang* period is valuable for them, for they can then undertake personal works. If they are assigned duty as *Mezetri*, they are also duty bound to attend to it but if there are emergencies, they can request others to replace them provided they have valid reasons. It is at this time that the Village Council too remains suspended and no official work is entertained except for very important or urgent works. If any official notification comes to the village the *Mezetri* can take the initiative in making decisions provided the tasks are simple and do not have too much governmental or official significance.

Even today it is after the period of *Ingkho Mapang* that all village collections and taxes are collected since the *Ingkho Mapang* period is regarded as the time when additional income is earned.

Market forces and its influence

As we observed people's inter-relationships in the course of their economic activities we find that the *Yangtep* system based on cooperation, friendship, support and inter dependence which provided the work force for jhum cultivation is on the wane for the *Yangtep* system is practiced by few people. Slowly most of the people are taking to daily wage work even in the *tsulu* or wet rice fields. This is coming about as old people as well as the school teachers and employees of government offices cannot give time to manage their fields on their own. Another reason is that the poorer section of the people in the village has taken to daily wage work even in the *tsulu* or wet rice fields for additional income.

As daily wage workers came into the market force the people realizing the practicality of hiring such workers slowly began to rely more on daily wage workers than on friends for the work was done faster and they would not be obliged to work their friends' fields. Moreover we find that competition is another factor that is eroding the *Yangtep* practice. As people compete to produce more, individualism becomes more pronounced and the traditional sense of community sharing, cooperation and support is becoming obsolete. Again as people prosper and have the means and resources, they look for convenience and paid labourers who will work as per their instructions.

Another factor that is reinforcing the rise of competition in the economic sphere is the role played by the government agencies such as the Horticulture Department, Government of Nagaland, NEDFI (North East Development Financial Institute), NHB (National Horticulture board) and so on. The incentives through subsidies and free resources for developing individual lands is leading to more people participating in the economy as individual entrepreneurs where profit is the driving force.

The salaried employees are contributing to the monetization of the economy too. Increasing use of hard cash for business transactions however minor is now the established norm and the barter system that was once the only form of exchange is all but obsolete.

Interestingly we find that the Village Council plays a major role in the economy by way of enforcing the rates of the wages, prices of paddy and rice, pigs, pork etc as well as setting the date for releasing the people for *Ingkho Mapang* from all village works and also recalling them back. The Village Council acts as the arbiter in the economic sphere so that there is uniformity in the business transactions as far as controlling wages and prices are concerned. But the final decision is made after the *Ayim Mungdang* (village general assembly) where the people discuss and debate the issue and come to a consensus on the prices.

We find that the economy of Changki village is closely linked to agriculture, mainly wet rice cultivation. The land holding system and land management is still based on traditional and customary laws that are enforced by the Village Council as well as the clans. The method of cultivation is still very simple technologically and manual labour is the only means for production.

As more and more people discard jhum cultivation, it has led to the loss of some of the indigenous variety of paddy. The old people in the village also told this researcher that as jhum cultivation started to be abandoned, the people began to lose the sense of unity and friendship for now people were not dependent on each other as much as in the olden days. They were of the opinion that the importance of sharing, giving and support has been eroded for with the new found prosperity brought about through the economic activity of wet rice cultivation and with the emergence of other occupations, the people have become more independent and business minded and therefore do not need each other as much as in the olden days. We find that conspicuous consumption is becoming a factor of social differentiation.

In the agricultural activity of wet rice cultivation we find that the people have taken to hiring outsiders to work on their fields some of whom work as casual labourers while there are those who work and live in the fields on a more or less permanent basis. As most of the young people go away from the village either to study or to work, the parents are left with no choice but to hire other workers who might be from the village itself or the Adivasi's from Assam. It is also noted that most of the parents do not want their children to become cultivators and have ambitions for their children to be educated and become more qualified and get on with life, with the ultimate goal being that of finding a government job.

We see that already there is a trend whereby agricultural work is shunned by quite a number of the educated younger generation. This is basically because their parents have sent them off to boarding school from a very young age to other towns such as Mokokchung, Kohima, Dimapur and even outside the state for those who can afford. In such circumstances then, the younger people never learnt the art and skills of agriculture and its allied works. Being exposed to other cultures through interaction with other people, the younger generations have also been pulled away from the village either through marriage, employment or simply the desire to live in a town or city where the attractions of the fast paced life is sought after.

It is also observed that many families moved out of the village and settled in other places but still retain houses in the ancestral home sites and fields. Some of these people have rented out their houses to others mostly non-local teachers working in the schools as well as newly married couples who have yet to build their own houses and the fields have been given out on sharecropping basis. So we find that another category of ownership is slowly emerging creating new relations between the owner and the renter of the houses.

The social standing of a person is reckoned in terms of occupation, education, wealth (both land and monetary) and in imperceptible ways a class structure is gradually emerging in Changki society. The government jobholders with a steady monthly income are differentiated from the daily wage earners and cultivators who depend on agricultural activity for their livelihood.

We find that the village is self-sufficient only in relation to the production of the staple food, which is rice. For other requirements the people have to rely on the markets in Mokokchung or in Mariani. Fresh vegetables, fruits, meat, poultry and other dairy products are not available in the village. The inconvenience brought about by the absence of a daily market in the village is felt greatly. This factor also means that there is no circulation of money within the village and the absence of banking facilities also hampers saving.

6

RELIGIOUS INSTITUTION IN CHANGKI

Smith (1980, reprint:74) wrote that 'the Ao Nagas, in common with the hill peoples of this section and in many other parts of India, have a simple religion.' The people believed that the universe was filled with a number of spirits with whom they must deal. He went on to say that 'the propitiation of the evil and capricious spirits is practically the sum and substance of their religion' (ibid:76). Their main concern was with the appeasement of these capricious spirits so that they would be favoured with an abundance of good rice. Mills (1926:215) on the other hand stated that 'the religion of the Ao is not a moral code'. However Imchen (1993:32) refuted this by saying that 'the Aos had a well-established and systematized form of religious belief and practice'. The concept of god was very much in the consciousness of the Aos whom they called *Tsüngrem*. Ao (2000:49) wrote that 'for the Aos, belief in the existence of a god or gods forms the core of their religion and is a guiding principle of their conduct in life'.

Imchen wrote that the Aos believed in various *Tsüngrem* or gods such as *Lichaba*, creator of earth, *Longtitsüngba*, lord of heaven, *Tiar/Tiaba*, god of providence and *Meyutsüngba*, lord over the dead and several other minor deities. The Aos believed that *Meyutsüngba* was the God of truth and justice and the final judge of the dead. *Meyutsungba* demanded a just life, pure and high moral and ethical standards; honesty and humility and as *Meyutsüngba* was unforgiving, therefore the fear of him was the guiding principle for the Aos to live an honest life on earth. 'His gate is the passage of the dead from the world of the living (Imchen, op.cit.:35). *Meyutsüngba* was believed to be the silent spectator of man's activities on earth and was judged accordingly and often an Ao would say "let us see at the gate of *Meyutsüngba*' when false accusations were leveled at others. 'no ceremonies and offerings are given to *Meyutsüngba* for there is no scope of bargaining with him for mercy by offering sacrifices because he is god of righteousness' (ibid:35). The Aos believed in the concept of life after death, for they believed in a place called '*Asü Yim / Diphu Yim'* or the village of the dead. They believed that on the way to the village of the dead they had to cross a stream called *Longritzü* – the lonely river. 'On reaching *Longritzü* the dead must wash their hands to drink. As they put their hands together to hold the water in the palm, they find their hands have holes. They then realize they are dead and thus cross the river never to return (ibid:47). After crossing *Longritzü* the dead find themselves at *Meyutsüngba's* gate where the dead carry the load of deeds while on earth along with a spear to test themselves at the gate. The Aos believed that there was 'a tree of righteousness called *Tsüngchidong / Asangdong*' (ibid:48) and it was here that the dead would throw their spears at the tree and only the honest and righteous people could hit the tree in the middle and were admitted to the village of the dead through *Meyutsüngba's* house. Women, it was believed, threw their weaver's baton. Those who did not live an upright and good life missed the tree and went to the village of the dead via the back of *Meyutsüngba's* house. It was believed that those who missed the tree of righteousness did 'not reach the ancestral land of the dead but instead roamed for eternity in a place called

Mata Yim, suffering sun burn and thirst in the midst of knife-edged grass called *Nasü ni*' (ibid:48). Imchen put forward the theory that when the Christian missionaries came preaching about heaven and hell, the Aos could relate to it for it was a 'confirmation of their ancient concept and belief and the fulfillment of their age long traditional belief and value system' (ibid:11).

The Aos also had a clear concept of one god above all deities, spirits and supernatural powers. The Aos believed that there was one Supreme Being called *Jungphodemdem* and as the Gospel of Christ taught about one god in heaven, it was also in keeping with the Ao traditional belief. Panger Imchen postulated that the ideas and belief system of the ancient Ao religion made a preparation for the acceptance of Christianity among the people. The Aos also observed certain days as '*genna*', (an Angami term for taboo), and called it '*amung*' when nobody could go to the fields and observed such days as scared. In the same token the Christians observe the Sabbath day on Sunday as holy and sacred. Imchen made such comparisons between the ancient Ao religion and christianity and said that factors such as the concept of god, the belief in the after life and reward according to one's conduct while on earth and observation of certain days as sacred contributed to the Aos finding an affinity with the new religion introduced. The Aos had their own world view, philosophy of life and an accepted assumption about the nature and existence of a god or gods, and of an after-life. Thus when the Christian missionaries came, although there was some resistance in the beginning, the Aos took to the new religion readily enough.

Advent of Christianity

Christianity was first introduced in Molungkimong village in the Changkikong range and Changki is one of the nine villages in this range. Rev. Dr. E.W. Clark was the first

American missionary to set foot in the Ao Naga Hills. He was born on 25th February 1830 in New York, U.S.A. After his post graduation and seminary studies, he was appointed by the American Baptist Missionary Union to the Assam mission on 28th July 1868. In October 1868, along with his wife Mary Mead Clark, he set sail from Boston and finally reached Sibsagar, Assam on 30th March 1869, where he took charge as missionary and also started a printing press. Sibsagar a small township east of Jorhat, located on the Dikho river, became a focal point for missionary activity. It was here that the Clarks came into contact with the Nagas, who came down from the hills to trade in the plains (ibid:150)

Rev. Dr. Clark was keen to take the gospel to the hills and in this endeavor Godhula, an Assamese evangelist and schoolteacher volunteered to go up to the hills and survey the prospects. Godhula was assisted by Supongmeren, from Dekhahaimong village (now Molungkimong village, in the Changkikong range under Mokokchung district) who acted as his interpreter as he could speak Assamese with a certain degree of fluency. After befriending some more Nagas from Dekhahaimong (Molungkimong) village, Godhula and his wife Lucy, made the first historic trip to the hills in 1872, where they stayed throughout the rainy season. It was a successful trip for by November 1872, Godhula brought down with him nine converts whom Rev. Dr. Clark then baptized on 11th November 1872. The nine converts prevailed upon Rev. Dr. Clark to go up to their village to which he readily agreed. So with sixty escorts and sentinels for the protection of Rev. Dr. Clark, they set forth and on 18th December 1872, Rev. Dr. Clark reached Dekhahaimong (Molungkimong), the first Ao village which embraced Christianity. Thus the advent of Christianity in Nagaland began. From Dekhahaimong (Molungkimong) the Clarks along with the converts shifted to Molung in 1876 due to hostilities from the non-converts. Molung thus became the first fully Christian village and it was here that the first American Baptist Mission centre was established. The first Ao primer was printed at Molung in 1877 and the first Christian marriage took place in 1878. It was from this centre that the christian mission began to expand, till due to its more ideal and central location, a new mission centre was set up in Impur, near Mokokchung, with the assistance of Rev. and Mrs. Haggard and Rev. and Mrs. Perrine on 1st October 1894 (ibid:150).

Establishment of the Baptist church in Changki

The Changki people are Christians of the Baptist denomination. The establishment of the Baptist church in Changki celebrated its 100th year in 2001. Although the Changki people practiced the indigenous religious and belief system before conversion to christianity, once they converted to christianity they gave up all the ancient religious beliefs, including the traditional Ao festivals such as *Moatsü* (before harvest) and *Tsüngremong* (after harvest), which are still being celebrated in other Ao villages. As such no one can recount the rituals and ceremonies of the ancient religion that were practiced in Changki. It is believed that before the advent of Christianity *Aodang* and *Putsülong* in the lower khel, and *Tekongkulem* and *Emsen kiong* in the upper khel were considered the most sacred religious sites in Changki.

Christianity was first introduced in the Naga Hills when Dr.E.W.Clark set up the Baptist mission in Dekhahaimong (Molungyimsen) in 1872, which was later shifted to Molung in 1876. Both these villages are in Changkikong range in close proximity to Changki. The first Christian evangelist to come to Changki was Godhula who was sent to the village with the purpose of spreading the Gospel as well as setting up a school in 1883. But the Changki villagers refused to give permission and he had to go back (Aonok, 1953:2).

When the Impur Mission opened in 1894, one Changki man called **Tzüdiyong**, went there to work in the Mission as a manual labourer and he became the first Changki to become a christian. However he was not baptized till much later, nor could he write or read. But he went to Changki village in 1896 and tried to spread the gospel but the villagers did not allow him. Even his own family and clansmen threatened to expel him from the village (ibid:3).

Meanwhile in the year 1897, during the Ao *Moatsu* festival (before harvest) in Changki, a quarrel between the lower and upper khel people erupted which escalated into a civil war with the villagers beheading fellow villagers. The SDO of Mokokchung sub-division at that time was A.E.H. Shuttleworth who sent troops to quell the trouble and rounded up the culprits, who were marched off to Kohima for rigorous imprisonment and hard labour (ibid:3).

The villagers had to undergo extreme deprivation and suffering as the British administration took punitive actions against the village for headhunting had been abolished. At the same time there was an outbreak of an epidemic, which forced many people to go away from the village. One such villager was **Odangba** who left Changki in 1897 and went to Impur to work as a cook with the missionaries. In 1898, Odangba brought his brother, Impokumba to Impur, where both of them converted to Christianity and learned to read and write. Odangba was baptized on 4th November 1899 at Impur by Rev. Perrine. His brother **Impokumba** who had also attended primary school was baptized in 1900 by Rev. Rivenburg. Thus Odangba became the first baptized christian among the Changki people (ibid:4).

Impokumba was first sent to Changki as a schoolteacher to teach the gospel and also to teach the people to read and write. The first four students who attended his classes were **Yalemchang, Yimkongchurong, Karidangchetba** and **Nikenmeri**. Impokumba also held Sunday services and in this way three persons namely **Nokchameri, Nokmechaba** and **Imtipokyim** converted to christianity and with these converts, the Changki Baptist church was established on 20th October 1901. However the converts were baptized only in 1903, for they had to go to Impur for the baptism. Impokumba was also appointed as a government L.P. teacher in 1903 when the mission school he had established was upgraded to that of a government primary school (ibid:4).

Odangba came to Changki from Impur as the first Pastor in 1905 and he continued till 1915. His wife **Rongsentula** of Molungyimsen village started the women department in the church in 1905. Thus christianity took root in Changki village (ibid:6).

An important feature of the church was the youth wing and during the time of Pastor **Nikenmeri** (1920 – 1924) a 'Central Hostel' was instituted, mainly for the boys, with the understanding that the youth studying in the mission school would sleep there (ibid:6). The idea was to foster camaraderie, cooperation, understanding and harmony between the youth of the upper and lower khel, as well as to teach the gospel. This came to be known as the 'Room' equivalent to the *ariju* (male dormitory) system only the 'Room' was based on Christian doctrines.

But this hostel, where both the upper and lower khel youth were to live in, proved to be inconvenient so each khel started its own hostel. Soon there was a 'Room' for the boys as well as the girls in both the khels and all the youth were directed to sleep there regardless of whether they attended school or not. The youth would go about their work as usual in the daytime but in the evening the youngest boys or girls of the lot would be sent to call all the others to come to the 'Room'. If some could not go to the 'Room' due to unavoidable circumstances, the message would be sent through the youngsters sent to call them.

The youth were taught to write, read, sing, pray and speak/preach in public. Strict discipline was enforced and the youth not following the rules and regulations of the 'Room' were giving harsh punishment. The punishment was to fetch a piece of wood measuring three feet in width and three feet in height. This meant that those punished would have to go to the jungles to find a tree measuring three feet wide and cut it to the required size.

The youth of the 'Room' were also responsible for pounding, winnowing and cleaning the rice belonging to the church when major events took place in the church and community feasts were given. The 'Room' boys and girls fetched water and firewood for their respective 'Rooms' which had to be kept immaculately clean. The youth were also responsible for keeping church premises clean and were the volunteers for all church activities. When a member of the 'Room' got married, the room mates would get together and carry out the necessary arrangements for the wedding.

The youth were also strictly prohibited to mingle with the opposite sex. This was most probably in keeping with the foreign missionaries' view of ensuring moral discipline and the 'Room' became taboo for the opposite sex to enter. Education as well as deportment was taught to all the youth in the village. The concept of the *ariju* (male dormitory) and the *züki* (female dormitory) was adapted into the Christian mould and it was successful for the 'Room' imparted education and strengthened the foundation of Christianity in the village.

Unfortunately in the early days church records were not maintained so the activities and functions are at best sketchy and based on stories told by old people of the village who went to such 'Rooms'. The exact date is not known but the 'Room' became defunct in the late 1960's and the reason given is that many of the villagers, especially the youth began to go out of the village for further studies and to look for jobs. The strict discipline of the 'Room' was also cited as one of the reasons.

Split in the church

In the earlier chapter on kinship we have touched upon the claims made by a clan as *the* original founding clan in the lower *khel*. The discord and disharmony created by this claim had direct fallout within the church. It is told that an Emrem Changki clan member had been allegedly caught stealing and this was reported to the village government and as per customary law he was fined as well as excommunicated from the church. However the person who had reported the theft retracted his statement and instead said that he had given permission to the Emrem Changki man to take the produce from his land. Despite this, the excommunication of the Emrem Changki clan member came about because one of the Changkiri clan member was an influential man in the church and soon the whole matter became a personal matter as the two men belonged to the rival clans. Refusing to accept the punishment, in retaliation, the Emrem Changki clan member along with his supporters left the church and established a parallel church in the lower *khel* in 1947. The "**Changki Yimlang Baptist church"** was thus established. Following this a school was also established at Aodang and along with it, their own student union was formed.

The two churches are independent entities each with its own treasury and congregation and the functioning of the two churches is along the same lines. A brief account of the organisation of the **Baptist church Changki** (mother church) and **Changki Yimlang Baptist church** (breakaway group) is given in the following passages:

The **Baptist church Changki** (mother church) has 1,249 baptized members. Baptism takes place when a boy or girl reaches the age of 14-15 and it is after baptism that a person is considered as a full-fledged member of the church for it is only after baptism that the name is entered in the church register. At present the Pastor is Imnachuchang and the secretary is Allen Amri. The congregation comprises of the upper and majority of the lower khel people.

The **Changki Yimlang Baptist church** (breakaway group) was established in 1947. The first Pastor was Temsumeren Aonok. There are a total number of 387 baptized members Changki Yimlang Baptist Arogo. At present the Pastor of the church is Tekachuchang and the Secretary is Toshimenba. The congregation comprises of a section of only the lower khel.

The Baptist church Changki (mother church) **and Changki Yimlang Baptist church** (breakaway group) **Organisation:**

In both the churches all powers and functions are vested on the **board of Deacons,** for the administration of the church and the **Pastor** is the overall in-charge of it. He presides over all the meetings connected with the church. The other committees all have heads of department and function separately but with the approval of the Deacon board. There is a treasurer each for the main church as well as the women's department. The secretary maintains all the official files of the church. The associate pastor, who helps the pastor in the administration of the church, takes over the charge when the pastor is out of station or is indisposed.

The pastor is required to have the minimum theological qualification of B.D. (Bachelor of Divinity). His main functions are to teach the gospel, through the Sunday devotional services, to give baptism classes and to baptize and to look after the spiritual well being of his congregation. He is also the administrative head of the church and all cash transactions and official documents require his signature. He is the chairman of the deacon board as well as the ex-officio member of all the committees under the main church. The annual report is presented by him and he is the official representative of the village for all programmes, activities and conventions connected with the church.

Deacon Board

The Deacon board of both the churches headed by the pastor comprises of only male members who are respected elders and active members of the village and church and also retired people such as teachers, government servants and Gaon Buras. There are 11 board members in the **Baptist church Changki** (mother church) and 10 board members in the **Changki Yimlang Baptist church** (breakaway group). The main function of the Deacon board is to make the annual programme for the church as well as the annual plan, budget and projects. The Deacon board also selects the auditors from the public to conduct the half yearly and annual audits of the church. The Deacon board is also responsible for selecting the Christian Youth Endeavor (CYE) office bearers and the heads of the various departments under the church. In all the various committees a representative from the Deacon board is mandatory. The members of the Deacon board are prohibited from active participation in the general political processes. The nomination of full time workers such as **Engkum** (cooks for church visitors from outside and for feasts organized by the church) and **Ajakmapang** (collectors of the 10% Tithe paddy and the one's who dry the paddy and take to the rice mills for husking and so on) for the church is done by the Deacon board.

Christian Youth Endeavor (CYE.)

The Changki CYE began in 1911 under the name Christian Endeavor (C.E) but discontinued in 1916. It was started again in 1921 with affiliation to Ao Baptist Arogo Mungdang (ABAM), the apex body of the Ao churches. Initially the youth services were held twice a month which was increased to a weekly basis in 1925. In 1932 the Senior Society of Changki Youth Endeavor was registered in the C. E Union of India, Burma (Myanmar) and Ceylon (Sri Lanka). The C.E. in 1934 had the senior and junior classes and in 1935 the Intermediate class was incorporated. The infant grade was also made a part of the C.E. in 1957. A compulsory enrolment of membership in the C.E. was enforced at a certain age group from 1959 in order to strengthen the Society. The office bearers and the executive committee were selected for a term of three years from 1961. The Sunday school came under the rules and regulations of the C.E. but in 1963, the Sunday school separated itself from the C.E. In 1969, the name C.E. was renamed Christian Youth Endeavor (CYE).

The various committees under the leadership of the youth director of the **Baptist Church Changki** (mother church) are as follows:

1. Executive committee
2. Programme committee
3. Look-out committee
4. Finance committee
5. Gospel committee
6. Good news committee
7. Music club
8. Sports committee
9. Beautification committee
10. Cross-road club
11. Cadet club
12. Crusader club

The main function of the CYE is to provide a forum for the youths to develop christian spirituality and their talents – be it singing, music, preaching or leadership qualities and so on. The CYE has a president, vice president and general secretary, CYE assistant general secretary and CYE treasurer. The CYE executive board members comprises of the following members:

1.	Youth director	–	Board chairman
2.	CYE officers	–	4 members
3.	Deacon board	–	1 member
4.	Main church	–	1 member
5.	CYE congregation	–	1 member
6.	Christian education director		
7.	CYE Treasurer	–	ex-officio member
8.	CYE advisor		

The Cadet club is comprised of students from Class IV – VII with a Squadron Leader heading it. The Cross Road club comprises of students from VII – IX with a leader called Banneret. The Crusader club comprises of class X students as well as college students with a chaplain as its leader. These various clubs have their own activities and are assigned tasks especially during special programmes organized by the CYE, the main church or the women's department.

The CYE functions independently of the main church but is subject to its approval and ratification. The main source of income for its various programmes and activities is from the main church. Other funds are raised through music concerts, sale of handicrafts made by the members, labour – that is, sometimes the members hire themselves out for doing work on a daily wage basis, service offerings, donations, entertainments, and projects. The CYE conducts weekly services from 3:30 pm to 4:30 pm on Sundays. The CYE generally organizes and conducts its programmes and activities as per the directives of the ABAM.

In 1947 when there was split in the church, the **Changki Yimlang Baptist church** (breakaway group) started its own CYE wing and the first CYE President was Nokchameri. The CYE has a president, vice president and general secretary, CYE assistant general secretary and CYE treasurer. The CYE executive board members comprises of the following members:

1.	Youth director	–	Board chairman
2.	CYE officers	–	2 members
3.	Deacon board	–	1 member
4.	church members	–	1 member
5.	CYE members	–	1 member
6.	CYE treasurer	–	ex-officio member

As the CYE members less than 100 students in number in this church, the various clubs such as the Cadet club, the Cross Road club and Crusader club function not according to the class or age of the students but are clubbed together for various programmes. The main activity of the CYE is social work through which they raise funds as well as do charity works.

The Women's Department

The women's department of the **Baptist church Changki** (mother church) began in 1905 under the leadership of Mrs. Rongsentola, wife of Odangba, the first pastor. She was given a pay of 8 annas (.50p) and had two treasurers and four other colleagues to assist her. The function of the women's department was to educate the women and to teach the gospel to them. The following are the women who served as leaders of the women's department.

1.	Rongsentola.	1905 – 1915
2.	Moasangla	1916 –1918
3.	Chenlinokchala	1919 - 1920
4.	Bendangsangla	1920 –1930
5.	Jongpongrepla & Aliangchetla	1931 - 1932
6.	Mesajenla	1932 - 1942
7.	Tiangsen	1942 – 1952
8.	Mariam	1953 – 1963
9.	Talisüjala	1964 – 1979
10.	Imtisangla	1980 - 1989
11.	B. Temsula	1990 – till date.

The main function of the women department is to look after the spiritual needs as well as fellowship and welfare of the women folk. The department conducts training, seminars and so on with the approval of the main church. Bible studies are also conducted regularly. The women department carries out charity work for the poor and needy through home visitations and by giving aid either in cash, prayer or kind. The department conducts worship service every Thursday from 5:30 am – 6:30 am.

The women department is headed by a woman leader also called the associate pastor (woman) and is comprised of a secretary, two key holders and 23 women elders. The women department is an independent department and it generates its own income for the upkeep of the department and the salaries of the workers. However the approval of the main church is required for any programmes that the women department undertakes.

The sources of income for the department are as follows:

1. Women service offering
2. Dedication of new born children thanksgiving offering
3. Pottery offerings
4. General thanksgiving offerings
5. Donations
6. Wages – 2 days wages of every woman is collected twice yearly @ Rs. 65
7. Poultry thanksgiving
8. Handful of rice (for every meal) is collected by each household for weekly donation to the department
9. Mother's day service offerings from the main church service are given to the department.
10. Some women give their tithe (10% of their monthly earnings) to the women department.

The associate pastor (women) or the women leader gets a monthly salary of Rs. 3535. The secretary gets a monthly salary of Rs. 1933. The women elders get a yearly lump sum of Rs. 600 while the key holders and treasurer get a yearly lump sum of Rs. 700.

The **Changki Yimlang Baptist Church** (breakaway group) women's department began functioning in 1948 with Aluenla as the first women leader. The following are the women who served as women leaders:

1.	Aluenla	1948 - 1958
2.	Benrongsangla	1960 – 1961
3.	Tekayangla	1962 – 1965
4.	Tekanochetla	1965 – 1970
5.	Temjensangla	1971 – 1982
6.	Merenkala	1982 – 1983
7.	Medemnokchala	1984 – 1997
8.	Imlila Amri	1998 – till date

This department is independent of the main church and it raises funds and generates income for the upkeep and salaries of the workers through activities such as the following:

1. Sale of bamboos
2. Sale of firewood
3. Collection of rice from each household
4. Charity box in each household
5. New born child dedication thanksgiving offerings
6. Chicken/vegetable thanksgiving
7. Donations
8. Household membership fees

The department conducts weekly devotional services every Thursday from 6 am – 7am. Every Tuesday a fellowship service of the women elders are held. The women department is headed by a women leader also called the associate Pastor (Woman) and is comprised of a secretary, two key holders and 15 women elders. The associate pastor is paid a salary of Rs. 3983 per month, the secretary Rs. 1000 while the key holders and women elders are paid a lump sum of Rs. 500 annually.

The Child Department

The **Baptist Church Changki** (mother church) Child Evangelism department was started in 1967 under the tenure of Rev. Ajangto who was then the pastor of the church. Mrs. Imtinekenla and Mrs. Imtikala were the one's who initiated and led this department. The child department was looked after by the women's department, however in 1975, the child department was handed over to the main church by the women's wepartment and in 1986, a full time child director was appointed. In 1987, the child department became a separate unit under the guidance of the church.

The child department as of now is headed by Miss. Temjenlila (B.Th), child director, and the children who are taught the Bible, songs, musical instruments and so on are divided into three groups. The children from class A to class VIII are divided accordingly:

Class A – B – Inok House

Class I - 2 – Abel House

Class 3 – 8 – Cain House

The child department conducts weekly Sunday services from 11 am – 12 pm, while the Bible study is conducted every Wednesday. At present there are 200 children registered in the child department. Many extra-curricular activities such as guitar lessons, visitations to other villages, children rallies, retreats, camps and so on are being carried out. They also do social work by giving special treats to the poor and needy such as cakes, clothes and so on during Christmas and Easter and so on. The only source of income for this department is from well-wishers in the form of offerings and donations but other requirements for various activities are given by the main church if it is approved by the deacon board. The annual report is given to the main church along with the financial statement and budget for the coming year.

The child department board members are:

1. Child director – chairman
2. Church members – 2
3. Associate pastor, (women)
4. Women department members – 1
5. Music director

6. Deacon board – 1
7. Sunday school secretary
8. Pastor – ex-officio

The **Changki Yimlang Baptist Church** (breakaway group) child department and Sunday school is headed by the child director, with a Sunday school superintendent to assist. As the children are less in number the activities of both the departments are combined in this congregation. The Sunday school has classes from beginner to intermediate, which follows the syllabi set by the ABAM, Impur centre. Final examinations are conducted every year and the marks sent to ABAM, Impur centre and the students awarded merit certificates according to their marks.

The board members are as follows:

1. Child director – chairman
2. Sunday school teachers – 2
3. Deacon board representative – 1
4. church members – 1
5. Youth director
6. Women leader
7. Sunday school superintendent

In addition to the Sunday school for children, an adult Sunday school is also conducted every Sunday, where Bible studies and commentaries on spiritual matters are discussed. The adult Sunday school is from 1 pm – 2 pm and approximately 30 – 40 adults attend the classes.

The Sunday school

The **Baptist Church Changki** (mother church) also conducts Sunday school for children separately. The exact date and year of the establishment of the Sunday school is not known but it has been a part of the church's programme for a long time. The department is under the Christian education director but presently, the child director heads it. The classes are being taught by school teachers on a voluntary basis. There are at present four classes:

1. Beginner – classes A, B, I, (four sections)
2. Primary – classes II, IV (five sections)
3. Junior – classes V, VI, VII (three sections)
4. Intermediate – classes VIII, IX, X (three sections)

The curriculum for the Sunday school is set by ABAM (Ao Baptist Arogo Mungdang) the apex body of all the churches in the Ao area and every year examinations are held and the marks sent to the ABAM Centre, Impur. The children are awarded merit certificates depending on their marks. The Sunday school is also looked after by the child director. Five teachers also help in teaching the Sunday school classes on a voluntary basis but the church gives them Rs.300/- as 'bonus' every month.

The board members of the Sunday school are:

1. Child director – chairman
2. Sunday school teachers – 1
3. church members – 1
4. Pastor ex- officio
5. Sunday school secretary
6. Deacon board – 1

Mission Board

The Mission board of the **Baptist Church Changki** (mother church) was established in 1978 to oversee the missionary activities of the church such as sponsoring of pastors, missionaries, evangelists and youth workers to various fields and also to sponsor teachers and headmasters. The pastor is the ex-officio chairman of the board. A general secretary, assistant secretary and a treasurer is chosen from among the board members. There are at present 18 members. The missionary work of the **Baptist Church Changki** is carried out from income of different sources such as:-

1. One rented house at Dimapur
2. Interests earned from bank deposits
3. Collection from devotional services
4. Collection from the observance of the annual Missionary Day
5. Donations from individuals, clans, societies and so on

The main function of the Mission board is to chalk out the annual plans and activities for the church as well as to draft rules and regulations for those in the mission filed, with due approval from the Deacon board.

The Mission board members are:

1.	Associate pastor	–	chairman
2.	Deacon board representative	–	1
3.	General congregation members	–	8
4.	Women department representatives	–	4
5.	Missionary	–	1
6.	Pastor	–	ex- officio
7.	Christian education director/ child director		
8.	Associate pastor (women)		

The **Changki Yimlang Baptist Church** (breakaway group) Mission board was established in 1988 and its main function is to oversee all the mission works that the church undertakes such as sending missionaries to the field. The board is responsible for collecting donations for such works.

The board members are the following:

1. Pastor – chairman
2. Deacon board representative – 1
3. Church members – 6
4. Women leader
5. Youth director
6. Child director

Evangelist committee

Both the churches have this committee and the main function of this committee is to visit the elderly, weak and sick people who cannot attend church to give them prayer support on behalf of the church. They also distribute paddy to the poor and aged who have no one to look after them. The Deacon board assesses the paddy revenue of the church and accordingly allots 10 – 15 tins of paddy annually for the poor and aged. They also visit other villages on preaching tours, representing the church in the outreach missionary tasks. All expenditure of this committee is borne by the church.

Theological Scholarship Committee

The **Baptist Church Changki** (mother church) has also instituted a Theological scholarship committee. There are five members in this committee with the pastor as the ex-officio member. This committee is responsible for helping those students who want to pursue higher studies in Theology by helping them find placements in the Senate of Serampore, the premier institute for Theology in India. Once the church recommends a student for B.D. a recommendation fee of Rs. 1000/- is given by the church. Those wanting to pursue post graduate degree (M.Th), the church will sponsor the deserving candidate. For instance, this year, the pastor is being sponsored by the church for M.Th degree in Bangalore, by giving study leave with full pay.

Mission School

The Mission School is run by the **Baptist Church Changki** (mother church) and celebrated its 100th year in 2001. The Mission School board comprises of the following:

1. Deacon board representatives – 2
2. Church members – 8
3. Headmaster ex-officio secretary
4. Pastor ex-officio
5. School teacher representative – 1

The board recommends and selects the headmaster/ headmistress and teachers and fixes the school fees and so on. The board also makes the plans and budget for the school year. All decisions are taken after 2/3 (two/third) majority votes of the board. The church controls all the financial and administrative function of the school.

Role of the Church in Changki

The rules and regulations of both the churches in Changki are very explicit and it is very strictly implemented and followed. It is only after Baptism that an individual becomes a full fledged church member with the name entered in the church registry. However as the organization, function and activities of the church shows, it is from a very young age that training and inculcation of the Christian tenets are imparted. From Bible studies beginning in the Sunday school to the CYE activities, the children and youth are trained and kept busy. It is mandatory that the children be enrolled in the Sunday school and CYE.

Attendance of the adults in the weekly Sunday church service is also considered important but more than that the giving of Tithe, that is, the 10% of one's earnings, is deemed to be most important. The philosophy of the villagers being "give unto god what is god's" is followed diligently. Anyone growing vegetables, poultry, pigs and who sell these give 10% of their profit, or if they have a surplus but do not sell, they will give as Thanksgiving a sum that they surmise to be equivalent to 10% of their produce. It may be noted that when the villagers give Thanksgiving contributions/donations of poultry, pigs or other produce, it is always in cash. It is only paddy that is accepted by the church as Tithe. The church is dependent on the tithe and the donations or thanksgiving for its maintenance and upkeep. The salaries and miscellaneous expenditure is drawn from these sources. The membership fees paid to the apex church body the Ao Baptist Arogo Mungdang is also from these sources. The church also organizes fund raising events and functions from time to time.

The church exercises control over its congregation by the rules and regulations laid down which also covers the personal life, lifestyle and behaviour of the individual. Anyone found guilty of promiscuity and causing public disturbance and bringing shame to the village are excommunicated from the church. Anyone caught stealing and being fined for "*Aomet*" (customary fine for stealing) of Rs.500/- and above are also excommunicated from the church. If a married person commits adultery, he/she is also liable to be excommunicated from the church, apart from being fined three pigs by the Village Council. There is also a rule that if an individual wants to marry someone who is not a Baptist Christian and if that person does not convert, the church will not only permit the couple to be married in the church, the individual who marries outside of the denomination/religion is also excommunicated from the church. In case of a divorce the one who is found to be guilty and responsible for the break up of the marriage is excommunicated from the church.

If a young girl has a child out of wedlock she and her partner are excommunicated from the church too. If the couple decides to marry they will not be able to marry in church. The pastor will bless them at home and declare them married. When a person gets excommunicated from the church, the person's name and the reason for the excommunication is announced in the Sunday weekly service to the congregation and the name is struck off the register. However, even if a person is excommunicated, he/she is not barred from attending the Sunday weekly services or other activities in the different departments. After a lapse of time, the minimum being three months, a person may ask pardon from the Deacon board and will be readmitted to the church as a regular member and the name re-entered in the church register.

In this way the lives of the people are controlled and regulated by the church. Excommunication is regarded as the maximum punishment that can be meted out to a person for wrongdoing. A person's social standing and role in society is tainted forever if he/she has been excommunicated from the church for any reason. The role of the church is more powerful in the village than in other urban towns as the community is smaller and more compact.

Impact of Christianity

The introduction of Christianity beginning in 1901 and in its wake, education, has played a major role in bringing about change among the Changki villagers. Along with the new religion, education was also accepted as beneficial for the people. Thus began an era where the old gave way to the new.

The establishment of schools opened new opportunities and changed the worldview of the people. Through education and opportunities presented in the form of employment outside the village many luminaries from Changki village emerged who were pioneers in various fields. Due to economic compulsions, the Changki people left the village and settled in other places and although links with the village were maintained in the beginning through relatives and due to ownership of home sites and rice fields, these linkages began to weaken with the passage of time. We find that some of the people who have settled outside have no association with the village at all.

Mills (1926) writing about the Ao tribe in general stated that the non- Christian Ao thought and worked for the welfare of his village and hated to live away from it. But with the conversion to Christianity there came about changes for "though the Christian still retains some of the love for his village and willingness to serve it, the feeling is undoubtedly less strong in him. Christians are often quite willing to live elsewhere than in their villages, and converts frequently refuse to take any part in its government. Attempts are often made to avoid little acts of social service on the most trivial excuses."(ibid:419) He observed that the personal convenience of the Christian was put above the common sentiments of their neighbours. He went to say that "in matters where their religion is concerned christians will work well together, but in secular matters they are inclined to rate the welfare of the individual far above that of the body politic, and if the process continues their villages will become mere collections of houses instead of highly-organised social units in which every man shoulders the burden of service and responsibility."(ibid:420)

Although Mills' observations on Christianity and conversion to the new religion and the changes brought about by it was on the whole Ao tribe in general, we find that such observations are also pertinent to Changki village. Christians brought in its wake a weakening of the strong bonds of community living and cooperation. Individualism and self interest began to assert itself and this can be seen in the fact that due to certain individuals' interests outside of the christian mould, a second church was established in 1947 thereby causing a rift among the congregation and villagers, particularly that of the lower khel as the breakaway church was established by some of the lower khel people.

With the advent of Christianity and education was also introduced changes in lifestyles and habits were also introduced. Smith (*op.cit.*:199) observed that such changes were "especially noticeable in the village of Changki, which has the largest number of better Christians, has better houses, is cleaner than other villages, and the people themselves are much cleaner than in many of the other villages."

As explained in Chapter II the Ao tribe comprises of three linguistic groups, Chungli, Mongsen and Changki. With the advent of Christianity and education in its wake, the Chungli language was adopted as the common language for all Ao people for the simple reason that the first missionaries lived in a Chungli speaking village and in the ensuing years the Bible was translated into Chungli and the first Ao primer was written in Chungli. All school work and religious work began to be carried out in Chungli. Smith observed that "the reduction of the language to writing is tending to unite the whole tribe."(ibid:199).

Through conversion to Christianity and education, the Changki people took up the Chungli language as the medium for school work and religious work and in such ways the people could make much headway for now communication were easier with the common language.

Changes also began to be brought about in material equipment such as fire-arms and metal cooking utensils, clothing and food habits. However such changes also led to the erosion of the traditional arts such as pottery, weaving of different cloths and with the introduction of fire-arms, random hunting led to extensive depletion of the wild life leading to environmental degradation.

The ban on the *Arju* (morung) dormitories and the loss of its significance in the lives of the people led to the deterioration of a powerful disciplinary agency. The social control exercised through the *Arju* and the concept of community participation began to be dissipated. With the new religion, the people rejected the traditional festivals and ceremonies and other cultural traits such as the oral tradition which was only means of recording history, legends and folklore and so on of the people.

The *Arju* or male dormitory system was abolished along with all aspects of the indigenous religion, even to the extent of giving up the *Moatsu* and *Tsüngremong* festivals, which are the two main festivals of the Ao. In fact none of the Changki villagers can recall any stories about the ancient religion. The people rejected all traditional customs and beliefs and wholeheartedly embraced the new religion. Superstitious beliefs and taboos were also weakened if not rejected. In thi way, we find that in Changki, the traditional aspects of the society such as indigenous festivals, dances and singing are absent.

At the empirical level a cross section of people have expressed the view that such total rejection of the traditions and customs has been a loss and the people feel a sense of something vital and vibrant missing. The other Ao villages also make jibes at the Changki people for not having any 'culture' which cannot be denied for much of the rich cultural legacy in the form of dance, songs, oral tradition, festivals, games and so on has been lost.

Although Christianity has been accepted and the population of the village comprises of only Baptist Christians, we also find that divisions have been formed, for in the village there are two parallel churches of the same denomination. The unity and solidarity of the village has been affected by this division for the loyalty of the people extends to their church only. For example, the members of the particular church will work for and consider as important only the church that they belong to. The year 2005 will commemorate the Centennial jubilee celebration of the women's department wing of the church but we find that in this too, the people belonging to the breakaway church have decided not to participate in the celebrations.

Some members of both the churches have made the effort to unite the two churches but so far this has not borne any results. The people are generally of the opinion that having two churches of the same denomination within a village diminishes the unity of the village but most people were careful about what they said and often told this researcher that some things are best left alone. As mentioned before, Changki has the dubious distinction of having two churches of the same denomination.

At the empirical level the older generations expressed disappointment that the younger people do not participate in the church activities as much as they did. The younger generation, on the other hand, were more cynical and said that the traditional mind set and the rigid ways of conducting the affairs of the church is something they cannot agree to but cannot voice out their opinions because it would mean censure of the worst kind.

Earlier in this chapter it was mentioned that the church had initiated 'Rooms' or separate dormitories for boys and girls where they learned the Scriptures, songs and christian tenets and also slept there. The rooms became defunct and its absence in the lives of the villagers is felt to be a general loss especially by the older generation. Those who had attended the 'Room' were of the opinion that it was through this 'Room' system that they learned the skills of praying, preaching and singing; discipline was strictly enforced and in this way social control was exercised.

The church in Changki may not be as strong as it was earlier on but it still plays an important role in the lives of the people. Its role as an agency of social control is evidently very important for any wrong doing committed against the rules and regulations of the church results in excommunication which is regarded as the ultimate social disgrace that can befall on anyone.

The church is also male dominated where the Deacon board composed of only males' exercise control over the functioning of the church. The patrilineal and patriarchal pattern of the society is reflected in the functioning of the church. This is also seen most visibly when women who belong to the mother church marry a man from the breakaway church or vice versa. In such cases the women switch membership to the church where their husbands have membership. There are no instances where the husband and wife belong to different congregations. We find that 43 women from the Baptist church Changki have been transferred to the Changki Yimlang Baptist church and 44 women from the Changki Yimlang church have been transferred to the Baptist church Changki.

The women's department in both the churches is under the control of the Deacon board and although the department can raise funds meant exclusively for programmes meant for women, the department requires the permission of the respective Deacon board to carry out any activities and is under the overall control of the main church. We find that the role that the church plays is still an important one for apart from membership to a clan church membership is also a vital factor in the lives of the people.

7

CONCLUSION

This study has been concerned very broadly with the Changki society and village life. In this work a sociological study of Changki located in Mokokchung district under the sub-division of Mangkolemba circle in Nagaland has been undertaken. The preceding five chapters discuss the various aspects of the village. The first chapter introduces the concept of 'village' as found in various literatures as well as in the census of India. The village as understood in the Naga context has also been dealt with. The second chapter describes the people and the setting of Nagaland in general, with particular reference to the Ao tribe and finally a detailed description of Changki village as well as the demographic characteristics of its population. The other four chapters discuss the various institutions – kinship and marriage; political institution; the economic institution and religious institution of Changki village.

In the present study of Changki we find that all the households are perched on the ridge of a hill and the agricultural lands are located far away in the surrounding hills and in the valley below the village. Changki village could be termed a nucleated village. The location of the houses in the village does not indicate any hierarchical order or social distance between different households or clans. Changki is a single tribe, multi clan village consisting of 422 households with a population of 1673, with almost an equal number of males and females. Although the people are engaged in various occupations, agriculture is the main occupation. Most of the people are literate and the village has four Primary schools and two High schools. However those who can afford, send their children out of the village for education in the towns within Nagaland or even outside of the state.

In Changki we find that the village is divided into two khels, *Süngdakba* commonly referred to as *luko* (upper) and *Ayim Anet* commonly known as *lulang* (lower) khel. Each khel is a separate entity with its own social and political organisation. Each khel has a *Samen Menchen* (village government) with its own rules and regulations and the people themselves clearly distinguish themselves as either belonging to the upper or lower khel. It is interesting to note that there is no hierarchical order or social distance between the households but there is differentiation on the basis of khel. The clans are also distinguished between the Mongsen and Chungli group. The founding clans and others who settled in the village later on belong to the Mongsen group while the last major group of settlers made up of five clans belongs to the Chungli group. This last group had come with a recognised village government (*Yimten*) and as such was allowed to settle in an area which came to be known as the Tsungli *kiong* in the lower khel.

Changki people are part of the Ao Naga society which follow the unilineal principle of patrilineal descent and are divided into large exogamous units which in Changki dialect is called kin (clans). There are three founding clans who enjoy certain rights and privileges and despite the assertions that all people in the village are equal the hierarchical ranking of the founding clans from the rest belie this. Land ownership is the main factor that differentiates the founding clan from the others. The people themselves call the founding clans *Kin Asem*, literally meaning 'the three clans' and the others

Kin Tebencha, meaning 'the rest of the clans'. Altogether there are thirteen clans in the village. Changki people follow the neolocal pattern of residence for when a couple gets married they have to set up their own independent household. It is considered a shame for a man to bring his wife and live with the parents after marriage.

The traditional political institutions is organised along two principles: firstly the village is divided into age-set grades which is mandatory for all males from the age of sixteen and secondly the control of the village affairs lies with the Village Council. The customary laws are the basis upon which the village is administered and the means of social control and maintaining law and order is by imposing 'fines'. All decision-making processes are carried out in the traditional manner which entail discussions and debates through which consensus is arrived at and matters settled amicably.

The Village Council composed of both the traditional '*Samen Menchen*' and the *Gaon Bura* look after the law and order, administration of justice, settlement of disputes, general welfare of the villagers, developmental schemes of the village and so on. The village as well as the various Changki unions outside the village affiliated to the *Senso Mungdang* or Changki general body comprising of all Changki males, wherever they may be residing, have been severely affected by claims of the Emrem Changki as the original clan over the Changkiri clan. The Mokokchung Changki Union Vs Changki *Yimten* case highlighted in chapter 4, shows how this rivalry has affected not only the village but also all other Changki unions found in other parts of Nagaland. The modern electoral process that was introduced with the formation of the state of Nagaland in 1963 has also brought about a new dimension to the polity of the village. Changki is part of the 29 Jangpetkong Constituency of Mokokchung district. This constituency comprises the villages of Changki, Chungliyimsen, Khar, Mongchen, Dibuai, Waromong and includes Alongkima, which is the area's administrative sub centre, Mangkolemba, the district sub-divisional centre and Longnak and Merakiong polling stations. In the electoral processes of party politics we find that divisions have been formed along party lines in the village with the founding clans deciding to support the regional party Nagaland People's Front (NPF) in the last election in 2001 and closing ranks against the Congress party. The village is divided into the regional party and the Congress party and this division is heightened during elections.

The economy of the village is based on the agricultural practice of wet rice cultivation and although there are many new occupations being practiced by the people, agriculture continue to be the mainstay of the village. Thus the village economy could be classified as agrarian as almost all the households were engaged in agricultural activities. Presently we find that the people have also taken to horticultural activities such as pineapple and orange cultivation as well as tea plantations. Arecanut plantation is also another economic activity taken up by the people. We find that the market forces and competition is making the people more individualistic where self interest and economic gains takes precedence over community life and participation. We find that a class structure is emerging in the village and conspicuous consumption is becoming the norm.

All the people of Changki are Christians belonging to the Baptist denomination. Christianity was introduced in the village in 1901 and with Christianity, education was also initiated. The introduction of education brought about immense changes for the villagers because through education new opportunities were opened and many of the Changki people went on to become pioneers in various fields. Although Christianity brought about positive changes; it also led to the loss of many cultural traits for with the advent of Christianity, Changki people gave up many of their festivals, rites, oral traditions and even songs and dances. The ancient religious beliefs and rituals have long been forgotten as the people rejected the traditional belief system as heathen practises. However certain traditional values have been adapted and incorporated into the Christian rites especially during weddings and funeral services.

Although the various institutions play important roles in the lives of the people of Changki, it is the clan membership which defines the identity and position of the members in the society. The family is considered as the smallest unit of the clan and the clan influences to a large extent the working of the various institutions especially that of the political institution.

The predominant theme of discord and dissension affecting all spheres of village life in Changki is the claim of the Emrem Changki clan as the original founding clan. Kinship ties and the network of relationships are established through marriage alliances and the web of social relations within the village is such that it is said that invariably each and every Changki person is related to each other in one way or the other. In this set-up we find that due to the clan rivalry, there are deep divisions within the village along clan lines that has affected the network of relationships.

The on-going rivalry is one that began almost eighty years ago, and through the decades the social, political and religious realms in the village has been affected to such an extent that this has pervaded the mind-set of the people and influences all aspects of the people's lives, especially in the lower khel.

The inter-clan dispute has divided the people and the solidarity of the village has been polarized along three aspects:

1. Clan
2. Church
3. Party politics

The divisions along these three aspects have created conflicts primarily between the two warring affecting their relationships with other clans. It has indirectly led to the split of the church and the congregation, further aggravating the situation and lastly it has entered the state electoral process of party politics contributing to the feud not only along clan lines but also party lines.

Although village life has been disrupted several times over the inter-clan rivalry, we also find that it has reinforced clan consciousness. The three founding clans, Longchari, Amri and Changkiri, have united and formed a front called the *Emkümri Kin Asem* thus asserting their hierarchical position in the village and the privilege that being the founding clan accords to them. Despite the inter and intra-clan rivalry we find that the clans do not become disorganised or break up easily because of the highly integrative character of the kinship system, which help to restrain and resolve conflicts between members of the same clan; as well as the importance that the people attach to the value of clan solidarity and the traditionally accepted authority of the clan elders. The founding clans of Changki village do not have the obvious trappings of power nor are they treated any differently by the others. But in subtle ways they are accorded deference and respect by the rest of the clans. This is most evident in the manner in which land is used in the village. Most of the land holdings belong to the founding clans; therefore if anyone wants to use the land or take out its produce, it is mandatory that they seek permission from the land owners. In matters of village affairs the founding clans are consulted and their decision sought. With regard to the village history and migration patterns, the founding clans have recorded the stories handed down through the oral tradition and it is only with their express permission that the same can be used. Even in the Village Council we find that it is the founding clans who dominate for the Village Council chairman has always been from one of these clans. The others who have occupied this seat belong to the Alingri clan and from the historical accounts of the village we find that this clan arrived at the village just a few days after the founding clans, therefore by virtue of their early arrival they are accorded the position as being next to the founding clans in the hierarchical order. We find that this traditional aspect of the village is very much adhered to and the concept of 'founding clan' is clearly ingrained in the psyche of the people.

Education has played a key role in ushering in changes and opportunities in the village. The importance that the Changki people attach to education can be observed in the number of schools that is found in the village (four government primary schools, one government high school and one private high school) and the strict vigilance that the Village Council keeps in monitoring the teachers and functioning of the schools. As education opened up new opportunities for employment and so on, the educated Changki people left the village to settle in other urban places. The rising aspirations and expectations of the people in the village were fuelled by the obvious trappings of 'modernity' that employment especially in the public sector could bring about. Thus the people in the village began sending their children to study outside in various towns of Nagaland and for those who could afford, outside the state. On one hand this has resulted in the placement of some of the educated youths in prestigious and respectable positions in government offices. But on the other hand it has led to rising frustration among the majority of the youth who cannot find employment and since they have been out of the village since childhood find the village too restricted and uninteresting. They also do not have the inclination to become cultivators, nor can they settle outside and it is this section of the educated, unskilled and unemployed youth who are causing concern for they are increasingly resorting to alcohol and drug abuse, petty theft to support the habit and creating trouble for the family, relatives and villagers in general.

Some of the educated unemployed youths have also joined the underground groups of Nagaland such as NSCN (IM) and NSCN (K) and so on. Although the Village Council exercises authority over the affairs of the village and acts on behalf of the people, the traditional authority mechanism is seemingly helpless with regard to the activities of the underground groups. The extortion of 24 per cent of pay from all government employees annually and house taxes levied on all by the underground groups continue to burden the people. In such ways we find that the power of the traditional authority is being undermined. The electoral process of party politics is another factor that has changed the equation of power and influence. The party politics has brought about disorganization of the traditional forms and brought about new re-alignments. This is most evident in the rivalry of the two clans in the lower khel spilling over into the modern political arena of party politics. The kinship networks and relationships has been decidedly influenced and disturbed by this rivalry and the ensuing conflict.

Changes in the material aspects of village life are evident and the outlook, aspirations and expectations of the villagers especially that of the younger generation is vastly different from that of their parents. However inspite of the changes in the lifestyle and entrepreneurial spirit of individualism overtaking the community sense of participation and living, we find that the institutional and organizational structure of the village is still based on tradition and customary usage. The clan system, age-set grades, the *Samen Menchen* (village government), *Senso* (Changki general assembly) and the linkages of the people living outside the village through the various Changki Unions established in urban areas are some aspects that still continue to be important and relevant for the people for it figure as the major focus of their collective identity. These traditional institutions are accepted and viewed as the cultural symbols that give a distinct identity to Changki people. All these indicate that the village as an entity is held as sacrosanct for it is only through the membership to the village that people get an identity and from this point of reference the cultural roots of an individual is derived.

In conclusion we may say that Changki village is a traditional village where the continuity of traditions is found in its institutions and social organisations. However the forces of change being brought in through the mass media, economic opportunities, government intervention in agro-based activities and by the people themselves who are educated, mobile and exposed to outside influences are gradually changing the lifestyle. The accelerated rate of development and the processes of change may be transforming the village but the pattern of change is adaptive in nature where most of the traditional institutions are retained. This is most evident in the general characteristics of concrete social relations and patterns of behaviour as well as in the customs practiced by the people of Changki village.

BIBLIOGRAPHY

Alemchiba, M. 1970. *A Brief Historical Account of Nagaland.* Kohima: Naga Institute of Culture.

Allen, B.C., Gait, E.A., C.G.H., Howard, H.F. 1979 (reprint). N. Delhi: *Gazeteer of Bengal and Northeast India.* Mittal Publications,

Ao, Tajen. 1980. *Ao Customary laws.* Jorhat: Annade Printing House.

Ao, Temsula. 2000. *The Ao-Naga Oral tradition.* Baroda: Bhasha Publications.

Aonok, Ajangto. 1953. *Changki Baptist Arogo Kum Tenem Otzü.* Mokokchung: Changki Arogo.

Baden-Powell, B. H. 1972 (reprint). *The Indian Village Community.* New Delhi: Cosmo Publications.

Bailey, F. G. 1957. *Caste and the Economic Frontier – A village in highland Orissa.* Manchester: Manchester University Press.

Beattie, John. 1966. *Other Cultures Aims, Methods and Achievements in Social Anthropology.* London: Routledge and Keagan Paul.

Beattie, J.H.M. & Lienhardt, R.G. 1975. *Studies in Social Anthropology – Essays in Memory of E.E. Evans-Pritchard by his former colleagues.* London: Oxford University Press.

Beteille, Andre. 1996. *Caste, Class and Power.* New Delhi: Oxford University Press.

Bhowmik, K. L. 1971. *Tribal India A profile in Indian Ethnology*. Delhi: World Press Private Ltd.

Burling, Robbins. 1963. *Rengsanggri Family and Kinship in a Garo Village*. Philadelphia: University of Pennsylvania Press.

Chacko, Pariyaram, M. 2005. *Tribal Communities and Change*. New Delhi: Sage Publications.

Clark, M. M. 1907. *A Corner in India*. Philadelphia: American Baptist Publication Society.

Dasgupta, Biplab. 1978. *Village Studies in the Third World*. Delhi: Hindustan Publishing Corporation (India).

Das, N. K. 1993. *Kinship Politics and law in Naga Society*.Calcutta. Director, Anthropological Survey of India.

Desai, A. R. 1961. *Rural Sociology in India*. Bombay: Popular Prakashan.

Dube, S. C. 1967. *Indian Village*. Bombay: Allied publishers Private Limited.

Eisenstadt, S. N. 1973. *Tradition, Change and Society*. New York: John Wiley & Sons.

Elwin, Verrier. 1961. *Nagaland*. Shillong: P. Dutta for the Research Department, Advisor's Secretariat.

__________ 1969. *The Nagas in the Nineteenth Century*. London: Oxford University Press.

Evans-Pritchard, E. E. 1951. *Kinship and Marriage among the Nuer*. London: Oxford University Press.

__________ 1978 (reprint). *The Nuer – A Description of the Modes of Livelihood and Political Institutions of a Nilotic People*. New York: Oxford University Press.

Fox, Robin. 1967. *Kinship and Marriage*. Harmondsworth: Penguin Books.

Fürer- Haimendorf, C.von. 1939. *The Naked Nagas*. London: Methuen & Co. Ltd.

____________ 1976. *Return to the Naked Nagas*. New Delhi: Vikas Publishing House Pvt Ltd.

Ganguli, Milada. 1984. *A Pilgrimage to the Nagas*. New Delhi: Oxford and IBH Publishing Co.

Ghosh, B.B. 1979. *Mokokchung District Gazetteer*. Kohima: Government of Nagaland.

Graburn, Nelson. 1971. *Readings in Kinship and Social Structure*. New York: Harper & Row Publishers.

Halpern, Joel, M.. 1969. *The Changing Village Community*. New Delhi: Prentice-Hall of India private Limited.

Hockings, Paul. 1999. *Kindreds of the Earth Badaga household structure and demography*. New Delhi: Sage Publications.

Horam, M. 1975. *Naga Polity*. New Delhi: B. R. Publishing Company.

____________ 1988. *Nagas – Old Ways New Trends*. New Delhi: Cosmo Publications.

Hutton, J. H. 1968 (reprint). *The Sema Nagas*. London: Oxford University Press.

____________ 1969 (reprint). *The Angami Nagas*. London: Oxford University Press.

Imchen, Panger. 1993. *Ancient Ao Naga religion and Culture*. New Delhi: Har-Anand Publications.

Jamir, Talitemjen, N. 1997. *Ao – Naga Cultural Heritage*. Mokokchung: Published by the author.

Leach, E. R. 1971. *Pul Eliya A Village in Ceylon. A Study of Land Tenure and Kinship*. London: Cambridge University Press.

Lerner, Daniel. 1958. *The Passing of Traditional Society*. New York: The Free Press.

Lewis, Oscar. 1965. *Village Life in Northern India*. New York: Random House, Inc.

Mackenzie, A. 1981 (reprint). *The Northeast Frontier of India*. New Delhi: Mittal Publications.

Maine, Sir Henry Sumner. 1974 (reprint). *Village Communities in the East and West*. New York: Arno Press.

Mair, Lucy. 1972 (second edition). *An Introduction to Social Anthropology*. Oxford: Clarendon Press.

Mandelbaum, David, G. 1972. *Society in India i) Continuity and Change ii) Change and Continuity*. Bombay: Popular Prakashan.

Marriot M[c]kim (ed). 1967 (reprint). *Village India*. Chicago: The University of Chicago Press.

Mayer, Adrian, C. 1960. *Caste and Kinship in Central India*. London: Routledge and Keagan Paul.

Mills, J. P. 1922. Lhota Nagas. London: Macmillan & Co Ltd.

__________ 1926. *The Ao Nagas*. London: Macmillan & Co Ltd.

__________ 1937. *The Rengma Nagas*. London: Macmillan and Co Ltd.

Misra, K. K. 1987. *Social Structure and Change among the Ho of Orissa*. New Delhi: Gian Publication House.

Nongkynrih, A. K. 2002. *Khasi Society of Meghalaya. A Sociological Understanding*. Delhi: Indus Publishing Company.

O'Malley, L. S. S. 1975 (reprint). *India's Social Heritage*. London: Curzon Press Ltd.

Patel, M. F. 1990. *Indian Village from Entity to Non-Entity*. New Delhi: Kanak Publications.

Puthenpurakal, Dr. Joseph, 1984. *Baptist Mission in Nagaland*. Calcutta: Firma KLM Private Limited.

Radcliffe-Brown, A. R. 1952. *Structure and Function in Primitive Society*. Routledge & Kegan Paul, London.

Radcliffe-Brown, A. R. & Forde, Daryll (eds). 1950. *African Systems of Kinship and Marriage*. London: Oxford University Press.

Sanyu, Visier. 1996. *A History of Nagas and Nagaland (Dynamics of Oral Tradition in Village Formation)*. Delhi: Commonwealth Publishers.

Sema, Piketo. 1992. *British Policy and Administration in Nagaland 1881-1947*. Delhi: Scholar Publishing House.

Sharma, Surendra. 1985. *Sociology in India: A Perspective From Sociology of Knowledge*. Jaipur: Rawat Publications.

Shimray, R. R. 1985. *Origin and Culture of Nagas*. Delhi: Mrs. Pamleiphi Shimray.

Singh, K. S. (ed). 1993. *Tribal Ethnography Customary Law and Change*. New Delhi: Concept publishing House.

__________ (gen. ed). 1994. *People of India – Nagaland. Volumn XXXIV*. Calcutta: Seagull Books.

Singh, Yogendra. 1988 (reprint). *Modernization of Indian Tradition*. Jaipur: Rawat Publications.

__________ 1989 (reprint). *Essays on Modernization in India*. New delhi: Manohar Publications.

__________ 2000. *Culture Change in India Identity and Globalization*. Jaipur: Rawat Publications.

Smith, W. C. 1980 (reprint). *The Ao Naga Tribes of Assam*. New Delhi. Gian Publications.

Srinivas, M. N. 1952. *Religion and Society among the Coorgs in South India*. London: Oxford University press.

__________ (ed), 1969 (reprint). *India's Villages*. Bombay: Asia Publishing House.

__________ 1976. *The Remembered Village*. Bombay: Oxford University Press.

__________ 1987. *The Dominant caste and Other Essays.* New Delhi: Oxford University Press.

__________ 1996. *Village, Caste, Gender and Method. Essays in Indian Social Anthropology.* New Delhi: Oxford University Press.

Srivastava, S.C. 1972. *Indian Census in Perspective.* Delhi Office of the Registrar General India, Ministry of Home Affairs.

Webster, Neil. 1992. *Panchayati Raj and the Decentralisation of Development Planning in West Bengal.* K. P. Calcutta: Bagchi & Company.

Wiser, William, H. & Wiser, Charlotte Viall. 1971. *Behind Mud Walls 1930 – 1960 with a sequel: The Village in 1970.* Berkeley, L. A.: University of California Press.

Yang, C. K. 1959. *Chinese Communist Society: The Family and the Village.* Massachusetts: The M.I.T. Press.

Yonuo, Asoso. 1974. *The Rising Nagas.* New Delhi: Vivek Publishing House.

GLOSSARY

Aba	–	*Father*
Abazemba	–	*Older father*
Aben	–	*Fish trap*
Achem	–	*Block of wood like trough with two hollows dug out for threshing paddy*
Achep	–	*West*
Aiengkho	–	*Basket used while traveling*
Ajakmapang	–	*Those who collect and disburse paddy belonging to Church*
Ajem	–	*Large container made of bamboo for storing paddy*
Ajen	–	*East*
Aki rongba	–	*Burning of house*
Ako	–	*Maternal uncle*
Akhang	–	*Common name for baskets*
Akhi	–	*Conical shape basket used for carrying paddy*
Akum	–	*Interchangeably respect and shade*

Akut	–	*Bigger conical shaped basket used for storing clothes*
Ala Chela	–	*Community fishing*
Aliban Aling	–	*Footpath leading to rice field to the east (upper khel)*
Aling	–	*Bamboo strips used to tie things*
Alu Athi	–	*Temporary house for shelter as well as storing paddy in the rice field*
Ama rakba mapang	–	*Season for planting rice seedlings*
Amung	–	*Genna/taboo*
Ani	–	*Traditional wrap around skirt*
Annala	–	*Close female friends of different clans but same age-set grade*
Anuzai	–	*Younger mother*
Aodang	–	*Sacred place in ancient times (lower khel)*
Aomet	–	*Fine for stealing*
Aonglu ajak	–	*Indigenous jhum paddy*
Aoow	–	*Grandfather*
Aowphu	–	*Bowl made out of bamboo*
Aphak	–	*Mat made out of bamboo*
Asu	–	*Cloth*
Asü Yim/Diphu Yim	–	*Village of the dead*

Athepdang	–	*Main room in the Changki traditional houses*
Athi	–	*Granary*
Awalong	–	*Powerful charm used to obtain love, wealth etc*
Awasu	–	*Manners*
Awhani	–	*Changki traditional skirt*
Ayah	–	*Weed scraper made out of metal*
Ayaktsungba		
Ayim Asem Senso Mungdang	–	*Village general assembly*
Ayim Charu		*Village tax*
Ayim Chencha	–	*Village fine*
Ayim Anet Salang	–	*Two village community hall (lower khel)*
Azzumo	–	*Mother's elder sister*
Azzu	–	*Grandmother*
Chakupa	–	*Rectangular shaped bamboo mat used for winnowing*
Changpang Aling	–	*Footpath leading to rice field to the west (lower khel)*
Changyangru	–	*Flat circular sieve made out of bamboo*
Chanakri	–	*Brother-in-law/Son-in-law*
Charong	–	*Walking stick*
Chenja Jano	–	*Fined*

Chentsu Chumang	–	*Inheritance*
Chungli	–	*Ao dialect*
Dao	–	*Naga machete*
Dobashi	–	*Government agent/interpreter*
Emchachari	-	*Rulers*
Emjangkhet	–	*Village community work by age-set grades*
Emjenri	–	*Latecomers*
Emkumri	–	*Founding clans*
Emli	–	*System of governance*
Emlu	–	*Village community land*
Emphi waba	–	*To clear village footpath*
Emsen Kiong	–	*Sacred place in ancient times (upper khel)*
Engkum	–	*Church workers entrusted with catering for guests*
Enki Tsuba	–	*To bar entry into village territory*
Gaon Bura	–	*Village elder who works as government agent*
Genna	–	*Taboo*
Ho	–	*Of same age-set grade*
Ho Tsungtepba	–	*Progressive change in age-set grading*
i emli teraksa	–	*Don't break our system of governance*
Ingkho Mapang	–	*particular period set annually*

		during which villagers engage in earning activities
Jangkhet	–	*Worth of one's service*
Jakla Liru	–	*Character*
Jungphodemdem	–	*Supreme Being*
Khat	–	*Land grants given to Naga villages by the Ahom kings*
Kharo	–	*Suspended bamboo shelf over fire place*
Khel	–	*Division of village into sectors such as upper and lower khel*
Kenu	–	*Younger sibling*
Keti	–	*Kinship term to address same age-set grade friends*
Kidong	–	*Several branches of lineage*
Kieo	–	*Small room in traditional Changki house*
Kilamet	–	*Fine for adultery*
Kilang	–	*Traditional fish trap*
Kilangmi	–	*Open platform made out of bamboo*
Kima Akumbok	–	*Small verandah in front of traditional Changki house*
Kin	–	*Clan*
Kin Asem	–	*Three clans*
Kin Emba	–	*To adopt or be attached to a particular clan*

Kin Tebencha	–	*Rest of the clans*
Kiong	–	*Locality*
Kuba	–	*Term used to address good friends among males of same age-set grade of different clans*
Kubok Waba	–	*To go camping*
Kumbalani Endi	–	*Footpath leading to rice field to the west (lower khel)*
Kumnak	–	*Term used to address a man's sisters' and clanswomen's sons*
Kuriko	–	*Term used to address best friends among females*
Langpa	-	*Ladder*
Lanuri Telongjem	–	*Students union*
Liba Liru yimya	–	*Norms of social behaviour*
Lichaba	–	*Creator of God*
Likhu	–	*Bamboo mat with slightly upturned ends used for drying paddy*
Longritzü	–	*Lonely river*
Longtitsüngba	–	*Lord of Heaven*
Longzak	–	*Stone used for sharpening dao etc*
Lokti Liba	–	*Community living*
Luko	–	*Upper khel*
Lulang	–	*Lower khel*
Lumelen	–	*Land tax*

Lusa	–	*Territory*
Manukhi	–	*Huge conical shaped basket used carrying jhum paddy*
Marok	–	*Cup*
Meraksa	–	*To lie*
Merokzukba	–	*Forest fire*
Meyutsüngba	–	*Lord over the dead*
Mezen	–	*Virgin forests*
Mezheu	–	*Summer*
Mezetri	–	*Village guards during Ingkho Mapang*
Mibenlangba	–	*Murder*
Milum	–	*Variety of fish*
Moatsu	–	*Ao spring festival*
Mongsen	–	*Ao dialect*
Morung	–	*Male dormitory*
Moutsujen	–	*Place where paddy is husked*
Mulok	–	*Basket used as container as well as measure for collecting funds such as paddy*
Mulok Emtepba	–	*Literally joining of two baskets; Socially merger of two clans as one*
Mungdang	–	*Meeting/Assembly*
Mungdang Kakba	–	*Violating general assembly decisions*
Mungphuo	–	*Onset of summer*

Naga Khat	–	*Land grants belonging to Nagas*
Namen Endi	–	*Footpath leading to rice field to the west (upper khel)*
Narokum	–	*Title*
Ningja Kuja	–	*Kinship terminologies*
Ning Menok	–	*Bringing a bad name*
Nubusu	–	*Cloth used to carry baby on the back*
Nuklubo	–	*Dao holder*
Nungtak	–	*Agenda*
Obang Utepba	–	*Consensus*
Orija Salang	–	*Changki Ayim Asem Senso hall*
Orirachet	–	*Another term for age-set system in Changki*
Pacha	–	*Term used to denote one's own clan among males*
Pachalari	–	*Term used to denote one's own clan among females*
Phenphuo	–	*Period when the cut jhum forests are left to dry*
Pok	–	*Demarcation of jhum land for cultivation*
Pusenru	–	*Ring made out of bamboo strips to keep the pots*
Puthia Mukojen	–	*Rice seedling nursery*

Putu Menden	–	*Village Government (Chungli)*
Putsuru	–	*Mushroom shaped stopper made out of baked clay*
Puyakru	–	*Double paddle made out of wood used in making clay pots*
Puzukru	–	*Shaping stick used for making clay pots*
Sachuk	–	*Bamboo skewers used for drying meat*
Sala Sana	–	*Exchange of views*
Samenthi	–	*Senior Councilors of Changki village government*
Samen Menchen	–	*Village Government (Mongsen)*
Samen Nuzaba	–	*Junior councilors of Changki village government*
Saniru	–	*Wooden slab used for cutting meat*
Sanen Luden	–	*Executive Committee*
Senso	–	*Citizen/Citizenship*
Senso Menchen	–	*General Body Office Bearers*
Senso Mungdang	–	*General assembly*
Senso Telongjem	–	*Solidarity of the people*
Sera Kipharu	–	*Broom made out of palm leaves*
Sungdakba	–	*Official name of the upper khel*
Sungden	–	*Wooden box*
Sungkho	–	*Firewood collection*

Sungkhokopok	–	*Bamboo basket used for carrying firewood*
Sungphu	–	*Wooden bowl with stand used for making chutney*
Suokzukba	–	*To cheat*
Taktepsu	–	*Traditional Changki shawl*
Teba	–	*The father*
Teba Emba	–	*To adopt or be attach to a particular clan by calling father*
Techempong	–	*Cylindrical bamboo jug used for grinding spices*
Tekong	–	*Hill*
Tekongkulem	–	*Ancient sacred place in the upper khel*
Temnakja	–	*Man's sisters' as well as clanswomen's sons*
Temnakri	–	*Nephews and Brother/son-in-law*
Tening tepong enerirong	–	*To bring good name*
Telakba	–	*Youngest male child*
Telakla	–	*Youngest female child*
Temokbasu	–	*Shawl*
Tenik	–	*Lineage*
Tepang Chenja	–	*Fine administered orally without taking the amount recorded*

Thatsu	–	*Ladle made out of bamboo*
Thiong	–	*Small room in Changki traditional houses where firewood, pigs and chickens were kept*
Tiar/Tiaba	–	*God of Providence*
Tinu Emba	–	*To adopt or be attached to a particular clan as a relative*
Tiuo Tukori	–	*Maternal uncles*
Tsuenkho	–	*Small conical shaped basket*
Tsukera	–	*Sickle*
Tsuki	–	*Female dormitory*
Tsukla	–	*Spring*
Tsulu	–	*Wet rice fields*
Tsulu Endi phiro waba	–	*To clean/clear village footpaths leading to wet rice fields*
Tsungba	–	*Priest*
Tsüngrem	–	*God*
Tsungremmong	–	*Ao harvest festival*
Tsüngtitong/ Asangdong	–	*Tree of Righteousness*
Tsutakhopok	–	*Baskets used to carry bamboo containers for collecting water*
Tukorang	–	*Hoe*
Tukonglu	–	*Jhum cultivation*

Tuktsu	–	*Small hoe used for weeding and planting of seedlings*
Utongdari	–	*Negotiator*
Ungkholulu	–	*Broom made out of wild grass*
Yanga	–	*Age-set system*
Yangtep	–	*Formation of working groups among age-set grades*
Yayang	–	*To earn*
Yimten	–	*Government*
Yimten Emli	–	*System of government*
Yimten Ozung	–	*Village government rule*
Yimten Kakba	–	*To violate village government rule*
Yimten Raksaba	–	*Crisis in village government*
Yimpuiri	–	*Village crier*
Zenba	–	*To winnow*
Zunga	–	*Age-set system (In Chungli dialect)*

INDEX

■■■